"It was a tragedy, to say nothing of an unmitigated foreign policy disaster, for the United States government to misdiagnose the Arab Spring as a democratic uprising rather than a windfall for Islamic supremacists. As Robert Spencer demonstrates with his signature blend of intellectual rigor and fearlessness, our continued refusal to grapple with the ideology that fuels jihadism has significantly increased the terrorist threat here at home. When you pretend your enemies are your friends, you don't get peace, you get terror."

—**ANDREW C. McCARTHY**, bestselling author of *Willful Blindness* and *The Grand Jihad*, policy fellow at the National Review Institute, and contributing editor of *National Review*

"Nothing is so important as telling the truth about Islam, especially in an age when few want to hear it because it is so disturbing. America is fortunate to have an indomitable truth-teller such as Robert Spencer. In this book, he explains how Islam is subverting America's freedoms and values. The Arab Winter will be upon America, unless America starts listening to people such as Robert Spencer. This is an extremely timely and important book by one of the West's most perceptive analysts of Islam."

—**GEERT WILDERS**, MP and leader of the Party for Freedom in the Netherlands and author of *Marked for Death: Islam's War Against the West and Me*

"Between 2010 and 2013, Robert Spencer relates, he has 'gone from being a trainer for the FBI and the U.S. military to being shunned by the U.S. government and a Roman Catholic bishop and banned from Great Britain'—even though his views have remained the same. What *has* changed is the willingness to discuss Islamism, jihad, and Shari'a. Written in response to this shift, Spencer's helpful survey of efforts to impose Islamic law on Americans irrefutably shows the dangers of succumbing to a medieval code."

—**DANIEL PIPES**, president of the Middle East Forum and author of *In the Path of God: Islam and Political Power* and *Militant Islam Reaches America*

"This book is a wake-up call that every one of our elected representatives and law enforcement and intelligence officials should heed. Robert Spencer shows the price of the prevailing refusal to study the ideology of Islamic jihad terrorists—and that price is only going to rise, unless the lessons of this book are heeded."

—**STEVEN EMERSON**, author of *Jihad Incorporated:*
A Guide to Militant Islam in the United States and
producer of *Jihad in America: The Grand Deception*

"Robert Spencer shows in this book just how serious the situation has become regarding the jihad against the U.S. Few people realize how much our government, law enforcement, and media elites have endangered us all with their denial of the jihad threat. But it's all in this book, along with a pathway back to sanity. If the West is to be saved, we will owe Robert Spencer an incalculable debt."

—**PAMELA GELLER**, popular blogger at Atlas Shrugs and
president of the American Freedom Defense Initiative

"Robert Spencer has been banned in Great Britain, canceled in Massachusetts, and shunned by the Obama administration. So what is it about Spencer's insights on Islam and the jihadist threat that has the Left and its smooth-talking Islamist allies in the West so eager to silence him? Look no further than *Arab Winter Comes to America*. Bold, eloquent, witty, and uncompromising in its assessment of the massive Islamic jihadi penetration of a feckless West, it is vintage Spencer. Snatch it up and give copies to your friends, family, and neighbors while you still can—and before the Spencer censors come to your town."

—**ERICK STAKELBECK**, author of *The Brotherhood:*
America's Next Great Enemy and host of CBN's *The Watchman* program

ARAB SP~~RING~~ WINTER COMES TO AMERICA

COMES TO AMERICA

ARAB SPRING WINTER COMES TO AMERICA

THE TRUTH ABOUT THE WAR WE'RE IN

ROBERT SPENCER

REGNERY
PUBLISHING

A Salem Communications Company

Library of Congress Cataloging-in-Publication Data

Spencer, Robert, 1962-
  Arab winter comes to America / Robert Spencer.
    pages cm
  Includes bibliographical references and index.
  ISBN 978-1-62157-204-6
  1. Terrorism--Religious aspects--Islam. 2.
Terrorism--Prevention--Government policy--United States. 3. Muslims--United
States. 4. Islamic fundamentalism--United States. 5. Subversive
activities--United States. 6. Islam and politics--United States. 7. Jihad.
8. United States--Politics and government--2009- I. Title.
  HV6432.S696 2014
  363.3250973--dc23
                                2014002639

Published in the United States by
Regnery Publishing
A Salem Communications Company
One Massachusetts Avenue NW
Washington, DC 20001
www.Regnery.com

Manufactured in the United States of America
1 2 3 4 5 6 7 8 9 10

Books are available in quantity for promotional or premium use. Write to Director of Special Sales, Regnery Publishing, One Massachusetts Avenue NW, Washington, DC 20001, for information on discounts and terms, or call (202) 216-0600.

Distributed to the trade by
Perseus Distribution
250 West 57th Street
New York, NY 10107

To those who are aware and resolute

CONTENTS

INTRODUCTION

WHY IT'S SO HARD TO FIND OUT THE TRUTH ABOUT THE WAR WE'RE IN

(Plus, How I Was Banned in Britain and Became an International Pariah)

When the "Arab Spring" revolutions began in Tunisia and Egypt in January 2011, the Western media reacted with unalloyed enthusiasm. Ignoring signs that the Muslim Brotherhood and other pro-sharia Islamic supremacist groups were likely to be the big winners in the uprisings, the media assured Americans that the "Arab Spring" heralded a new flowering of democracy and pluralism in the Middle East.

The fruits of the "Arab Spring" are now clear. By September 2013, less than three years after this movement began amid such hope, North Africa and the Middle East were in flames. The Muslim Brotherhood took over Egypt and then so alienated its citizens that it was driven from power after a year, ushering in a new era not of democracy and pluralism, but of uncertainty, violence, and strife. In Libya, where President Obama gave military aid to the anti-Gaddafi rebels, a U.S. consulate was attacked, and a U.S. ambassador was murdered. And

Islamic jihad terrorists from all over the globe were flocking to the bloody civil war engulfing Syria—where military aid from the United States of America supported the side for which those jihadists were fighting.

It quickly became apparent that the illusory "Arab Spring" had given way to a very real Arab Winter. It wasn't strictly an Arab phenomenon at all, but a new and aggressive global resurgence of the Islamic jihad that had already struck the United States on September 11, 2001.

And on April 15, 2013, at the Boston Marathon, the Arab Winter came to America.

The jihad attack in Boston shows that our future in this country could be just as bloody as the present of the Muslim world. The violence at the Boston Marathon—and many similar recent plots across the United States, as this book will demonstrate—had exactly the same cause as the ongoing violence in Syria, Egypt, and Libya. Tragically, the United States is completely unprepared.

The ideology behind the Boston Marathon bombing was the same ideology ascendant in the Arab Spring uprisings that were hailed by the media and the Obama administration as a new flowering of pro-Western sentiment and political and societal freedom in North Africa and the Middle East. It is no different from the ideology that motivated a Muslim U.S. Army psychiatrist to slaughter thirteen Americans at Fort Hood in November 2009. It is identical to the belief system that inspired the 9/11 hijackers.

Yet in the face of this renewed jihad has come, from both the U.S. government and the mainstream media, denial, obfuscation, and worst of all, sympathy with those who have sworn to destroy the United States as a free nation and establish an Islamic state in its place.

Heads in the Sand

In this book I detail the pervasiveness of that denial and illustrate just how destructive it is, as well as explaining the driving forces behind the jihadists operating now in the United States: their beliefs, their associations, and the international jihad network that has been working for the same goals around the globe.

I also expose the details of the belief system of the jihad terrorists in the United States and explain the relationship between those beliefs and the agenda of "moderate Muslim" advocacy groups also operating here. This is essential information for Americans to have in the wake of the Boston bombings, the Fort Hood shooting, and other jihad terror activity on American soil. For almost incredibly, even as Islamic terror activity is increasing, the Obama administration has systematically removed any mention of Islam and jihad from counterterror training manuals for the FBI, the Department of Homeland Security, and other law enforcement and intelligence agencies. That whitewashing is playing a large part in the intelligence failures that make continuing jihad activity in the United States possible.

Thus it is crucial for every patriotic American—and every lawmaker who wishes to counter the Obama administration's suicidally politically correct counterterror policies—to be fully informed about this dangerous belief system, so as to be able to formulate strategies to counter it realistically and effectively.

The denial goes back a long way—all the way back to the beginning of the last round of the Islamic jihad against the United States, when George W. Bush went to the Islamic Center of Washington, D.C., on September 17, 2001, and proclaimed, "Islam is peace." The September 11 terrorist attacks, he explained, "violate the fundamental tenets of the Islamic faith."[1] In an address to Congress on September 20, 2001, he added, "The terrorists practice a fringe form of Islamic extremism that has been rejected by Muslim scholars and the vast majority of Muslim clerics—a fringe movement that perverts the peaceful teachings of Islam."[2]

This claim doesn't become any truer for being oft repeated. But at least during the Bush administration it was still possible to tell the truth about the motives and goals of jihad terrorists, and many who trained FBI agents and other counterterrorism officials about the nature and magnitude of the jihad threat did just that.

I was one of them. For several years I gave semi-regular briefings on Islam and jihad to the FBI and its Joint Terrorism Task Force, as well as to the United States Central Command (CENTCOM), the United States Army Command and General Staff College, the U.S. Army's

Asymmetric Warfare Group, and the U.S. intelligence community. I spoke to rooms full of agents who were so deep undercover that only their first names were given on their nameplates. I received certificates of appreciation from CENTCOM and the Asymmetric Warfare Group.

But all that changed in 2010, as Islamic advocacy groups in the United States began claiming that counterterror training was "Islamophobic" and demanding that the Obama administration scrub training materials of all mention of Islam and jihad in connection with terrorism and stop bringing in "Islamophobic" trainers, including me. The Obama team quickly complied—at what cost, we will see.

Banned in Britain

Just as quickly, the international public discourse began to focus more on Muslims as victims than on Muslims as terrorists and to portray those who spoke out against jihad violence and Islamic supremacism as "bigoted," "hateful," and "Islamophobic." What had begun as a wild claim of U.S. Islamic groups with ties to Hamas and the Muslim Brotherhood became mainstream conventional wisdom.

So mainstream that in June 2013, I was barred from entering Great Britain. The UK Home Office explained why in a letter to me:

> You are reported to have stated the following:
>
> [Islam] is a religion and is a belief system that mandates warfare against unbelievers for the purpose for establishing a societal model that is absolutely incompatible with Western society because media and general government unwillingness to face the sources of Islamic terrorism these things remain largely unknown.

I said no such thing, of course. I generally speak and write in coherent English. But the point is clear enough. I certainly have pointed out that Islam mandates warfare against unbelievers. This claim is not really controversial to anyone who has studied Islam at all, as we shall see. But saying it was enough to get one banned from entering Britain in the summer of 2013.

Interestingly, the week before I had planned to enter the United Kingdom, the British Home Office allowed in a Saudi sheikh named Muhammad al-Arefe, who has said, "Devotion to jihad for the sake of Allah, and the desire to shed blood, to smash skulls, and to sever limbs for the sake of Allah and in defense of His religion, is, undoubtedly, an honor for the believer. Allah said that if a man fights the infidels, the infidels will be unable to prepare to fight."[3]

So, apparently one can enter Great Britain if one believes that violent jihad is a tenet of Islam—as long as one is in favor of it.

The Hit-and-Run Bishop

But I had begun to be established as a pariah before the British ban. In February 2013, Robert McManus, the Roman Catholic bishop of Worcester, Massachusetts, canceled my scheduled appearance at a Catholic men's conference on the grounds that my appearance would harm interfaith dialogue: "My decision to ask Mr. Spencer not to speak at the Men's Conference resulted from a concern voiced by members of the Islamic community in Massachusetts, a concern that I came to share. That concern was that Mr. Spencer's talk about extreme, militant Islamists and the atrocities that they have perpetrated globally might undercut the positive achievements that we Catholics have attained in our inter-religious dialogue with devout Muslims and possibly generate suspicion and even fear of people who practice piously the religion of Islam."[4]

All this appeared bitterly ironic two months later, when the Boston Marathon bombings were perpetrated by two members in good standing of the Islamic Society of Boston, near McManus's bailiwick. And as a fitting coda to the story, the bishop himself called his own judgment into question three months later by being arrested for drunk driving, leaving the scene of an accident, and refusing a chemical test. Apparently he smashes up cars, as well as reputations, with a Daisy Buchanan–like confidence that someone else will clean up the mess. Bishop McManus later confessed to a "terrible error in judgment"—not with regard to a relentless ideology murdering his fellow Christians around the globe, but in regard to his drinking and driving.[5] I could have saved him a lot of trouble by buying him a drink, talking with him about his terrible errors in judgment, and driving him home safely.

But in banning me, McManus wasn't taking a fringe position of cowardice and appeasement, but rather expressing a view that has become mainstream: that to discuss jihad terror and Islamic supremacism was somehow wrong and to ignore and deny the evil actions of Islamic jihadists was preferable and a surer path to peace.

From 2010 to 2013, I had gone from being a trainer for the FBI and the U.S. military to being shunned by the U.S. government and a Roman Catholic bishop and banned from Great Britain—all without changing my positions one iota. Fortunately, the turnaround was not total: all through the period of this change, others courageously insisted on having me speak.

This is not a book about me, although inevitably I enter as a character here and there. But what happened to me is indicative of a larger phenomenon: the demonization and marginalization of resistance to jihad terror—with the entirely predictable result that today jihad terrorists are bolder than ever, both in the United States and around the world. That boldness manifests itself in ever more jihad attacks and plots, even as Barack Obama has repeatedly assured the nation that al Qaeda is "decimated" and "on the path to defeat" and John Brennan, the president's top counterterrorism advisor, has dismissed it has "a mortally wounded tiger that still has some life left in it."[6]

It's as if the flames of the burning Twin Towers just keep spreading and spreading until they threaten to engulf the entire world, while the guardians of our safety insist that there is no fire, no fire at all. That fire is raging hotter than ever. It's time we sound the alarm.

CHAPTER ONE

WORLD WAR WHO?

America is at war, and has been since at least September 11, 2001, but no one is really sure who with. The politically correct establishment blames America itself, and even conservatives are not at all united in their assessment of the threat we are facing.

The U.S. government seems determined not only to obscure the nature and magnitude of that threat, but in many ways to aid and abet those who have sworn to destroy the United States. Its officials act this way this not because they have collectively decided to commit treason, but because they underestimate and misunderstand the problem they are facing and thus choose the wrong remedies to deal with it.

The only people who seem to have perfect clarity about who they are and what they hope to accomplish are the nation's foes.

A Soldier of Allah in the U.S. Army

Consider the Fort Hood killer, Nidal Malik Hasan.

At a pretrial hearing before his military trial on July 9, 2013, one of the most notorious recent assassins inside the United States explained his creed, allegiances, and intentions clearly. Hasan, a major in the U.S. Army who admitted to having deliberately killed thirteen people and wounded thirty at Fort Hood on November 5, 2009, complained that he was being made to wear an army uniform. "I can't take any pride in wearing this uniform," he explained. "It represents an enemy of Islam. I'm being forced to wear this uniform."[1]

During Hasan's trial it was revealed that not long after the attack he told a panel of mental health professionals, "I'm paraplegic and could be in jail for the rest of my life. However, if I died by lethal injection I would still be a martyr."[2] He didn't mean a martyr like St. Sebastian or Thomas More. Hasan hopes to be the kind of martyr who kills on behalf of Islam and is killed in the process, in accord with the Qur'an's promise of Paradise to those who "fight in the cause of Allah" and "kill and are killed" (9:111).

During the pretrial phase, Hasan quizzed potential jurors about their opinions of the Taliban, sharia (Islamic law), and the Islamic faith. It came out during his trial that after the shootings he had told the mental health panel, "I don't think what I did was wrong because it was for the greater cause of helping my Muslim brothers."[3] The United States, he said, was targeting those Muslim brothers in an "illegal war."[4]

The war he was referring to was the one in Afghanistan, where Hasan was about to be deployed. Dr. Tonya Kozminksi, who had worked with Hasan at a hospital in Fort Hood, testified that several weeks before Hasan's jihad attack, Hasan warned that if the army ever decided to send him to Afghanistan, "They will pay."[5] Considering the war against the Taliban to be a war against Islam, he realized that—in his own words—he "was on the wrong side." So, as explained, he simply "switched sides."[6]

While many Americans, both Muslim and non-Muslim, opposed the Afghan war, Hasan's expression of support for the Taliban was unusual. The U.S. government and mainstream media generally take it for granted that no Muslims in the United States or, indeed, anywhere else in the world, support the likes of the Taliban except "extremists" who have hijacked and misinterpreted Islam—and that there are no "extremists" among Muslims in the United States, or at most an insignificant number. Yet Hasan, a naturalized American citizen (until he renounced his citizenship shortly before his trial), was obviously an "extremist" who had somehow, despite his "extremism," had not only joined the U.S. Army, but even risen to the rank of major.

He achieved that promotion, moreover, despite the fact that his "extremism" was on abundant display for years before he opened fire at Fort Hood. Hasan had been raising eyebrows for a considerable time, with his declarations about his own allegiances—he proclaimed that he was "Muslim first and American second"[7]—and his routine harassment of his colleagues with harangues about Islam. His business card read "SOA," a well-known acronym among jihadists for "Soldier of Allah."[8]

Making Himself Perfectly Clear

In June 2007, Hasan gave a PowerPoint presentation to his coworkers, in which he proposed to show "what the Qur'an inculcates in the minds of Muslims and the potential implications this may have for the U.S. military." He said, "It's getting harder and harder for Muslims in the service to morally justify being in a military that seems constantly engaged against fellow Muslims."[9]

An official who spoke to some of those who attended the presentation recounted, "Hasan apparently gave a long lecture on the Qur'an and talked about how if you don't believe, you are condemned to hell. Your head is cut off. You're set on fire. Burning oil is burned down your throat."[10] According to the Associated Press, "he gave a class presentation questioning whether the U.S.-led war on terror was actually a war on Islam. And students said he suggested that Shariah, or Islamic law, trumped the Constitution and he attempted to justify suicide bombings."[11]

Hasan argued that Muslims must not fight against other Muslims (something prohibited by Qur'an 4:92), and that the Qur'an mandates both defensive and offensive jihad against unbelievers to impose Islamic law on those unbelievers. He quoted the Qur'anic verse calling for war against the "People of the Book" (that is, mainly Jews and Christians) until they "pay the tax in acknowledgment of [Islamic] superiority and they are in a state of subjection" (9:29). Hasan seems to have been telling the assembled (and no doubt stunned) physicians, who had been expecting a lecture about psychiatry, that Muslims have a religious obligation to make war against non-Muslims and subjugate them under their rule. The clear implication was that Americans—and the United States itself, as the world's foremost infidel polity—were included in this.

In line with that idea, Hasan warned that Muslim soldiers should not be sent to fight for the United States in Muslim countries, invoking—as evidence of what could happen if Muslims were sent to Muslim countries—the earlier jihad murders by another Muslim serviceman, Sergeant Hasan Akbar, who threw grenades into a tent full of American soldiers and killed two of his commanding officers in Kuwait in March 2003, in an attack also motivated by his Islamic faith.[12]

"Good Work for God"

Then, on November 5, 2009, Hasan illustrated that same point himself. That morning he attended prayers at a mosque in Killeen, Texas.[13] Returning home, he gave a neighbor a copy of the Qur'an and told her, "I'm going to do good work for God."[14] Later on the same day, he entered a center at Fort Hood in Texas where soldiers receive medical examinations before deploying overseas. Then, shouting "Allahu akbar" (Allah is greatest—with the implication that Islam is superior to other religions), he drew a pistol and began firing.[15]

During his trial, prosecutors showed that several days before his attack, and even just a few hours before he started shooting, Hasan searched the internet for "jihad" and specifically for articles about Islamic jihadists and Muslim clerics calling for jihad attacks on Americans.[16]

Just Another Case of Workplace Violence

Yet despite these abundant indications that Hasan was engaged in act of Islamic jihad akin to the September 11, 2001, attacks on the World Trade Center and the Pentagon, albeit on a smaller scale, the

Defense Department has classified Hasan's shootings not as a terrorist act, but as "workplace violence."[17]

Hasan himself contradicted this classification at his trial, when he pointedly registered his agreement with the prosecution's contention that, unlike some others who had opened fire in public places, he hadn't just suddenly snapped or been overcome by an overwhelming paroxysm of rage: "I would like to agree with the prosecution that it wasn't done under the heat of sudden passion. There was adequate provocation, that these were deploying soldiers that were going to engage in an illegal war."[18]

Nonetheless, the U.S. government has so far continued to ignore repeated requests from the victims' families to reclassify the killings and make the victims eligible for the Purple Heart and benefits that are normally accorded to combatants killed or injured in the line of duty.[19]

Even during his trial, as Hasan was making his motives absolutely clear, the military judge, Colonel Tara Osborn, barred prosecutors from introducing evidence that Hasan had corresponded with al Qaeda leader Anwar al-Awlaki and was inspired to carry out his attack by the example of Sergeant Hasan Akbar, whose grenade attack on his own commanding officers Major Hasan had featured in his PowerPoint presentation.[20] To introduce such evidence, Osborn said, would "only open the door to a mini-trial" of Akbar and lead to a "confusion of issues, unfair prejudice, waste of time and undue delay."[21]

Unfair prejudice against what or whom? Osborn didn't say. Akbar was already convicted, and Hasan had admitted he was the shooter, so it seems unlikely that she meant unfair prejudice against either of them. But disallowing this evidence did obscure the Islamic character of Hasan's motive. The only way Osborn's statement made sense was if she meant that that this evidence would have created "unfair prejudice" against Islam or Muslims—a strange concern for a military judge in a trial of a mass murderer inspired by Islam's jihad doctrine.

In any case, Hasan's was the oddest of murder trials, in which the murderer openly and repeatedly confessed that he had committed the murders, and his motive was deemed irrelevant, with discussion of it severely circumscribed.

Saving the U.S. Army from "Islamophobia"

The disconnect from obvious reality has grown ever wider. The Obama administration's official unwillingness to face the full reality of the Islamic jihad is all-pervasive, affecting both foreign and domestic policy. Echoed in the mainstream media, it has contributed to an atmosphere in which, during Barack Obama's second term, Americans are arguably less safe and less informed about the threat they face than ever before. Those who are informed about the threat, or who find themselves confronted by it in one form or another, are often intimidated into silence by the politically correct backlash that is sure to come against them if they dare to speak out.

Nidal Hasan's own coworkers during his tenure as an army psychiatrist were subject to that intimidation, and their choices illustrate show how deadly effective it is. Although Hasan's jihadist tendencies were well known, clearly fear that they would be accused of "Islamophobia" prevented his army superiors from acting upon signs of his incipient jihadist tendencies. Instead, they kept promoting him. The AP reported in January 2010 that "a Defense Department review of the shooting rampage at Fort Hood, Texas, has found the doctors overseeing Maj. Nidal Hasan's medical training repeatedly voiced concerns over his strident views on Islam and his inappropriate behavior, yet continued to give him positive performance evaluations that kept him moving through the ranks."[22]

And so Hasan rose through army ranks and did so with extraordinarily positive recommendations, even as he justified suicide bombing and spouted hatred for America while wearing its uniform. In an evaluation dated March 13, 2009, just short of eight months before his jihad attack, Hasan's superiors wrote that he displayed "outstanding moral integrity" and praised his project topic for his master's of public health degree: "the impact of beliefs and culture on views regarding military service during the Global War on Terror." They even praised him specifically as a Muslim, in passages that their authors must have remembered with stinging regret after his jihad murders: one said that he should be put into a position "that allows others to learn from his perspectives" and declared that his "unique insights into the dimensions of Islam" and his "moral reasoning" could be of "great potential interest and strategic importance to the U.S. Army."

A July 1, 2009, report went even further, saying that Hasan had "a keen interest in Islamic culture and faith and has shown capacity to contribute to our psychological understanding of Islamic nationalism and how it may relate to events of national security and Army interest in the Middle East and Asia." Among his "unique skills" were listed "Islamic studies" and "traumatic stress spectrum psychiatric disorders." The report concluded, "Maj. Hasan has great potential as an Army officer."[23] At this point his murders were only four months away.

Even during the time when they wrote these effusive recommendations, Hasan's superiors and the others around him were aware of his pro-jihad statements and were worried by them. "Yet no one in Hasan's chain of command," reports the AP, "appears to have challenged his eligibility to hold a secret security clearance even though they could have because the statements raised doubt about his loyalty to the United States."[24]

Not Daring Not to Praise the Muslim Officer

The reason for the silence in the face of all these warnings is obvious. Hasan's superiors were neither stupid nor incompetent. But they no doubt knew what would happen if they removed Hasan from his position or even simply reprimanded and disciplined him for his statements about Islam. They could have been accused of bigotry, intolerance, even racism (despite the fact that Islam is manifestly not a race)—or of "Islamophobia," the politically correct label used to suggest that any criticism of Islam must arise from irrational fear of and prejudice against Muslims.

That charge is regularly made by Hamas-linked Muslim Brotherhood front groups that pose as Muslim civil rights organizations in the United States, such as the Council on American-Islamic Relations (CAIR) and the Islamic Society of North America (ISNA). Army officers who raised questions about Hasan's loyalty to the United States could easily have found themselves in the midst of a firestorm. It isn't hard to imagine how events might have played out: the mainstream media would have embarked upon a full-bore witch hunt for the alleged witch hunters of Muslims in the military, interviewing the weeping mothers of Muslim soldiers killed in the line of duty while fighting for the United States in Iraq or Afghanistan. Army generals would have had to answer questions about alleged discrimination against Muslims in the military on the Sunday morning talk shows. And ultimately the president of the United States would have ordered a special effort to make Muslims in the military feel at home and welcome.

Those who complained about Hasan would almost certainly have faced public abuse, media smearing by CAIR and ISNA as "Islamophobes," and possibly even disciplinary action from their superiors. Chris Matthews, Stephen Colbert, Jon Stewart, and Bill Maher would have subjected them to nationally broadcast ridicule. All army personnel would have been ordered into sensitivity training, perhaps run by CAIR itself.

For years now CAIR, ISNA, and other Islamic groups in the United States have done all they could to demonize everyone who speaks honestly about the threat of jihad. Since 2009, CAIR has published annual "Islamophobia Reports" that portray everyone who examines how Islamic jihadists justify their violence and make recruits by pointing to Islamic texts and doctrines as sinister, well heeled, and driven by an unrelenting bigotry and hatred.[25] The most recent of these reports contains highly tendentious profiles of virtually everyone who has ever written or spoken critically of jihad terror, combined with fantastical attempts to portray them all as part of an organized anti-Muslim cabal, a veritable "Islamophobia network."

"Moderate" Muslim groups such as CAIR and ISNA have issued numerous pro-forma denunciations of terrorism, but the Fort Hood massacre was an indication of how successful their shielding of Islamic supremacism and its most dangerous proponents from any criticism has been: Nidal Hasan was not removed from his post, and no steps were taken to protect anyone else from him. "Islamophobia" was duly avoided.

Seeking Guidance from the Imam

As if all that weren't appalling enough, those communications with al-Awlaki that Osborn excluded from the evidence at Hasan's trial had been intercepted by the FBI long before Hasan's jihad attack at Fort Hood. They showed that the bureau could have prevented the massacre—but, like Hasan's superiors, FBI agents, too, did nothing.

These communications were known about long before Hasan opened fire at Fort Hood. Five days after the shootings, ABC News reported that while Hasan "came under scrutiny by officials beginning last year for communicating with Anwar al-Awlaki," agents had "determined that the communications were benign and contained no threat. Given the results of the review, the FBI did not have enough information to open a full-field investigation."[26]

In reality, Hasan's emails to al-Awlaki show that the FBI had ample reason to keep a close eye on the army psychiatrist. Hasan first came to FBI attention when he emailed al-Awlaki on December 17, 2008. Hasan wrote (spelling and punctuation as in the original),

> Assalum Alaikum Wa Rhahmutallahi Wa Barakatu [May the peace, mercy, and blessings of Allah be with you], There are many soldiers in the us armed forces that have converted to Islam while in the service. There are also many Muslims who join the armed forces for a myriad of different reasons.
>
> Some appear to have internal conflicts and have even killed or tried to kill other us soldiers in the name of Islam i.e. Hasan Akbar, etc. Others feel that there is no conflict. Previous Fatwas seem vague and not very definitive. Can you make some general comments about Muslims in the u.s. military.
>
> Would you consider someone like Hasan Akbar or other soldiers that have committed such acts with the goal of helping Muslims/Islam (Lets just assume this for now) fighting Jihad and if they did die would you consider them shaheeds [martyrs]. I realize that these are difficult questions but you seem to be one of the only ones that has lived in the u.s. has

a good understadning of the the Qur'an and Sunna and is
not afraid of being direct.

Jazaka'Allah Khair [May Allah reward you with good-
ness].[27]

Asking al-Awlaki whether he considered someone like Hasan Akbar,
who had murdered two of his commanding officers, to be an Islamic
martyr should have been enough to get Hasan onto the FBI's radar and
keep him there. It did not. Notices about Hasan traveled through various bureaucracies, but nothing was done.

Meanwhile, Hasan kept writing to al-Awlaki. In one email, he noted
that Hamas's practice of "firing unguided rockets into Israel has the
potential of indiscriminately killing civilians." But after some consid-
eration, he invoked several Qur'an verses to justify the practice: "So
whoever has assaulted you, then assault him in the same way that he
has assaulted you" (2:194), and "the retribution for an evil act is an evil
one like it, but whoever pardons and makes reconciliation—his reward
is from Allah.... And whoever avenges himself after having been
wronged—those have not upon them any cause for blame. The cause
is only against the ones who wrong the people and tyrannize upon the
earth without right. Those will have a painful punishment" (42:39–42).[28]

In a subsequent email Hasan concluded definitively, based on these
passages, that Hamas's actions were justified: "Hamas and the Muslims
hate to hurt the innocent but they have no choice if their going to have
a chance to survive, flourish, and deter the Zionist enemy. The recom-
pense for an evil is an evil. So, to claim that these rocket attacks go
against the spirit of Islam is false. The blame is only against those who
oppress men wrongly and insolently transgress beyond bounds through
the land defying truth and justice."[29]

Al-Awlaki began responding to Hasan not long after that, and Hasan
continued to ask him for guidance, writing, "During my workig [sic]
career I have been a bus boy, a dishwasher, a cook, a cashier, a lab
technician, a researcher, and entrepreneur. Allah (SWT) [Glorified and
Exalted be He] lifted the veil from my eyes about 8–9 years ago and I
have been striving for Jannat Firdaus [the highest level of Paradise] ever

since. I hope, Inshallah [Allah willing], my endeavor will be realized. If you know someone that you feel that will be compatible and complement my endeavors to please Allah (SWT) please let me know."[30]

"Not a Product of Interest"

Asking a known jihad terror leader for guidance on how to reach Paradise should have been enough for the FBI at very least to question Hasan. In fact it should have been sufficient for him to be removed from active duty as an army psychiatrist—his loyalties were so clearly to America's enemies. But nothing was done. Counterterror analysts scrutinizing Hasan's messages to al-Awlaki labeled each "Not a Product of Interest."[31]

Hasan persisted, even though al-Awlaki had stopped answering his emails. On May 31, 2009, Hasan wrote to al-Awlaki, "I heard a speaker defending suicide bombings as permissible and have been using his logic in debates to see how effective it really is." He explained why he agreed with the unnamed speaker's reasoning and added, "I don't want to make this to [sic] long but the issue of 'collateral damage' where a decision is made to allow the killing of innocents for a valuable target. I[n] the Qur'an it states to fight your enemies as they fight you but don't transgress. So, I would assume that suicide bomber whose aim is to kill enemy soldiers or their helpers but also kill innocents in the process is acceptable. Furthermore, if enemy soldiers are using other tactics that are unethical/unconscionable than [sic] those same tactics may be used."[32]

Once again, however, even though Hasan was discussing why it was permissible according to Islam to kill innocents in suicide attacks, this was "Not a Product of Interest." The FBI agent in San Diego who was monitoring Hasan's communications was reasonably upset by this designation and contacted the Washington Field Office (WFO) of the Joint Terrorism Task Force (TFO) to ask why. He was told that the Washington Field Office "doesn't go out and interview every Muslim guy who visits extremist websites. Besides, this guy has a legitimate work related reasons to be going to these sites and engaging these extremists in dialogue. WFO did not assess this guy as a terrorism threat."

The Washington Field Office also told the San Diego agent that Hasan was "politically sensitive for WFO."[33] How and why Hasan was "politically sensitive" was left unexplained, but it may have been a reference to how politically sensitive it would have been to investigate a Muslim who was a major in the U.S. Army. And certainly interviewing "every Muslim guy who visits extremist websites" would have entangled the bureau in charges of "Islamophobia" that it appeared intent on avoiding.

Nothing to Do with Islam

And yet when asked about the emails from Hasan to al-Awlaki, FBI director Robert Mueller said in August 2013 that "given the context of the discussions and the situation that the agents and the analysts were looking at, they took appropriate steps."[34]

Mueller's statement followed a long train of denial and obfuscation from government officials. Not long after the massacre, Homeland Security secretary Janet Napolitano declared, "This was an individual who does not represent the Muslim faith."[35] U.S. Army chief of staff George Casey declared, "Our diversity, not only in our Army, but in our country, is a strength. And as horrific as this tragedy was, if our diversity becomes a casualty, I think that's worse."[36] The U.S. government's report on the massacre doesn't mention Islam even once.

All this politically correct denial cost was thirteen dead and thirty wounded.

"Racism" at Fort Dix

Napolitano, Casey, and the rest were just reflecting a political correctness that has been entrenched for years, and that is only getting worse. On December 22, 2008, five Muslims were convicted of plotting to enter the U.S. Army base in Fort Dix, New Jersey, and murder as many soldiers as they could.[37] A sixth got five years in prison for weapons offenses, and the group became known as the "Fort Dix Six."

Like Hasan's, this was a jihad plot. One of the plotters, Serdar Tatar, told an FBI informant late in 2006, "I'm gonna do it.... It doesn't matter to me, whether I get locked up, arrested, or get taken away, it doesn't matter. Or I die, doesn't matter, I'm doing it in the name of Allah."[38]

Another plotter, Mohamad Shnewer (the only American citizen among the convicted men), was caught on tape saying, "They are the ones, we are going to put bullets in their heads, Allah willing."[39]

The men trained "for jihad," according to informant Besnik Bakalli, while on a trip to the Pocono Mountains in Pennsylvania, where they bought guns and practiced with them at firing ranges.[40]

The plot was uncovered in January 2006, when two of the plotters entered a Circuit City outlet in New Jersey and asked a clerk to convert a videotape to DVD. The video showed men shooting automatic weapons and crying out, "Allahu akbar."

Although the clerk, Brian Morgenstern, was alarmed, he hesitated over what to do. Years of politically correct indoctrination from the mainstream media made him wonder if it would be wrong to stop these men. Finally he asked a coworker "Dude, I just saw some really weird s---. I don't know what to do. Should I call someone or is that being racist?"[41] His concern was ironic, given that the Fort Dix plotters were all white European Muslims from the former Yugoslavia. Fortunately, Morgenstern's coworker urged him to contact police, and he ultimately did.

Morgenstern's hesitation is yet another indication of how successful American Muslim advocacy groups have been in portraying resistance to the global jihad as "racism" and honest discussion of the elements of Islam that jihadists use to justify acts of violence and other acts in service of Islamic supremacism as "bigotry"—and ultimately, in confusing huge numbers of Americans about just what we're up against.

We can be grateful that Brian Morgenstern came forward anyway. But it isn't hard to imagine what could happen if the next young person in his position decides that it is better to keep silent than to do anything that might appear to be "racist." Now that this is—as we shall see—largely the policy of the U.S. government, that possibility is likelier than ever.

Telling the Truth about the War We're In

It is long past time for a searching reevaluation of the politically correct shibboleths that could have kept Brian Morgenstern from blowing the whistle on the Fort Dix jihadists, and that did prevent the U.S. government from recognizing the danger posed by Major Nidal Hasan.

This book supplies the information that the government and mainstream media are deliberately ignoring. It explains what men like Nidal Malik Hasan and the Fort Dix Six and many others like them believe, what they have against the United States, and what they hope to accomplish. Armed with this information, no more Brian Morgensterns need ever fear being "racist" for standing against jihad terror.

None of these things is difficult to find out, if you know where to look. But they've been obscured by years of denial and obfuscation—which have become weapons themselves in this war. Until we understand the motives and goals of our enemies, we will never be able to overcome them. That has been a basic axiom of warfare since time immemorial—and that's no doubt why our foes in this great conflict have made it a central part of their battle plan to make sure that as many Americans as possible, including (and especially) policymakers in Washington and the top opinion-formers in the mainstream media, have no clue as to what this war is really about.

And it has worked. But the truth cannot be successfully obscured forever. Bringing it to light is essential to the survival of this free republic.

CHAPTER TWO

MISUNDERSTANDING ISLAM
WITH A MEAT CLEAVER

slamic jihadists insist they're acting on Islamic imperatives embed-
ded within the Qur'an and Muhammad's teaching. Non-Muslim
leaders in the West insist that this is not the case, that Islamic teaching is peaceful, benign, and even beneficial for society, and that violence
in the name of Islam is committed only by those who misunderstand
its true teachings.

But why do jihadists continually misunderstand Islam in this particular way? Nidal Hasan was a case in point. But there are many, many
others. In May 2013, a convert to Islam who called himself Mujaahid
Abu Hamza (formerly Michael Adebolajo), his hands scarlet with the
blood of Drummer Lee Rigby, the British soldier he had just brutally
hacked to death on a London street, and still holding the meat cleaver,
calmly began explaining himself on camera.

In the course of his explanation, Abu Hamza invoked the Qur'an's
ninth chapter (Surat at-Tawba), which enjoins Muslims to make war

against and subjugate Jews and Christians, declaring "we are forced by
the Qur'an, in Sura At-Tawba, through many ayah [verses] in the
Qur'an, we must fight them as they fight us." He added, "I apologize
that women had to witness this today but in our lands women have to
see the same."

Abu Hamza's reference to "our lands" may have appeared odd, as
he was born in England to Nigerian parents who had immigrated to
England in the early 1980s. But he meant neither English nor Nigerian
lands, of course; Abu Hamza converted to Islam around 2003, and that
meant that in his mind he was no longer English, if he ever had been.
He understood his commitment to Islam to supersede everything else,
requiring a loyalty above national allegiances and even ties of blood.
The Qur'an commands Muslims to "be good to parents" (17:22). However, even in that relationship, the overarching principle is that Muslims
must be "hard against the unbelievers, merciful one to another" (48:29).

And so Mujaahid Abu Hamza committed murder on a street of the
land where he grew up, in defense of those he considered to be his only
true kith and kin: Muslims worldwide. He did so, moreover, in obedience to what he considered to be the commands of his holy book.

British government and media elites, however, were sure that he
had gotten his religion all wrong. They rushed to assure the public that
Islam had nothing to do with his action. He was, they said, an "extremist" who misunderstood the clear and peaceful teachings of Islam.
British prime minister David Cameron summed up the mainstream
view when he said in the House of Commons, "What happened on the
streets of Woolwich shocked and sickened us all. It was a despicable
attack on a British soldier who stood for our country and our way of
life and it was too a betrayal of Islam and of the Muslim communities
who give so much to our country. There is nothing in Islam that justifies
acts of terror and I welcome the spontaneous condemnation of this
attack from Mosques and community organisations right across our
country."[1]

Muslim organizations did indeed condemn the murder, but that in
itself hardly establishes that it was a betrayal of Islam; Muslim organizations may have simply thought it an inopportune act, or they may
have condemned it out of political expedience. Whatever their genuine

sentiments about the atrocity, however, their condemnations reinforced Cameron's core belief that Islam was a peaceful religion that was not represented by its "extremists."

Denial in Wichita

The same phenomenon played out in Wichita, Kansas, in December 2013, when—if an Islamic jihadist had gotten his way—jihad would have struck again in America. Instead, Terry Lee Loewen, an avionics technician at Wichita's Mid-Continent Airport, was arrested as he tried to drive a van that he thought was full of high explosives onto the tarmac at that airport, where he was planning to trigger it, causing what he hoped would be (as he put it in a letter to his wife) "maximum carnage + death."[2] Loewen wanted this to be yet another jihad massmurder attack on American soil, in which he would be, as he wrote in the same letter, "martyred in the path of Allah." In this and other statements, Loewen made his motivations absolutely clear.

He said that he wanted to "commit an act of violent jihad on behalf of al Qaeda" against the United States, even though he himself is an American: just as for many other converts to Islam who turn to jihad, his conversion meant his rejection of his nation and people as infidel, and a new loyalty instead to the supranational Islamic umma.[3]

Loewen also freely acknowledged that he would be classified as an Islamic "extremist": "Let me preface the bottom line by saying I have become 'radicalized' in the strongest sense of the word, and I don't feel Allah wants me any other way."[4]

In the same vein, he expressed frustration with Muslims who didn't see the jihad imperative as he did: "I don't understand how you can read the Qur'an and the sunnah of the Prophet (saw)[5] and not understand that jihad and the implementation of Sharia is absolutely demanded of all the Muslim Ummah. I feel so guilt-ridden sometimes for knowing what's required of me but yet doing little or nothing to make it happen. I love my Muslim brothers and sisters, whether they agree with me or not, it's just hard to deal with the denial that some of them appear to be going through."[6]

Some of Loewen's statements suggested that he had come into some conflict with those "Muslim brothers and sisters": "As time goes on I care less and less about what other people think of me, or my views on Islam. I have been studying subjects like jihad, martyrdom operations, and Sharia Law…I believe the Muslim who is labeled 'a radical fundamentalist' is closer to Allah…than the ones labeled 'moderates'. Just my opinion; if I'm off base, please set me straight."[7]

Apparently, no one did. Loewen continued looking for "someone who is active in jihad and could use an occasional influx of 'help'…I just hate the kaffar government and those who are following it to the Hellfire, and the sooner it and its followers get there, the better."[8]

Yet just as in the case of the Woolwich beheading, law enforcement officials were anxious to dispel any impression that Loewen's attempt at mass murder and mayhem had anything remotely to do with anything genuinely Islamic. Kansas U.S. attorney Barry Grissom said that there was "no indication that the defendant was involved or working with any member of any religious community in Wichita."[9] A *Wichita Eagle* editorial noted that Grissom "and FBI Special Agent in Charge Mike Kaste made the important point that Loewen's alleged actions in no way should reflect on any religious group. Too many continue to forget that those who plan or carry out terrorist acts in the name of Islam have twisted that faith to unrecognizable extremes."[10]

Blind Faith in Peaceful Islam

Belief that Islam is a fundamentally peaceful religion and that Islamic terrorists have "twisted that faith to unrecognizable extremes" is a cornerstone of both British and American foreign policy—in fact, of that of the entire Western world.

The Obama administration's foreign policy toward Islamic states, as well as its domestic policy toward Muslims in the United States, is predicated on the unshakeable assumption that what Barack Obama has called the "holy Qur'an," the supreme guide to Muslim doctrine and practice, teaches peace, tolerance, nonviolence, and other fashionable virtues. "America and Islam are not exclusive," the president said during his outreach speech to the Muslim world in Cairo in June 2009, "and need not be in competition. Instead, they overlap, and share common principles of justice and progress, tolerance and the dignity of all human beings."[11]

But is this a fair summation of Islamic teaching? If so, it would be hard to explain how people such as Mujaahid Abu Hamza, Nidal Hasan, Osama bin Laden, Tamerlan Tsarnaev, and all the other Muslims who have invoked Islam—often quoting specific verses of the Qur'an—to justify violence could possibly have come to misunderstand their own religion so drastically. Contrary to the conventional wisdom that all religions are equally capable of inciting their adherents to violence, Muslims committing violence in the name of Islam are a daily feature of life in many parts of the world, and armed Islamic movements exist in numerous countries, while Christians committing violence and quoting the New Testament to justify it exist today largely just in Hollywood movies.

Pining for White Right-Wing Bombers

On April 15, 2013, a brilliantly sunny Monday afternoon, the Boston Marathon was drawing to a close, and a large crowd had gathered at the finish line to greet friends and family members among the runners. Then two nail bombs exploded in quick succession, killing two people and wounding well over two hundred, maiming some of them for life. Before the identity of the bombers became known, the mainstream media was full of hope that the Bible-quoting Christian killers that inhabit their imaginations would finally materialize.

Media reports were full of speculation about how the bombings appeared to be the work of "right-wing extremists," "Tea Partiers," and the like. On the day of the bombings, Charles P. Pierce in *Esquire* was one of the first of many to caution people against thinking that the marathon had just been the site of a jihad attack ("foreign terrorism") and to try to link the bombings to the Right: "Obviously, nobody knows anything yet, but I would caution folks jumping to conclusions about foreign terrorism to remember that this is the official Patriots Day holiday in Massachusetts, celebrating the Battles at Lexington and Concord, and that the actual date (April 19) was of some significance to, among other people, Tim McVeigh, because he fancied himself a waterer of the tree of liberty and the like."[12]

Likewise, CNN national security analyst Peter Bergen speculated that if "conventional explosives" had been used, "that might be some other kind of right-wing extremists," as opposed to al Qaeda. He reminded viewers that "we've also seen other extremist groups attacking, right-wing groups, for instance trying to attack the Martin Luther King Jr. Day parade in Oregon in 2010."[13]

Most egregiously of all, David Sirota of Salon hoped that the bomber would turn out to be a "white American."[14]

Sirota got his wish. The killers, two brothers named Tamerlan and Dzhokhar Tsarnaev, were white—indeed, literal Caucasians—and Dzhokhar Tsarnaev was a naturalized American citizen.

Defending Islam in Boston

The Tsarnaev brothers were two Muslims from southern Russia near the breakaway Muslim republic of Chechnya. Their motivations quickly became clear. CNN reported a week after the bombings that "Dzhokhar Tsarnaev, wounded and held in a Boston hospital, has said his brother—who was killed early Friday—wanted to defend Islam from attack."[15]

Just before he was captured, when he was hiding out inside a pleasure boat, Dzhokhar wrote a long self-justification on the inside of the boat, including the line: "When you attack one Muslim, you attack all Muslims."[16]

It came to light soon after the bombings that on a Russian-language social media page, Dzhokhar had featured a drawing of a bomb under the heading "send a gift," and just above links to sites about Islam.[17] Tamerlan's YouTube page contained two videos by Sheikh Feiz Mohammed.[18] According to a report published in the *Australian* in January 2007, in a video that came to the attention of authorities at the time, Feiz Mohammed "urges Muslims to kill the enemies of Islam and praises martyrs with a violent interpretation of jihad."[19]

Tamerlan also said, "I'm very religious."[20] His friend Donald Larking affirmed this. "Tamerlan Tsarnaev was my friend and we talked about everything from politics to religion," according to Larking. "He was very, very religious. He believed that the Qur'an was the one true word and he loved it."[21] Tamerlan did not drink alcohol because Allah forbade it—"God said no alcohol"—and his Italian girlfriend had converted to Islam, as his American wife did later.[22] Even his name indicated the world he belonged to. Apparently Tamerlan Tsarnaev was named for the warrior Tamerlane, the fourteenth-century conqueror of much of Asia, who was as noted for his brutality as for his piety. In 1398, he massacred a hundred thousand Hindus in Delhi, and he killed ninety thousand more people in Baghdad in 1401, all the while adhering devoutly to the religion of Muhammad.

The Boston Marathon bombs were similar to IEDs that jihadis used in Afghanistan and Iraq, and Faisal Shahzad, who tried to set off a jihad car bomb in Times Square in the summer of 2010, also used a similar bomb. The instructions for making such a bomb had even been published in al Qaeda's online Inspire magazine.[23] Not only were the motivations of the Tsarnaev brothers abundantly clear; it is likely that the Tsarnaevs were actually tied in somehow to the international jihad network—as was indicated by how they fought off Boston police early on the Friday after the Marathon bombings with military-grade explosives. The question of where they got those explosives has never been answered. Nor has it ever been explained where the brothers got the military training that they reportedly displayed during the fight against police before Tamerlan was killed and Dzhokhar was captured.

The Clueless and the Craven: Defending Islam in the Mainstream Media

Yet despite the manifest evidence connecting the Tsarnaevs to violent Islamic jihad, the mainstream media continued to obfuscate the truth. On July 15, 2013, three months after the bombings and long after the Tsarnaev brothers' motivations had become crystal clear to anyone who was interested in the evidence, PBS expressed hope that the surviving brother's trial would "shed more light on the motive behind the bombing."[24] The rather clueless report failed to mention either Dzokhar's explicit written statement of his intentions or any of the other copious evidence of what actually motivated both brothers.

NBC's profile of the Tsarnaevs made scant mention of their connections to Islam, only getting around to noting eight paragraphs down in a lengthy story that "Tamerlan had a YouTube page that featured videos about Islamic radicalism" and making some cursory references after that to the brothers' possible jihadist ties.[25] CNN's initial profile of the bombers never mentioned Islam at all, suggesting instead that the immigrant bombers had decided to blow up the marathon because Americans had not extended them a welcoming hand, and quoting a comment Tamerlan had made on a social media site: "I don't have a single American friend. I don't understand them."[26]

When journalists did deign to examine the brothers' Islamic identity, they downplayed it. The *Atlantic* ran a piece entitled "The Boston Bombers Were Muslim—So?" The article complained that "we confuse categories—'male,' 'Muslim'—with cause," and cautioned against stereotyping all Muslims, painting them with a broad brush.[27]

Meanwhile, MSNBC's Chris Matthews had on his show an FBI agent who asked about the bombers, "Where was their inspiration? Where did they get the guidance?" To that, Matthews responded, "Why is that important? Why is that important to—is that important to prosecuting? I mean, what difference does it make why they did it if they did it? I'm being tough here."[28] Also on MSNBC, Martin Bashir lamented how these Muslim bombers were "burying the 'peace, compassion and kindness of the Qur'an.'"[29]

Even many months after the attack, the media was still attempting to exonerate Islam of any responsibility for the bombings. In December 2013, the *Boston Globe* published a major study that purported to show that the Tsarnaev brothers "appear have been motivated less by Islamist ideology and more by their own personal failings and inner demons."[30]

The obfuscation was not limited to the media. The Roman Catholic archbishop of Boston, Cardinal Sean O'Malley, cautioned at a prayer service, "We must be a people of reconciliation, not revenge.... The crimes of the two young men must not be the justification for prejudice against Muslims." So far so good: revenge and prejudice are never justified. But then O'Malley added, "It is very difficult to understand what was going on in the young men's minds, what demons were operative, what ideologies or politics or the perversion of their religion."[31]

It is impossible to say for certain why Cardinal O'Malley was so confident that the bombers were perverting Islam, despite the Qur'an's many commands to Muslims to commit acts of violence against unbelievers.[32] It is likely, however, that he simply believes what he has been told over and over again: that Islam is a religion of peace, and that those who commit acts of violence in its name are twisting and hijacking the beautiful, peaceful teachings of the religion. In reality, the Qur'an exhorts Muslims to use the "steeds of war" to "strike terror into the hearts of the enemies of Allah" (8:60)—and not long before the Boston Marathon bombings, al Qaeda specifically recommended bombing sporting events as an effective way to do just that.[33]

Alternative History

Imagine for a moment if the attackers in the Boston Marathon bombing had indeed turned out to be "right-wing extremists," as the media so clearly hoped they would. Imagine that they were even that mother lode of leftist media fantasy, Christian "extremists"—think Robert De Niro in *Cape Fear*, his body tattooed all over with biblical quotes, muttering about the wrath of God and determined to terrorize not just a single family, but an entire city, an entire nation. Just to make it really interesting, imagine that the people these Christian terrorists had killed with their bombs were Muslims.

In such a case, one thing is absolutely certain—the media coverage would have been, to put it mildly, quite different. There would have been no anxiety to exonerate Christianity from responsibility, no careful reminders not to confuse categories with causes, no speculation about what could possibly have led the hapless bombers to misinterpret their own religion. Instead, the media feeding frenzy would have been intense. The airwaves would have been crowded with earnest examinations of all the biblical material that could possibly be construed as incitements to violence, recommendations of what churches and Christian leaders must do to make sure that this kind of attack never happens again, and story after story about bright, attractive young people who got mixed up with church groups and ended up with their lives and the lives of everyone around them tragically in ruins.

Instead, the bombers were Muslims, acting explicitly in the name of Islam. But the mainstream media has no interest in how the Qur'an may incite those who believe it is the word of Allah to commit acts of violence against those who do not believe it is. The *Atlantic* asked why it mattered that the bombers were Muslim. It's a fair question, but there's a fairly obvious answer. It matters because the fact that they were Muslims is not incidental to what they did. Jihad, behind all the obfuscation and denial, is in fact primarily an Islamic doctrine of warfare against unbelievers. It is not fortuitous that devout Muslims have violently attacked Americans in the past. And it is all too likely that others will want to wage jihad against Americans in the future. And so the more we know about it, the better we can prepare to defend ourselves.

But the more we lie to ourselves and each other, and allow our government to lie to us, on the issue of what this jihad is really all about, then the more we enable people like Tamerlan and Dzhokhar Tsarnaev. We cannot possibly defeat an enemy whom we refuse to understand, refuse to study, refuse to listen to because he explains why he is our enemy in terms that we can't bear to hear. Media obfuscation of the connection between Islam and violence attacks on America is nothing short of criminal. And it will bear much more fruit of the kind it bore on the sunny day of the Boston Marathon.

The Glamorization of Evil

That media obfuscation combined with the mainstream Left's increasingly open anti-Americanism and its ongoing infatuation with the superficial to reach its apotheosis in July 2013, when the pop music magazine *Rolling Stone* featured a doe-eyed, tousle-haired Dzhokhar Tsarnaev on its cover, looking for all the world like the latest rock star to set adolescent girls swooning. The tagline on the cover read: "THE BOMBER: How a Popular, Promising Student Was Failed by His Family, Fell into Radical Islam and Became A Monster." Tsarnaev was cast as the victim: his family let him down, and then he somehow "fell" into "radical Islam." The magazine did not accord Tsarnaev's victims the same sympathetic treatment. (The *Rolling Stone* cover, as appalling as it was, was not singular. When a Syrian jihad warrior cut out the heart of a fallen enemy and took a bite out of it, the BBC ran a sympathetic interview with him, quoting him as pleading for understanding—"put yourself in my shoes.")[34]

Even before the *Rolling Stone* cover, the surviving Tsarnaev brother had already become a heartthrob to numerous young girls, who even began to circulate the hashtag "#FreeJahar"—the simplified version of

Dzhokhar—on the social media site Twitter. "Thousands of American teen girls," reported the *New York Post*, "are crushing on Boston Marathon bomber Dzhokhar 'Jahar' Tsarnaev, 19—and leading a social-media movement to exonerate him."

One girl wrote, "Yes i like Justin Bieber and i like Jahar but that has nothing to do with why i support him. I know hes innocent, he is far too beautiful."[35] Demonstrators chanting "Free Jahar" even appeared at Boston's Moakley Federal Courthouse on July 10, 2013, when the bomber made his first court appearance.[36]

Boston mayor Thomas M. Menino was indignant over the *Rolling Stone* cover, writing to *Rolling Stone* publisher Jann Wenner that it "rewards a terrorist with celebrity treatment," and adding, "The survivors of the Boston attacks deserve *Rolling Stone* cover stories, though I no longer feel that *Rolling Stone* deserves them."[37]

A Pervasive Unreality

Symptomatic of the general inability to deal realistically with the jihad threat, however, was the fact that Menino himself was a major patron of the Islamic Society of Boston, which operates the mosque the Tsarnaevs attended. Menino, according to a 2008 *Boston Phoenix* exposé, "in a fit of multicultural ecumenicalism, approved the sale of city-owned land to the mosque for the bargain basement—and still controversial—price of $175,000, plus the promise of in-kind services, including upkeep of nearby parks. The predictable uproar that arose in the wake of not only selling land well below market rates, but also selling it to a religious institution in contravention of the supposed separation of church and state, was supposed to be muffled by making the complex available for community use. But oops—that never happened. The promised community facilities for non-congregant use still have not been built."[38]

Not only that, but although it was "originally intended to minister to an urban congregation of African-American Muslims, the mosque project was turned over by the city, with no fanfare and little notice, to the control of suburban-based Muslims of largely Saudi Arabian heritage: the Islamic Society of Boston (ISB), which more recently became the Muslim American Society of Boston (MAS-Boston). Perhaps city officials believed that one Muslim community was pretty much like any other Muslim community. In fact, the two groups are quite different."[39]

The Muslim American Society is the principal name under which the Muslim Brotherhood operates in the United States.[40] According to a captured internal Muslim Brotherhood document, the Brotherhood's "work in America is a kind of grand Jihad in eliminating and destroying the Western civilization from within and 'sabotaging' its miserable house by their hands and the hands of the believers so that it is eliminated and Allah's religion is made victorious over all other religions."[41]

So Menino was instrumental in the construction of a Muslim Brotherhood mosque in Boston, which the Tsarnaevs attended. His indignation at *Rolling Stone*'s glamorization of evil looks quite different in that light. Were it not for Menino and so many others like him in prominent positions all over the country behaving as if Muslim Brotherhood ties were a matter of no consequence, it might not be so culturally unacceptable in America today to oppose jihad terror or so easy to glamorize mass killers and enemies of American society and freedoms. *Rolling Stone*'s sympathy for the devil was just the final stage in a long process—the culminating point of over forty years of nationwide indoctrination into self-hatred and contempt for Western culture and uncritical acceptance of anything that appears to be "other."

Learning from Boston

On April 30, Barack Obama promised that he would be taking lessons from the Boston Marathon jihad bombing. "When an event like this happens," the president said, "we want to review every step that was taken, we want to leave no stone unturned, we want to see if there is [sic] in fact additional protocols and procedures that could be put in place that would further improve and enhance our ability to detect a potential attack."[42]

Yet it did not inspire confidence that the man Obama charged with the task of ferreting out the lessons of Boston was his director of national intelligence, James Clapper, who had gained notoriety for the absurd claim that the Muslim Brotherhood was "largely secular."[43] According to Obama, "part of what Director Clapper is doing is to see if we can determine lessons learned from what happened" in Boston.

Ironically, one of the foremost of those lessons is that people like James Clapper are woefully ill-equipped to be entrusted with the nation's intelligence-gathering apparatus.[44]

The FBI Discovers a Jihadi...and Lets Him Go

The administration's missteps can't just be chalked up to innate incompetence. The essential problem is willful ignorance—a refusal to face the reality of Islamic jihad. The depth of the denial is made clear by the fact that the Russian government actually had Boston jihad bomber Tamerlan Tsarnaev under surveillance and even shared concerns about his contacts with jihad terrorists with the FBI.[45] (According to a Homeland Security official, the Saudis had also warned the FBI in writing about Tsarnaev, a claim that the Saudi ambassador in Washington immediately and heatedly denied.)[46]

Yet even after the bombing should have awakened the authorities to the glaring shortcomings of their investigation of Tamerlan Tsarnaev, President Obama seemed at a loss to imagine how the FBI might have made better use of the Russian intelligence: "It's not as if the FBI did nothing. They not only investigated the older brother, they interviewed the older brother ... are there additional things that could have been done in the interim that might have prevented it?"[47]

One additional thing—among many—that could have been done was an investigation of the mosque attended by the Tsarnaevs. And not just by them. The Tsarnaev brothers were not the only jihad terrorists to attend the Islamic Society of Boston (now the Muslim American Society of Boston) mosque. Aafia Siddiqui, aka "Lady al-Qaeda," who was convicted of trying to murder American soldiers and may also have been plotting a jihad terror attack against an American city, was also a member of that mosque, as were convicted jihad terror plotter Tarek Mehanna and his accomplice, Ahmad Abousamra. The renowned Muslim Brotherhood sheikh Yusuf al-Qaradawi, who has praised Hitler and called upon Muslims to finish the führer's job of putting the Jews "in their place," was a trustee of the Islamic Society of Boston and has addressed the mosque congregation during fundraisers. Another imam who has addressed the Boston congregation, Yasir Qadhi, has called for the replacement of the U.S. Constitution with Islamic law and said that the "life and prosperity" of Christians "holds no value in the state of Jihad."

Making Mosques into Sanctuaries

On June 12, 2013, as the scandal of the Obama administration's massive surveillance of law-abiding Americans was breaking, it was revealed that while the National Security Agency was listening to every phone call and reading every email, there was one place where people could be safe from surveillance: inside a mosque. *Investor's Business Daily* reported that "the government's sweeping surveillance of our most private communications excludes the jihad factories where homegrown terrorists are radicalized.

"Since October 2011, mosques have been off-limits to FBI agents. No more surveillance or undercover string operations without high-level approval from a special oversight body at the Justice Department dubbed the Sensitive Operations Review Committee."

This panel "was set up under pressure from Islamist groups who complained about FBI stings at mosques. Just months before the panel's formation, the Council on American-Islamic Relations teamed up with the ACLU to sue the FBI for allegedly violating the civil rights of Muslims in Los Angeles by hiring an undercover agent to infiltrate and monitor mosques there."

And specifically: "The FBI never canvassed Boston mosques until four days after the April 15 attacks, and it did not check out the radical Boston mosque where the Muslim bombers worshipped."[48]

The day after the *Investor's Business Daily* report, Republican representative Louie Gohmert of Texas confronted FBI director Robert Mueller, saying,

> The FBI never canvassed Boston mosques until four days after the April 15th attacks. If the Russians tell you that someone has been radicalized and you go check and see the mosques that they went to, then you get the articles of incorporation as I have for the group that created the Boston mosque where these Tsarnaevs attended, and you find out the name Alamoudi—which you'll remember because while

you were FBI director, this man who was so helpful to the Clinton administration with so many big things, he gets arrested at Dulles Airport by the FBI and he's now doing over twenty years for supporting terrorism. This is the guy that started the mosque where your Tsarnaevs were attending, and you didn't even bother to go check about the mosque? And then when you have the pictures, why did no one go to the mosque and say, "Who are these guys? They may attend here." Why was that not done, since such a thorough job was done?

Mueller initially disputed Gohmert's assertions, saying, "Your facts are not altogether well—." In a heated exchange, Gohmert shot back, "Sir, if you're going to call me a liar, you need to point out specifically where the facts are wrong."

Mueller responded, "We went to the mosque. Prior to Boston," he said vehemently. "Prior to Boston happening, we were in that mosque talking to imams several months beforehand as part of our outreach efforts."

Gohmert asked, "Were you aware that those mosques were started by Alamoudi?"

"I've answered the question, sir," Mueller replied.

Not satisfied with this, Gohmert pressed, "You didn't answer the question, were you aware that it was started by Alamoudi." Mueller then admitted that he had not been.[49]

So the Federal Bureau of Investigation was warned by at least one foreign government that Tamerlan Tsarnaev was a jihadist. Tamerlan Tsarnaev was attending a Muslim Brotherhood–linked mosque founded by a principal al Qaeda financier. And the FBI sent agents to that mosque—not to investigate Tsarnaev or any other possible jihad activity there, but to engage in "outreach" to Muslims and spend time "talking to imams."

If anything illustrated the Obama administration's abject failure to take the jihad threat seriously, that was it. The only thing that would have completed the picture would have been if Robert Mueller had been holding Dzhokhar Tsarnaev's photo on the cover of *Rolling Stone*.

CHAPTER THREE

WE WUZ FRAMED!

The denial of the reality of Islamic jihad in the United States increasingly takes the form of a claim that jihad plotters are victims of FBI entrapment. Some Muslim spokesmen in the United States have even gone so far as to assert that there is no significant jihad against the United States at all—just the FBI fabricating plots and victimizing young Muslims. It's all the fault, you see, of an "Islamophobic" political culture and an intelligence agency bent on justifying its counterterror budget by manufacturing some terrorists when they can't find any.

The career of one FBI informant has contributed significantly to the impression that the jihadis arrested for plotting acts of violence in the United States were entrapped by agents provocateurs. Craig Monteilh spent a year as a "convert to Islam" named "Farouk al-Aziz," infiltrating mosques in southern California for the FBI but has now repudiated his earlier actions and brought suit against the FBI. Monteilh charges, "The way the FBI conducts their operations, it is all about entrapment … I know the game, I know the dynamics of it. It's such a joke, a real joke. There is no real hunt. It's fixed." He thinks the FBI should apologize for operations like the ones in which he played a part, but, he says, "they don't have the humility to admit a mistake."[1]

The financial stakes are high, as the FBI's critics point out. A 2011 exposé in the Far-Left publication *Mother Jones* asserted, "Ever since 9/11, counterterrorism has been the FBI's No. 1 priority, consuming the lion's share of its budget—$3.3 billion, compared to $2.6 billion for organized crime—and much of the attention of field agents and a massive, nationwide network of informants. After years of emphasizing informant recruiting as a key task for its agents, the bureau now maintains a roster of 15,000 spies—many of them tasked, as Hussain was, with infiltrating Muslim communities in the United States."[2] (Shahed Hussain was an FBI informant whom Islamic jihadist Abdul Rahman, aka James Cromitie, took to be a member of a jihad terror group.)

The primary purpose of this infiltration, according to the *OC Weekly*, was to "create and facilitate fake terrorist plots."[3] Martin Stolar, an attorney for a Muslim accused of plotting a jihad attack at the Herald Square subway station in New York City, is adamant: "The problem with the cases we're talking about is that defendants would not have done anything if not kicked in the ass by government agents. They're creating crimes to solve crimes so they can claim a victory in the war on terror."[4]

Fox Protests against Closure of Henhouse Door

All over the country, Muslim leaders have expressed surprise and outrage that law enforcement agencies would send informants into mosques. In April 2010, Farhana Khera, the executive director of Muslim Advocates, a Muslim legal advocacy organization, added her voice to a growing chorus of Muslim and leftist voices that were claiming that U.S. government sting operations were "entrapment operations" targeting innocent Muslims with no ties to terrorism, in order to fuel "anti-Muslim sentiment" and draw attention away from "actual threats."[5] She accused the FBI of "planting informants" in mosques in the United States, "without evidence of wrongdoing."[6]

Khera even claimed that U.S. officials (whom she did not name) had threatened to deport South Florida cleric Foad Farahi if he refused to "spy on his congregants."[7] But Farahi's case was hardly a good example of FBI harassment of an innocent Muslim with no prior ties to terrorism. Though Khera somehow neglected to mention it, there is evidence that he had associations with several jihad terror suspects: al Qaeda operative José Padilla reportedly worshiped at Farahi's mosque,[8] and Farahi has allegedly told the FBI that he had had contact with al Qaeda jihadist Adnan Shukrijumah,[9] as well as with Imran Mandhai, who was sentenced to prison after pleading guilty to involvement in a jihad plot to bomb a National Guard armory and other targets.[10] On his Facebook page, under "Activities and Interests," Farahi listed at least three Muslim Brotherhood individuals and organizations.[11]

Khera herself did not shy away from association with Muslim Brotherhood–linked groups, such as the Islamic Society of North America. At an ISNA convention in July 2010, she warned Muslim community members about FBI infiltration of mosques, "Sometimes community members don't even think of themselves as a[n] [FBI] source. They might just think [to] themselves, 'Well, I have a good relationship with the head of the FBI office. He comes by my office from time to time and we have tea, or we go to lunch, and he just talks to me about the community.' But what may seem like an innocuous set of conversations in the FBI's mind they may be thinking of you as an informant, as a source. And the repercussions and the harm that that can cause can be pretty serious."[12]

During the same ISNA conference session, Nura Muznavi, a staff attorney at Muslim Advocates, urged the audience not to share information with the FBI: "I said earlier, any information you provide as a community leader to the FBI can be the basis for further surveillance and investigation of your community. So you really don't want to be putting yourself in a situation where you're providing anybody with information about people in your community that the FBI now is gonna follow up and start investigating those people."[13]

Why Would Anyone Want to Conduct Surveillance inside a Mosque?

Khera's Muslim Advocates group not only advises Muslims not to speak with law enforcement; the organization has also complained in a press release that a Senate Homeland Security and Government Affairs Committee report "falsely characterized Muslims in America as susceptible to 'radicalization.'"[14]

Many American Muslims take the position that there is really no necessity to look for possible terrorists in their community. After a local convert to Islam had been exposed as an FBI informant, Dr. Hamed Baig, president of the Islamic Center of Des Moines, Iowa, said in 2012, "That was really surprising, very sad that somebody would come or the FBI or Homeland Security would send somebody here to pretend to be Muslim and try to find out what goes on here. I feel there is no need for that."

Anis Rehman, the mosque's executive board treasurer, was angry: "When we saw that he was not actually a member but a pretender then it made me more angry. I find that to send an impostor into our community which is so small where not only we know each other but (where) the law enforcement agents can perhaps pick each one of us by name and by family, I don't think that the incident [on] 9/11 could warrant such action in a small community like ours."

Another local Muslim, Basim Bakri, declared, "I think the FBI owe[s] us an apology because they did violate our civil rights. It wasn't right at all, it wasn't right from the beginning and they have no right to do that."[15]

The Council on American-Islamic Relations (CAIR) reacted strongly to the revelations about Monteilh and other mosque informants: "Law-abiding Muslims at mainstream mosques and Islamic centers are being incited and entrapped by former criminals with questionable characters.... The American Muslim community has never waivered [sic] from its commitment to keeping America safe, nor has it hesitated from cooperating with various law enforcement agencies, including the FBI, in ensuring the security of all U.S. citizens."[16]

Snitches Get Stitches

In reality, however, CAIR itself, while it poses as a civil rights organization for Muslims—in the words of its spokesman Ibrahim Hooper, "a Muslim NAACP"—has not exhorted Muslims in the United States to cooperate freely and fully with law enforcement, but often just the opposite.[17] In January 2011, it came to light that a CAIR chapter in California had circulated a poster reading "Build a Wall of Resistance" and "Don't Talk to the FBI."[18] Cyrus McGoldrick, a former official of CAIR's New York chapter, even threatened informants, tweeting with brutal succinctness, "Snitches get stitches." Zahra Billoo of CAIR-San Francisco regularly tweets that Muslims have no obligation to talk to the FBI and should contact CAIR if the FBI asks to talk to them.[19]

Worst of all, when federal investigators began looking into the disappearances of Somali Muslim men in Minnesota, and it turned out that they had returned to Somalia to wage jihad with the al Qaeda–linked group Al-Shabaab, Muslims who opposed this jihad accused CAIR of hindering the investigation and trying to prevent from them speaking with law enforcement officials.

In June 2009, a Somali Muslim named Abdirizak Bihi, whose nephew, Burhan Hassan, was killed in Somalia, held a protest against CAIR in Minneapolis, denouncing it for encouraging Muslims not to speak with the FBI. "We don't want anyone to come into our community and tell us to shut up," said Bihi. "Law enforcement will not be able to do anything without information from the community." Protesters chanted, "CAIR out! Doublespeak out!" Another protester, Osman Ahmed, said he and other relatives of Burhan Hassan thought CAIR, for all its claims of moderation, was actually on the side of the jihadists: "They are supporting the groups we suspect of recruiting our kids. We refuse to be silent."[20]

Bihi later told the House Committee on Homeland Security that "CAIR held meetings for some members of the community and told them not to talk to the FBI, which was a slap in the face for the Somali American Muslim mothers who were knocking on doors day and night with pictures of their missing children and asking for the community to talk to law enforcement about what they know of the missing kids."[21]

CAIR's interference bore bitter fruit in September 2013, when Al-Shabaab jihadists, including several Muslims from the United States, stormed an upscale mall in Nairobi and murdered upwards of seventy people after freeing the Muslims and declaring that they only wanted to kill non-Muslims. In a case of spectacularly poor timing, just two days before the massacre CAIR had released a report on "Islamophobia" entitled *Legislating Fear: Islamophobia and its Impact in the United States*, in which it harshly criticized Republican representative Peter King of New York for holding a series of hearings on Muslim radicalization in the United States, including one on Al-Shabaab recruitment in America. "In his opening statement for the hearing," the CAIR report said, "King cited an incident in Minneapolis, saying, 'When one cleric spoke out against Al-Shabaab inside the Minneapolis mosque where many of the missing young Somali-American men had once worshiped, he was physically assaulted, according to police.' This statement is noteworthy as it continued King's line of factually inaccurate attacks on the Muslim community." The report complained that King had painted Somali Muslims in Minneapolis as uncooperative with investigators, when really, "law enforcement officials had indicated a Somali community in Minnesota that was concerned and helpful"—an ironic claim, given how the truly "concerned and helpful" Somali Muslims in Minnesota such as Abdirizak Bihi had protested against CAIR for trying to stop the Muslim community at large from cooperating with the FBI.[22]

Bihi lamented after the Kenya mall jihad murders, "I tried to warn America." CAIR had worked hard to stop him, even branding him an "Islamophobe" in their "Islamophobia" report released two days before the massacre. Bihi explains CAIR's tactics against American Muslims who oppose them, "They say that I am a bad person, that I am anti-Muslim, and that I don't represent a hundred percent the Somali community. They lie about my life most of the time and try to destroy my character, my capability, and my trust in the community."[23]

Closing Ranks

The uncooperative attitude toward law enforcement is not confined to CAIR. Even the Islamic Society of Boston closed ranks after two of its members murdered two people and wounded and maimed 260 with a jihad attack at the Boston Marathon. On April 22, 2013, a week after the bombings, the mosque sent an email advising its members to lawyer up: "We have been informed that the FBI may be starting to question some of the community members about the two suspects. Insha'Allah [Allah willing] we want to help as much as we can, but of course not put ourselves at risk either. Seeking representation does not imply any guilt on your part but is simply a way of protecting your own rights. Please do not hesitate to use the information listed below or contact the ISB Cambridge Mosque for any other resources." Instead of telling members to cooperate fully with law enforcement investigating the terrorism for which their fellow members were responsible, the email gave contact numbers for the ACLU.[24] Why did mosque authorities assume mosque members would need legal representation? Wouldn't innocent citizens ordinarily be eager to help the authorities in their investigation of a horrific act of terrorism?

All this made Barack Obama's prescription for ending jihad terrorism appear bitterly ironic. Just a few weeks after the Boston bombing, on May 23, 2013, in a major speech on terror-related issues, the president said, "The best way to prevent violent extremism is to work with the Muslim American community—which has consistently rejected terrorism—to identify signs of radicalization, and partner with law enforcement when an individual is drifting towards violence."[25]

In fact, as we have seen, mosques and prominent national Muslim groups were coaching the Muslim-American community precisely on how not to partner with law enforcement and not to identify those Muslims who were becoming likely to engage in violence. Consider Muslims Advocates' labeling the very notion of "Muslims in America as susceptible to 'radicalization'" as a false characterization. Even the Muslim Public Affairs Council (MPAC), which is generally less aggressive than Muslim Advocates and CAIR and has even called on mosques to "have a relationship that involves public meetings with the FBI's regional office and local law enforcement" and recommended arrangement of programs "in cooperation with local law enforcement agencies to educate and train the community on how to really detect criminal activities,[26] assures Muslims that they are not asking them to "'spy' on each other": "Absolutely not. The thought is anathema to our purpose as an organization."[27] But if Muslims are not to be looking at what others in the mosque are doing, they will never be able to spot or report terror plotting. Faced with this level of cooperation, it's easy to see why the FBI has opted to use informants inside mosques rather than rely on what the Muslim community, advised by leaders like these, would choose to tell them.

MPAC seems to view partnership with law enforcement more as a way to disabuse the authorities of their assumptions about Islam, and convince them that Muslims have no more proclivity to commit terrorist acts than any other group, than to help the FBI identify terrorists before they kill people: "Engagement of local law enforcement and local FBI field offices is absolutely critical in protecting our civil liberties. It counters the basic human weakness to make assumptions about a person/community which they have never been in contact with before." But what if there are real jihadis in one's local mosque?

Innocent People Don't Plot Jihad Terror Attacks

Perhaps Monteilh and other infiltrators and informants were overzealous, even unethical. If so, they themselves deserve to be prosecuted. Nevertheless, the alleged victims now crying entrapment did agree to participate in plots involving the mass murder of Americans. Peter Ahearn, a retired FBI special agent, explains, "If you're doing a sting right, you're offering the target multiple chances to back out. Real people don't say, 'Yeah, let's go bomb that place.' Real people call the cops."[28]

That's the rub. While there may have been some abuses in the FBI infiltration programs (as there are in all human endeavors), if someone agrees to set off a bomb in the cause of jihad at the behest of an FBI undercover agent, there is no guarantee that he wouldn't agree to set one off prompted by a genuine jihadist. The leftist journalists and Islamic advocates who have decried what they see as FBI entrapment have never explained, or even attempted to explain, why it is that there are people so willing and even eager to commit acts of violence in the name of Islam that they allow themselves to be ensnared in these plots.

Despite what Farhana Khera's and Muslim Advocates group pretends, there is abundant evidence that Muslims in America can be susceptible to "radicalization," as can be seen from jihad terror plots Muslims in the United States have mounted in recent years, including those of Naser Abdo, the former U.S. Army enlistee who attempted a second terror attack at Fort Hood; Khalid Aldawsari, who plotted a terror attack in Lubbock, Texas; Amine Mohamed el-Khalifi, who planned a suicide bombing at the U.S. Capitol; Muhammad Hussain, who plotted terror attacks against high-profile targets in Baltimore; Abdulhakim Mujahid Muhammad, who murdered a U.S. soldier outside an Arkansas military recruiting station; Faisal Shahzad, who attempted a car bombing in Times Square; and many others.

Eager to Kill

Even from the leftist exposés decrying entrapment, it's clear that the supposed victims were eager to do violence against non-Muslims in the name of Islam. The initial *Mother Jones* piece about FBI informants, which author Trevor Aaronson later expanded into a book, *The Terror Factory*, opens with a convert to Islam, James Cromitie (who changed his name to Abdul Rahman upon his conversion to Islam), thundering that "the worst brother in the whole Islamic world is better than 10 billion Yahudi [Jews]."

And Rahman was ready to act upon his hatred. He told a man who he thought was a member of an Islamic jihad group but who was actually an FBI informant that he wanted to "do something to America" and was planning to bomb a bridge.[29] When told that bridges were undesirable targets because they were made of steel and thus hard to destroy, Rahman responded, "Of course they're made of steel. But the same way they can be put up, they can be brought down." But ultimately he settled on a plot to bomb several New York synagogues and fire Stinger missiles at airplanes.

The trial judge believed that Rahman and his co-defendants had been entrapped: "The government made them terrorists. I am not proud of my government for what it did in this case."[30]

Would Rahman have embarked on this plot without the informant? That is arguable. It's obvious, however, that if the informant had never come into his life, Rahman would still not have been a peaceful, law-abiding American citizen, free of the seething hatreds that Islamic jihadists and supremacists find exhorted and justified in the Qur'an. And so appeals court judge Jon O. Newman, referring to Rahman's statements about wanting to bomb a police car, "hit the bridge," and "get a synagogue," concluded, "From everything that Cromitie said, the jury was entitled to find that he had a pre-existing 'design' and hence a predisposition to inflict serious harm on interests of the United States, even though government officers afforded him the opportunity and the pseudo weapons for striking at specific targets."[31]

Likewise, Quazi Mohammad Nafis, whom Aaronson profiled in a January 2013 follow-up piece. Nafis, he says, was "a 21-year-old student living in Queens, New York, when the U.S. government helped turn him into a terrorist."[32]

Even by Aaronson's account, it couldn't have been all that hard. Nafis, says Aaronson, told an FBI informant that "he wanted to wage jihad in the United States, that he enjoyed reading Al-Qaeda propaganda, and that he admired 'Sheikh O,' or Osama bin Laden." He later told another informant, who he thought was an al Qaeda member, that he was "ready for action," and that "what I really mean is that I don't want something that's, like, small. I just want something big. Something very big. Very, very, very, very big, that will shake the whole country."[33]

Nafis embarked upon a plot to bomb the New York Stock Exchange and later changed the target to the Federal Reserve Bank in New York City. Eventually he was arrested after trying to detonate what he thought was a thousand-pound bomb in front of the Federal Reserve Bank— which he wanted to do, he said, "for the Muslims," to "make us one step closer to run the whole world."[34]

Almost immediately after his arrest, however, Islamic supremacists claimed that Nafis was a victim of entrapment. Former CAIR official Cyrus McGoldrick tweeted, "FBI leads idiot in an #entrapment case. Thank God we give them so much money to manufacture crimes." And CNN journalist Mona Eltahawy claimed, "We've seen many other entrapments here in U.S."[35]

The same claim has been made in connection with numerous other jihad cases in the United States, including that of Mohamed Mohamud, a Muslim in Portland, Oregon, who tried to murder those who had gathered for the city's Christmas tree–lighting ceremony. Mohamud's case is similar to Nafis's, in that both involved Islamic jihadist attempts to explode bombs that they did not know were harmless decoys supplied to them by FBI agents, rather than the real thing. Islamic advocacy groups such as the Hamas-linked CAIR have taken up the claim of Aaronson and others that the jihad plots thereby thwarted would never even have existed in the first place if undercover agents hadn't started meddling.

Yet Nafis himself said that he had come to the United States from Bangladesh to engage in jihad activity; his goal was to "destroy America." Blowing up the Federal Reserve Bank was not something he had to be enticed into doing.

Nafis at one point told an FBI informant, "We are going to need a lot of TNT or dynamite."[36] Aaronson complains that Nafis didn't know where to get explosives, and that the FBI was helping his plot go farther than it ever would have without the agency's participation; how he can be certain that Nafis never would have figured out how to get explosives any other way is left unexplained. Both Nafis and Mohamud were willing to do whatever was necessary to enable them to murder large numbers of Americans. We should count ourselves fortunate that they were supplied with fake bombs by the FBI before either other jihadis or their own ingenuity armed them with real ones.

"We Are Going to Put Bullets in Their Heads, Allah Willing"

Leftists and Muslims have also claimed that the Fort Dix plot was another entrapment case. "In the case of the Fort Dix Five," writes Paul

Harris in the UK's *Guardian*, "which involved a fake plan to attack a New Jersey military base, one informant's criminal past included attempted murder, while another admitted in court at least two of the suspects later jailed for life had not known of any plot." Harris doesn't explain how these apparently rogue convictions were obtained. Meanwhile, Mohamed Younes, president of the American Muslim Union, offered another theory: "I don't think they actually mean to do anything. I think they were acting stupid, like they thought the whole thing was a joke. They don't look like the type of people to do something like this."[37]

The reporter who took down these remarks missed the opportunity to follow this up by asking Younes exactly what "the type of people to do something like this" actually do look like. Would a Muslim leader in the United States engage in the "racial profiling" that Islamic advocates constantly complain is being used against them?

Others pushed the entrapment theme as well. Faten Shnewer, Fort Dix plotter Mohamad Shnewer's mother, said of the verdict, "It's not right, it's not justice." Why not? Because the government "sent somebody to push him to say something; that's it."[38] Jim Sues of CAIR's New Jersey chapter echoed Faten Shnewer's lament: "Many people in the Muslim community will see this as a case of entrapment. From what I saw, there was a significant role played by the government informant."[39]

But what the government may have pushed Mohamed Shnewer into saying was hardly benign and belied Younes's claim that the whole thing was a joke. When he showed a fellow plotter, who turned out to be a government informant, some DVD files featuring Osama bin Laden calling Muslims to wage jihad warfare and containing the last will and testaments of some of the 9/11 hijackers, Shnewer said of American soldiers at Fort Dix, "They are the ones, we are going to put bullets in their heads, Allah willing."[40] One of the other plotters, Serdar Tatar, added, "I'm gonna do it.... It doesn't matter to me, whether I get locked up, arrested, or get taken away, it doesn't matter. Or I die, doesn't matter, I'm doing it in the name of Allah."[41]

Entrapment?

"A Gentle, Misguided, Autistic Teenager"

Similarly farfetched was the entrapment claim in the case of another accused jihadist, a convert to Islam known (at least among non-Muslims) as Justin Kaliebe. The eighteen-year-old from Long Island pled guilty in early 2013 to trying to join Ansar al-Sharia (Partisans of Islamic Law), a Yemeni group affiliated with al Qaeda. He faced a thirty-year prison sentence.[42]

Kaliebe's lawyer Anthony LaPinta, however, urged leniency. "Justin Kaliebe," LaPinta insisted, "is a gentle, misguided, autistic teenager who does not have the ability to fully understand the magnitude and consequences of his actions." In other words, in the immortal words of the "Officer Krupke" song from *West Side Story*, he was depraved on account he was deprived.

According to Bilal Hito, who attended the same mosque Kaliebe frequented in Bay Shore, Long Island, Kaliebe's parents divorced when he was just three or four years old. A news report identified Kaliebe as hailing from "Babylon and Bay Shore, N.Y.," intimating a dreary home life shuttling back and forth between parents engaged in a polite cold war.[43] Hito said, "There was something about Justin that made you feel you were around a little boy. Mentally he was very young. He was more like a kid brother."[44]

Kaliebe's friend Ahmad Deib, who also knew Kaliebe from the Bay Shore mosque, vehemently dismissed the jihad terror charges against Kaliebe. "That, to me, is a bunch of garbage. This is a case of entrapment. This kid, he couldn't hurt a fly. He is one of the most kindhearted kids you would ever know."[45]

As gentle and autistic, mentally young, and kindhearted as he may have been, Kaliebe seemed to be fully aware of what he was doing. Undercover officers caught him pledging allegiance to al Qaeda and jihad leaders: "I pledge my loyalty, allegiance and fidelity to the Mujahedeen of Al-Qaa'idah in the Arabian Peninsula and its leaders, Shaykh Abu Baseer Nasir Al-Wuhayshi and Shaykh Ayman Al-Zawahiri, hafidhahum Allah [may Allah protect them]! May Allah accept this from me and may he allow me to fight in his cause til the day that I leave this dunya [world]."[46]

Far from being a simple soul, Kaliebe was aware that he might be dealing with undercover agents, asking for assurances that the man he thought was an al Qaeda operative was not going to "rat him out" and assuring him in turn that he wanted to wage jihad "for the sake of Allah."[47] He spoke about "the crime that they would charge people like us with," which involved plotting "to kill, maim and kidnap in foreign countries."[48]

Nonetheless, he wanted to charge ahead, declaring, "There is no way out for me.... The only way out is martyrdom."[49] When asked if he wanted to die, he said, "I wanna ... it's what anyone would want, any believer would want."[50] He was aware that he was going to be waging hot warfare against "those who are fighting against the Sharia of Allah ... whether it's the U.S. drones or the, their puppets, in the Yemeni army ... or, who knows, if American agents or whatever, U.S. Special Forces ... who they got over there."[51]

Was this hatred of his own country and desire to fight and die for Islam really a product of divorce and autism? Millions of children grow up in broken homes, and millions are autistic, and yet they don't take the path Justin Kaliebe chose. Was he really entrapped? He went ahead enthusiastically. Law enforcement agents cannot justly be held accountable for his choices.

Depraved on Account They're Deprived

More than twelve years after 9/11, we have yet to see a sincere and effective effort within mosques to expose and report those who hold to the beliefs that led to those attacks—including at Justin Kaliebe's Bay Shore mosque, where investigators should (in a sane world) have investigated what he was taught that led him to embark upon his jihad path. Instead, we got the "Officer Krupke" defense. But Justin Kaliebe wasn't depraved on account he's deprived. He was depraved because he was indoctrinated into a violent, supremacist ideology.

No one wants to face the implications of that.

American Muslim advocacy groups have turned the allegations that the FBI is creating these crimes in order to solve them into demands that law enforcement agencies stop sending informants into mosques altogether, end surveillance of Muslim communities, and stop profiling Muslims—which they aren't really doing in the first place. Muslims have successfully shifted the onus from their own communities to law enforcement, so that officials take it for granted that it is their responsibility to "build trust" with Muslims, not Muslim communities' responsibility to demonstrate (not just enunciate) their opposition to jihad terror Islamic supremacism.

Islamophobia and the New York Subway Jihad Plot

They have changed the subject to the supposed profiling of Muslims even in the context of jihad mass murder plots. In September 2009, Najibullah Zazi, Adis Medunjanin, and Zarein Ahmedzay, three Muslims who had trained in an al Qaeda camp in Pakistan, hatched a plot to build bombs and plant them in New York City subways.[52] The New York Police Department conducted a series of raids of Muslim homes in Queens, looking for evidence about the plot—whereupon in October 2009, Muslims demonstrated outside the Flushing Public Library, denouncing what they claimed was racial profiling. "I was so scared and I was so nervous," said Naiz Khan, one young man whose apartment was searched by FBI agents. "I have been so affected by this."

The FBI search was understandable, as Khan had let Najibullah Zazi stay in his apartment; yet Khan still assumed the role of the victim, claiming he had been unable to find work since the incident. Monami Maulik of a South Asian immigrant advocacy group, Desis Rising Up and Moving, declared, "An entire community of people and religion should not be profiled or characterized as terrorists because of [one] certain investigation." Sultan Faiz, a local mosque official, added, "People are scared."[53]

Bizarrely, they seem more scared by the investigation of terrorist plots than by the plots themselves. Zazi's plot was real: ultimately he and Ahmedzay pled guilty to terror charges. Medunjanin pled not guilty but was found guilty and sentenced to life imprisonment.[54] Rather than complaining about profiling, local Muslims might have been expected to cooperate with law enforcement, anxious to root bad elements out of their community. Instead, they assumed the stance that all investigation of their community was unjustified and was hurting the good relations between Muslims and law enforcement—a relationship that hadn't been much use in ferreting out the plot in the first place or even the securing the authorities much cooperation with the investigation after the fact. Good relations between Muslims and law enforcement were only invoked to complain about investigations.

Hence CAIR's complaint when it was revealed that the FBI had sent informants into mosques in Los Angeles and San Diego: "The use of an informant to infiltrate mosques in southern California, has re-ignited feelings of anger, disillusionment and mistrust among American Muslims toward the FBI."[55]

Anger and Distrust

Leftist academics have eagerly taken up this point of view. New York University's Center for Human Rights and Global Justice issued a report early in 2012: *Targeted and Entrapped: Manufacturing the "Homegrown Threat,"* claiming that the FBI and New York Police Department were violating the civil rights of Muslims by sending informants into mosques and Muslim communities.

A particularly piquant example of this strangely selective indignation came from James Yee, a former Muslim chaplain for the U.S. military and an Obama delegate to the 2008 Democratic National Convention, in the wake of the Fort Dix verdicts. Yee expressed sorrow over the verdicts not because of the potential loss of life at Fort Dix, but because the convictions would anger Muslims in the United States. "All of this doesn't help build trust with the American Muslim community," he complained, "and that is vital if our law enforcement is going to fight terrorism. If anyone can improve security, it's our community, but we need to be seen as trusted partners, not potential suspects."

Yee had managed to become a Democratic convention delegate even though he had been investigated in 2004 for mishandling classified material at Guantanamo. The charges were dismissed in March 2004, but Yee was not exactly cleared. The AP reported that "in dismissing the charges, Maj. Gen. Geoffrey D. Miller, commander of Joint Task Force Guantanamo, which operates the detention center, cited 'national security concerns that would arise from the release of the evidence' if the case proceeded." Not a resounding affirmation of Yee's innocence.

But that didn't appear to matter to Democratic Party leaders. Politicians have generally been more concerned with courting Muslim communities for votes and joining their calls for an end to surveillance and infiltration programs than with protecting Americans from future jihad attacks. At an October 2011 hearing about the New York Police Department's counterterror activities in Muslim areas, New York City councilman Brad Lander asserted, "It looks like we are targeting Muslim neighborhoods and communities. That's not good for us. We have people out there who are partners who feel the trust is betrayed."[56]

New York police commissioner Raymond Kelly defended the NYPD programs, saying, "What we're doing is following leads."[57] Judging from the statements of the supposed victims of entrapment above, the leads were worth following.

Becoming an Orwellian surveillance state in order to protect Americans from terrorism would be a cure worse than the disease. Certainly all surveillance and infiltration programs must be subject to strict oversight and close examination to ensure they do not transgress Constitutional bounds. Still, the increasingly common charges of entrapment should be seen for what they are: yet another attempt to divert attention from the ugly reality of Islamic jihad activity in the U.S. and around the world and to place the responsibility for jihadist misdeeds upon non-Muslims—in particular, the very ones who are trying to thwart the jihadists' plans.

After 9/11, we were assured again and again that the vast majority of Muslims in the United States and worldwide were peaceful and sincerely condemned such violence perpetrated in the name of their religion. Yet over twelve years later, we still have yet to see a sincere and effective effort within mosques to expose and report those who hold to the beliefs that led to those attacks.

Instead, we get more finger-pointing. And that means we will also get more jihad.

CHAPTER FOUR

THE JIHAD AGAINST COUNTERTERRORISM

uslim groups and their leftist allies didn't just complain about entrapment and surveillance; they took their battle to the courts.

In February 2011, the Council on American-Islamic Relations (CAIR) joined forces with the American Civil Liberties Union (ACLU) in a suit against the FBI over the activities of Craig Monteilh as an informant in mosques. The suit claimed that Monteilh—and hence the FBI—had violated the First Amendment rights of the Muslims in those mosques with his "indiscriminate surveillance" of "people who were more devout in their religious practice, irrespective of whether any particular individual was believed to be involved in criminal activity."[1]

Although virtually all Islamic jihadists are, in fact, devout in their Islamic faith and practice, CAIR and other Islamic groups have been working strenuously since 9/11 to obscure this connection and to tar

49

as "Islamophobic" anyone who dares to note its existence. The suit takes particular umbrage at Monteilh's efforts to engage the more devout Muslims in the mosques he frequented in discussions of jihad and warfare. CAIR's national spokesman, Ibrahim Hooper, branded Monteilh an "agent provocateur," pointing out that "he was the one suggesting all these kinds of bizarre activities to the extent that community itself turned him in."[2] This was true: the Muslim community in Orange County, California, actually contacted the FBI about Monteilh, not realizing that he was an FBI informant.[3]

Hooper and other CAIR officials, unwilling to see Monteilh as one out-of-control operative in an otherwise sound program, complained that all such surveillance only alienated law-abiding Muslims. "When Muslims perceive that they are viewed as a suspect community by law enforcement or the FBI," Hooper explained, "it really has a devastating effect on relations between law enforcement authorities and American Muslims."

CAIR took aim at other counterterror efforts as well. In April 2012, the organization filed another suit, this time against the federal government, claiming that the feds had violated the First Amendment rights of Muslims in Michigan by subjecting them to excessive questioning at the Canadian border. Here again, they were offended by officials' apparent assumption that devout observance of Islam could be an indicator of involvement in jihad terror activity. CAIR asserted that Muslims attempting to cross the border were asked questions such as "How many times a day to you pray?," "Do you pray your morning prayer in the mosque?," and "Who else prays in your mosque?"[4]

CAIR-Michigan's Dawud Walid suggested that his indignation over all this stemmed from his concern that law enforcement officials weren't making the best possible use of their time and budget: "Invasive religious questioning of American citizens without evidence of criminal activity is not only an affront to the Constitution, but is also a waste of limited resources."[5]

Then in June 2013, the ACLU joined the New York Civil Liberties Union and City University of New York (CUNY) Law School's Creating Law Enforcement Accountability (CLEAR) project to sue the NYPD for profiling Muslims and conducting unwarranted surveillance of Muslims in the New York area.

Ace Dandia's Frightening Houseguest

One of the victims of this profiling, and plaintiffs in the lawsuit, was a Muslim college student named Asad "Ace" Dandia, who was befriended by another student, Shamiur Rahman—who turned out to be an informant. After Dandia discovered that Rahman was working for the NYPD, Dandia recalled that he had once invited Rahman to spend a night at his home, and the informant had accepted. "I was terrified and I was afraid for my family," said Dandia, "especially for my younger sister. I felt betrayed and hurt because someone who I took as a friend and a brother was lying to me."

Dandia asked a crowd outside NYPD headquarters after the suit was filed, "How would you react if you found out that someone who spent a night in your house was an informant for the police department? I was shocked that the police who were supposed to protect and serve me were spying on me, although I did nothing wrong."[6]

Scared to Preach the Word

Another plaintiff in the case, a Brooklyn imam named Hamid Hassan Raza, complained, "I have for years, taped the sermons I give because I am afraid an NYPD officer or an informant will misquote me or take a portion of a sermon out of context. I stopped mentioning in my sermons, or even as I counsel worshippers, current affairs or religious subjects that I fear the NYPD might object to." He said that he had avoided discussing the Boston Marathon jihad bombings for this reason. "I never know what the NYPD might question and I don't want to subject myself or my community to further police scrutiny or worse," he said. "Because of NYPD spying, I'm not able to fulfill my duty as an Imam. I'm constantly falling short of my obligations to my congregation."[7]

These are curious statements. What did the imam want to say about the Boston bombings that he couldn't say? It is hard to see how a full and unequivocal condemnation of those bombings would have aroused any suspicion at the NYPD.

Hina Shamsi of the ACLU's National Security Project sounded the same notes, of loss of trust and indignation that Muslim religious practice would be a cause for suspicion, that so many Muslim leaders had sounded before her: "The NYPD has betrayed the expectations and violated the rights of New York's Muslims and it has betrayed, also, the expectations of all New Yorkers.... Since 2002, the NYPD has carried out a policy and practice based on the false and unconstitutional premise that Muslim religious belief and practices are a basis for law-enforcement scrutiny. That is a premise rooted in bias and ignorance, not good law enforcement or fact."[8]

It's hard to see how any real harm was done in these cases. What exactly were the plaintiffs worried about, if they weren't doing anything wrong? Dandia may understandably be dismayed to find that someone he thought was his friend was anything but, yet he had no reason to be worried "especially" for his younger sister or anyone else. Assuming Dandia couldn't be persuaded to push down a detonator for a bomb planted in a crowd of infidels, Shamiur Rahman would pass in and out of his life with little note.

And if Raza hadn't planned on praising the Boston bombers as glorious mujahedin, why did he have need to worry about what the NYPD might think? It would seem a hard sell for him to convince a court that taping his sermons was a hardship—many preachers of all faiths sell taped copies of their sermons, and Raza's congregation may ultimately appreciate the service, whatever its origins.

Abundant Reason to Send In Informants

The NYPD, the FBI, and other law enforcement agencies have abundant reason to send informants into mosques and conduct surveillance of Muslims. Four separate studies conducted independently of one another since 1998 have all found that 80 percent of U.S. mosques were teaching jihad, Islamic supremacism, and hatred and contempt for Jews and Christians. There are no countervailing studies that challenge these results. In 1998, Sheikh Muhammad Hisham Kabbani, a Sufi leader, visited 114 mosques in the United States. Then he testified before a State Department open forum in January 1999 that 80 percent of American mosques taught the "extremist ideology."[9]

Confirming this same percentage were the Center for Religious Freedom's 2005 study of material taught in mosques in Los Angeles, Oakland, Dallas, Houston, Chicago, Washington, and New York, and the Mapping Sharia Project's 2008 study.[10] Each separately showed that between 75 and 80 percent of mosques in America were preaching hatred of Jews and Christians and the necessity ultimately to impose Islamic rule. And in the summer of 2011 came another study showing that only 19 percent of mosques in the United States *don't* teach jihad violence and/or Islamic supremacism.[11]

A Good Imam Is Hard to Find

Thus the Islamic Society of Boston is not remotely the only mosque in the United States with questionable ties to jihadists and Islamic supremacists. Another notorious U.S. mosque is the Dar Al-Hijrah Islamic Center in Fairfax County, Virginia, which has had a string of unsavory imams. Mohammed al-Hanooti, the mosque's imam from 1995 to 1999, was named an unindicted co-conspirator in the 1993 World Trade Center bombing. Then, in 2001 and 2002, the mosque's imam was none other than Anwar al-Awlaki, who later became a notorious al Qaeda operative and one of the most wanted men in the world—until he was ultimately killed by a U.S. drone strike in Yemen on September 30, 2011.

Al-Awlaki was targeted because of his extensive contacts with numerous jihadis who committed mass murders of Americans, including three of the 9/11 hijackers and Fort Hood jihadi Nidal Malik Hasan, who had also attended the Dar Al-Hijrah mosque. Al-Awlaki was also in contact with Umar Farouk Abdulmutallab, who tried to blow up an airliner over Detroit with a bomb hidden in his underwear on Christmas Day 2009. These actions are not inconsistent with the teachings al-Awlaki imparted as imam. Among other things, he said, "The hatred of kuffar [unbelievers] is a central element of our military creed."

Shaker Elsayed, Dar Al-Hijrah's current imam, took over in 2005. He has also served as secretary general of the Muslim American Society, a Muslim Brotherhood group. Johari Abdul-Malik, the mosque's director of outreach since 2002, has publicly defended the Islamic Society of Boston's founder, Abdulrahman Alamoudi, now in prison for financing al Qaeda. Ahmed Omar Abu Ali taught Islamic studies at Dar Al-Hijrah and also served as a camp counselor; he is now in prison for plotting to assassinate then president George W. Bush. Abdelhaleem Hasan Abdelraziq Ashqar, a member of the mosque's executive committee, is now serving an eleven-year prison sentence for contempt and obstruction of justice for refusing to testify regarding the jihad terror group Hamas.

Yet another mosque that should cause concern for Americans is Columbus, Ohio's, Noor Mosque. Its leader, Dr. Hany Saqr, previously served as the imam of another Columbus-area mosque that was at the time the headquarters of the largest known al Qaeda cell in the United States since the 9/11 attacks. Its members included three convicted Islamic jihad terrorists: Iyman Faris, Nuradin Abdi, and Christopher Paul. Saqr is also one of the leaders of the Muslim Brotherhood in North America.[12]

Active at the Noor Mosque for several years, until he moved to Bahrain in 2007, was Dr. Salah Sultan. A protégé of Sheikh Qaradawi, the internationally renowned Muslim Brotherhood spiritual leader and popular Al Jazeera TV preacher, Sultan has appeared on Egyptian television approvingly quoting the notorious hadith, or tradition of Muhammad, about how the end times will not come until Muslims kill Jews, and the Jews will hide behind trees that will then call out to the Muslims, "O Muslim! A Jew is hiding behind me, come and kill him." Sultan has also appeared at events in support of Hamas. The Noor Mosque has been directly linked to the Somali Muslims who have traveled from the United States back to Somalia for training with the al Qaeda–linked group Al-Shabaab, perpetrators of the Kenya mall jihad massacre on September 23, 2013.[13] The popular American imam Siraj Wahhaj, a friend of the "Blind Sheikh" Omar Abdel Rahman and himself named a potential unindicted co-conspirator in the 1993 World Trade Center bombing, has spoken at the Noor Mosque. Mosque members threatened the life of Rifqa Bary, a teenage girl who left Islam for Christianity and became the center of a heated custody case in 2009.

Islam Made Them Do It

At the time of the Boston bombings, some commentators said that it was the first jihad attack on U.S. soil since September 11, 2001. Even aside from the Fort Hood massacre, however, this was not true. There have been a good many jihad plots in the United States over the last few years. Many of these were not reported as jihad or classified by law enforcement as having anything to do with Islam and jihad, even when it was painfully obvious that the motivation of the perpetrators was substantially the same as that which moved the 9/11 plotters or Nidal Hasan.

The 9/11 plotters avowed their Islamic motivations proudly. Khalid Sheikh Mohammed and his fellow defendants facing charges of having masterminded the 9/11 attacks issued a statement in 2009 that explicitly grounded their actions in Islamic religious terms: the very motive that neither the media nor the government showed any inclination of wanting to acknowledge or examine. The statement was even entitled "The Islamic Response to the Government's Nine Accusations."

"Many thanks to God," they wrote about the attacks, "for his kind gesture, and choosing us to perform the act of Jihad for his cause and to defend Islam and Muslims. Therefore, killing you and fighting you, destroying you and terrorizing you, responding back to your attacks, are all considered to be great legitimate duty in our religion. These actions are our offerings to God. In addition, it is the imposed reality on Muslims in Palestine, Lebanon, Afghanistan, Iraq, in the land of the two holy sites [Mecca and Medina, Saudi Arabia], and in the rest of the world, where Muslims are suffering from your brutality, terrorism, killing of the innocent, and occupying their lands and their holy sites. Nevertheless, it would have been the greatest religious duty to fight you over your infidelity. However, today, we fight you over defending Muslims, their land, their holy sites, and their religion as a whole [emphasis added]."[14]

Their statement that "it would have been the greatest religious duty to fight you over your infidelity," in contrast to fighting the United States because of its alleged atrocities against Muslims, reflects a key distinction in Islamic theology. Ordinarily, jihad warfare is *fard kifaya*, an obligation of the community as a whole but not of every individual believer. However, jihad becomes *fard ayn*, obligatory on every individual Muslim to aid in some way, when a Muslim land is attacked.

In "The Islamic Response," the defendants were saying that they were waging a defensive jihad against the United States because of its supposed misdeeds in "Palestine, Lebanon, Afghanistan, Iraq, in the land of the two holy sites, and in the rest of the world, where Muslims are suffering from your brutality," but that it would have been an even greater thing to wage an offensive jihad against the United States solely because it was a non-Muslim government, for that would have been something they took on voluntarily and not as a matter of fulfilling a religious requirement.

Other jihad plotters, including many who have plotted attacks inside the United States or against U.S. interests, have made similar statements over the years, explicitly tying Islam to violence in a way that Islamic organizations and even some in the media generally claim is only done by "Islamophobes." In January 2007, Taliban jihad leader Baitullah Mehsud declared that "Allah on 480 occasions in the Holy Koran extols Muslims to wage jihad. We only fulfill God's orders. Only jihad can bring peace to the world. We will continue our struggle until foreign troops are thrown out. Then we will attack them in the U.S. and Britain until they either accept Islam or agree to pay jazia."[15]

"Jazia," or jizya, is the tax that the Qur'an requires to be paid by the "People of the Book" (primarily Jews and Christians), who are subjugated under the rule of Islamic law and denied basic rights: "Fight those who believe not in God nor the Last Day, nor hold that forbidden which hath been forbidden by God and His Apostle, nor acknowledge the religion of Truth, (even if they are) of the People of the Book, until they pay the Jizya with willing submission, and feel themselves subdued" (9:29). Mehsud was revealing the truth about the Afghan conflict that no analyst in either Bush or Obama administrations has ever acknowledged: that even when the last American soldier leaves Afghanistan, there will be no peace, for some Muslims who believe like Mehsud will pursue the conflict to the United States and Britain (as well as other infidel polities) and fight them until they convert to Islam or submit to its rule.

Smoking in Times Square

That jihad is already being waged in the United States. On May 1, 2010, a naturalized American citizen from Pakistan and former financial analyst named Faisal Shahzad tried to detonate a car bomb in Times Square; since it was a Saturday evening, the area was extremely crowded. The car was smoking when two street vendors noticed it and notified police, and the bomb was disarmed before it exploded. Shahzad was arrested after he boarded a plane on his way back to Pakistan and sentenced to life imprisonment after showing no signs of remorse at his trial.

Shahzad explained why he wanted to commit mass murder in Times Square in a video he made shortly before the attack. In it, he says that "jihad, holy fighting in Allah's course, with full force of numbers and weaponry, is given the utmost importance in Islam.... By jihad, Islam is established.... By abandoning jihad, may Allah protect us from that, Islam is destroyed, and Muslims go into inferior position, their honor is lost, their lands are stolen, their rule and authority vanish. Jihad is an obligation and duty in Islam on every Muslim."

Shahzad warned that there would be many more attacks such as the one he tried to set off in Times Square, all to advance the cause of Islam: "You will see that the Muslim world has just started.... Islam is coming to the world, inshallah, Islam will spread on the whole world. And the democracy will be defeated, and so was Communism defeated, and all the others isms and schisms will be defeated, and the word of Allah will be supreme, inshallah. And Muslims are gonna do that. And as Allah says in sura 3, verse 110 [of the Qur'an]...." Then the video cuts to footage of some mujahedin walking around. Qur'an 3:110 says to the Muslims, "You are the best nation produced (as an example) for mankind. You enjoin what is right and forbid what is wrong and believe in Allah. If only the People of the Scripture had believed, it would have been better for them. Among them are believers, but most of them are defiantly disobedient."

A Devout Muslim

Just about a year before the failed Times Square bombing, another warrior of jihad in the United States had been more successful. An African American convert to Islam named Abdulhakim Mujahid Muhammad staged what he later called a "random and unplanned attack" on a military recruiting center in Little Rock, Arkansas. Seeing two soldiers standing outside the center, Muhammad recalled, "I did not want them to see me coming. I had the SKS with me and put it out the window. I rolled by and started shooting. I was trying to kill them."

Muhammad managed to kill Private William A. Long, twenty-three, and to wound Private Quinton Ezeagwula, eighteen. In a series of letters he later described the religious motivations for his attack, explaining how "step by step I became a religiously devout Muslim, Mujahid meaning one who participates in jihad." He explained that "in Islam there's a call to duty—jihad—and it's of different types but the one I'm mentioning is a defensive struggle or fight with weapons against those who attack, kill, maim the Muslims. And this is a part of Islam." (Several years later, Dzhokhar Tsarnaev would invoke exactly the same doctrine in explaining his bombings at the Boston Marathon.)

Speaking of his larger goals, Muhammad explained, "Far as Al-Qaeda in the Arabian Peninsula I won't say much but yes, I'm affiliated with them. And it's more of a Islamic Revivalist Revolutionary Movement than an organization. Same with other Al-Qaeda fronts. Our goal is to rid the Islamic world of idols and idolaters, paganism and pagans, infidelity and infidels, hypocrisy and hypocrites, apostasy and apostates, democracy and democrats and relaunch the Islamic caliphate ... and to establish Islamic law [sharia]—Allah's law on earth and anyone who strives for this is affiliated with the movement. So yes I'm Al Qaeda and proud to be."

Dropping the Ball

Muhammad expressed pride in other jihad attacks and plots and noted triumphantly that even though he had been under law enforcement surveillance, the CIA and the FBI had not been able to head off his shooting outside the recruitment center: "In regards to the CIA & FBI yea they followed me, yea they tapped my phone, read my emails, interrogated me not once, not twice but three times before my jihadi attack on the crusader recruiting center but what good did it do? I outsmarted them and they know it."

Muhammad struck a sharply different tone from that of Ace Dandia and the other Muslims who professed to be personally devastated by law enforcement surveillance. For his part, Muhammad was not dev- astated at all; instead, he was exultant that such efforts had not man- aged to prevent jihad attacks, writing of law enforcement officials, "I know the real reason why they're so [quiet]. And it's because they dropped the ball with me and not just me. Nidal [Nidal Malik Hasan, the U.S. Army major charged in the Fort Hood shootings), Umar Farouk [the Nigerian charged for trying to detonate plastic explosives on a Northwest Airlines flight], Faisal [Faisal Shahzad, the Pakistani- American sentenced to life in prison for his failed attempt to bomb Times Square] and others who evaded their agents and devices and paid-informants posing as Muslims. They can't catch us all."[16]

Muhammad had half a dozen Molotov cocktails in the back of his truck and had hoped to carry out a larger-scale attack, saying of his shootings, "compared to what I had planned originally it was like a grain of sand. One crusader dead, one wounded, 15 terrorized, big deal. Nidal Malik is the real Islamic warrior, and my plan A was on that scale." And he offered a chilling warning: "I'm just one Muhammad. There are millions of Muhammads out there. And I hope and pray the next one be more deadlier than Muhammad Atta!! (peace be upon him) commander of the blessed raids in NY and D.C. on 9/11."[17]

"It Is Time for Jihad"

There has not been a "blessed raid" in the United States deadlier than 9/11, or at least not yet. But there have been other instances of Islam-motivated violence and murder, including some attacks that got virtually no media attention. A Saudi national named Khalid Ali-M Aldawsari, for example, came to the United States on a student visa specifically for the purpose of staging a jihad attack. In an email, he asserted that "one operation in the land of the infidels is equal to ten operations against occupying forces in the land of the Muslims."

Once enrolled at South Plains College in Lubbock, Texas, Aldawsari set about amassing materials for a bomb. According to the Justice Department, he bought, among other things, "a gas mask, a Hazmat suit, a soldering iron kit, glass beakers and flasks, wiring, a stun gun, clocks and a battery tester." He also began to assemble lists of targets that included hydroelectric dams, nuclear power plants, and President George W. Bush's Texas home—which Aldawsari referred to as "Tyrant's House."

Aldawsari kept a diary, in which he confided that he had tried to get—and succeeded in getting—a particular scholarship because he thought it would "help tremendously in providing me with the support I need for Jihad.... And now, after mastering the English language, learning how to build explosives and continuous planning to target the infidel Americans, it is time for Jihad." He prayed to Allah, "You who created mankind and who is [sic] knowledgeable of what is in the womb, grant me martyrdom for Your sake and make jihad easy for me only in Your path."[18]

Yet another Muslim who appeared to believe that his duty to Allah involved killing infidels was a convert to the faith named Reshad Riddle, who on Easter Sunday 2013 shot his father outside of the Hiawatha Church of God in Christ in Ashtabula, Ohio, entered the church waving a handgun, and placed a copy of the Qur'an on the podium. Police officer Thomas Clemens, who was called to the church to subdue Riddle, recounted that inside the church Riddle "referred to the Qur'an and Allah, quoting passages" and saying that he had "served his purpose." Detective William Felt, who later questioned Riddle about the crime, also noted that he quoted the Qur'an.[19]

Suing to Protect the Jihad?

There have been numerous other plots and attacks similar to these in the United States in recent years. All of them establish that law enforcement officials have been perfectly justified in sending informants into mosques and scrutinizing devout Muslims more closely than, say, Methodist grandmothers.

But if the leftist and Muslim legal initiatives against law enforcement counterterror operations directed at Muslims succeed, the inevitable result will be less surveillance of mosques, less monitoring of Islamic jihadist internet chatter, and less vigilance all around in the face of an obvious and persistent threat. Americans will be rendered less safe and more vulnerable to Islamic jihad attacks.

There are numerous good reasons to suspect that that may be the ultimate objective of these legal challenges.

CHAPTER FIVE

THE JIHAD AGAINST
TALKING ABOUT JIHAD

There has been a concerted effort in recent years to rule all discussion of jihad violence and Islamic supremacism beyond the bounds of acceptable public discourse. Much of this effort has centered on the idea of "Islamophobia," a word used to give the impression that resistance to jihad is some kind of pathology, an irrational hatred of Muslims and Islam.

The hysteria over "Islamophobia" got its primary impetus in 2005, when Muslims around the world rioted, killing over one hundred people in Nigeria alone, over the publication in Denmark of cartoons depicting the Islamic prophet Muhammad.[1] The Organization of Islamic Cooperation (OIC), known at that time as the Organization of the Islamic Conference, a multinational organization made up of fifty-six Muslim nations (plus the Palestinian Authority) that since the collapse of the Soviet Union make up the largest voting bloc in the United Nations, began a large-scale effort to compel Western governments, including the United States, to criminalize criticism of Islam, including analyses of how jihadists use the texts and teachings of Islam to justify violence—classifying it all as "hate speech."

At the OIC's international meeting in Senegal in March 2008, it adopted the goal of crafting a "legal instrument" to combat criticism of Islam from "political cartoonists and bigots."[2] The secretary general of the OIC, Ekmeleddin Ihsanoglu, went so far as to liken the Danish cartoons to the 9/11 jihad attack: "The Islamic world took the satirical drawings as a different version of the September 11 attacks against them." He claimed that Muslims were "being targeted by a campaign of defamation, denigration, stereotyping, intolerance and discrimination," and urged European legislators to criminalize "Islamophobia."[3]

According to the Associated Press, Ihsanoglu gave the assembled OIC members "a voluminous report by the O.I.C. that recorded anti-Islamic speech and actions from around the world. The report concludes that Islam is under attack and that a defense must be mounted."[4] He said nothing about the hundred-plus deaths and other attacks on non-Muslims in the wake of the publication of the Muhammad cartoons.

Ihsanoglu declared, "Islamophobia cannot be dealt with only through cultural activities but [through] a robust political engagement." Political engagement meant attempts to restrict the freedom of speech, as Abdoulaye Wade, president of Senegal and OIC chairman, made clear: "I don't think freedom of expression should mean freedom from [sic] blasphemy. There can be no freedom without limits."[5]

In 2007, Doudou Diène, the UN special rapporteur on contemporary forms of "racism, racial discrimination, xenophobia and related intolerance," suggested that even quoting the Qur'an accurately but critically was an act of bigotry that needed to be proscribed: "One may note that a number of Islamophobic statements have been falsely claimed to be scientific or scholarly, in order to give intellectual clout to arguments that link Islam to violence and terrorism. Furthermore, the manipulation and selective quoting of sacred texts, in particular the Qur'an, as a means to deceptively argue that these texts show the violent nature of Islam has become current practice."[6]

"Shut Up!" "Yes, Sir!"

All this was disturbing enough, but the worst aspect of the international campaign against free speech was the readiness of European and American leftist politicians, including government leaders, to support restrictions on free speech about Islam. Already in 2008, Ihsanoglu was noting with satisfaction that the OIC's campaign against free speech had made "convincing progress at all these levels mainly the UN Human Rights Council in Geneva, and the UN General Assembly. The UN General Assembly adopted similar resolutions against the defamation of Islam." He added, "In confronting the Danish cartoons and the Dutch film *Fitna*, we sent a clear message to the West regarding the red lines that should not be crossed. As we speak, the official West and its public opinion are all now well aware of the sensitivities of these issues. They have also started to look seriously into the question of freedom of expression from the perspective of its inherent responsibility, which should not be overlooked."[7]

Fitna was a short film by Dutch politician Geert Wilders featuring passages from the Qur'an exhorting Muslims to violence and then showing scenes of contemporary violence that those passages had inspired. The OIC condemned *Fitna* in "the strongest terms," characterizing it as a "deliberate act of discrimination against Muslims," claiming that it was intended only to "provoke unrest and intolerance."[8] The OIC didn't claim that the Qur'an quotes were inaccurate or dispute the film's accuracy in any other way. Nonetheless, a Dutch court ultimately indicted Wilders for having "intentionally offended a group of people, i.e. Muslims, based on their religion." Wilders had, the indictment said, "incited to hatred of people, i.e. Muslims, based on their religion," and had "incited to discrimination ... against people, i.e. Muslims, based on their religion." It also claimed that Wilders had tried to incite people to hate Muslims because of their race—despite the fact that that Muslims are of all races.[9]

Wilders was acquitted in June 2011. On hearing the verdict, he said, "Today is a victory for freedom of speech. The Dutch are still allowed to speak critically about Islam, and resistance against Islamization is not a crime."[10] Wilders also added some comments akin to those that had gotten him prosecuted in the first place, declaring that it was his "strong conviction that Islam is a threat to Western values, to freedom of speech, to the equality of men and women, of heterosexuals and homosexuals, of believers and unbelievers." The OIC's attempts to criminalize criticism of Islam, and the willingness of the Dutch legal system to go along with this initiative in a clear attempt to mollify its Muslim population, bore out these assertions.

Free Nations Agree to Silence Themselves

By 2010, the OIC's campaign had achieved notable success. In November of that year, the UN General Assembly voted to condemn what it called the "vilification of religion."[11] Every majority-Muslim state, without exception, supported the resolution. A Reuters report claimed that the resolution's language had been softened from its initial form: the term "defamation" had been changed to "vilification" in order to win more support from Western nations.

But the two words are essentially synonyms, and both are dangerously subjective. What actually constitutes "defamation" or "vilification" would presumably be left up to some UN body to determine—in other words, in practice to the Islamic states, the largest voting bloc in the United Nations. And that would mean that counterterror analyses of the motives and goals of jihad terrorists that delved into the teachings of Islam would be considered "vilification."

The resolution was a step towards making criticisms of "matters regarded by followers of any religion or belief as sacred" into criminal acts.[12] It was essentially a call for an anti-blasphemy law, bringing Islamic law's prohibition of material offensive to Islam to the West. To sugarcoat this, the UN resolution against "vilification" condemned not only "Islamophobia," but "Judeophobia and Christianophobia" as well.

This, however, was merely a sop to Western sensibilities and bothersome notions of free speech, not something that the Muslim framers of the resolution took seriously. After all, massacres of Christians in Egypt, Iraq, Pakistan, and Indonesia, and jihad terror attacks against Passover seders in Israel, along with other acts of Muslim hatred towards adherents of other religions, never led to calls for UN censure from the OIC or anyone else. When Andres Serrano's "Piss Christ" became a cause célèbre or a thousand anti-Semitic caricatures appeared in the government-controlled media of Muslim countries—the *Protocols of the Elders of Zion* ran as an eleven-part mini-series on Egyptian TV—neither the OIC nor the UN expressed any outrage or issued any formal condemnations.

Obama Discovers a New Presidential Duty

And as many Western European nations began to crack down on what was characterized as "Islamophobic hate speech," the United States under Barack Obama joined the effort as well. In his celebrated address to the Muslim world at Cairo in June 2009, Obama seemed to endorse the OIC's anti–free speech agenda: "I consider it part of my responsibility as President of the United States to fight against negative stereotypes of Islam wherever they appear."[13] He didn't explain where in the Constitution he had found this awesome new responsibility.

Instead, in October 2009, Obama showed that this wasn't mere empty rhetoric, as his administration joined Egypt in supporting a resolution in the UN's Human Rights Council to recognize exceptions to the freedom of speech for "any negative racial and religious stereotyping."[14] Approved by the UN Human Rights Council, the resolution called on states to condemn and criminalize "any advocacy of national, racial or religious hatred that constitutes incitement to discrimination, hostility or violence."

"Incitement" and "hatred" are in the eye of the beholder—or, more precisely, in the eye of those empowered to make such determinations. The powerful can decide to silence the powerless by classifying their views as "hate speech." The Founding Fathers knew that the freedom of speech was an essential safeguard against tyranny. The ability to dissent, freely and publicly and without fear of imprisonment or other reprisal, is a cornerstone of any genuine republic. If some ideas cannot be heard because they are proscribed from above, the ones in control are tyrants, however benevolent they may be.

With this UN resolution, no less distinguished a personage than the president of the United States gave his imprimatur to this tyranny; the implications were grave. But Hisham Badr, Egypt's ambassador to the United Nations, was delighted. He praised the resolution and observed that "freedom of expression has been sometimes misused" and that an understanding of the "true nature of this right" would require government restrictions. Instead of taking issue with his attack on free speech, the American ambassador to the United Nations, Douglas Griffiths, praised "this joint project with Egypt" as an attempt to achieve "tolerance and the dignity of all human beings."[15]

Legal expert Eugene Volokh explained why the measure was so disturbing: "If the U.S. backs a resolution that urges the suppression of some speech," he explained, "presumably we are taking the view that all countries—including the U.S. —should adhere to this resolution. If we are constitutionally barred from adhering to it by our domestic constitution, then we're implicitly criticizing that constitution, and committing ourselves to do what we can to change it." In order to be consistent, Volokh continued, "the Administration would presumably have to take what steps it can to ensure that supposed 'hate speech' that incites hostility will indeed be punished. It would presumably be committed to filing amicus briefs supporting changes in First Amendment law to allow such punishment, and in principle perhaps the appointment of Justices who would endorse such changes (or even the proposal of express constitutional amendments that would work such changes)."[16]

In March 2011, OIC general secretary Ekmeleddin gave a speech to the UN Council on Human Rights, calling upon it to set up "an Observatory at the Office of the High Commissioner to monitor acts of defamation of all religions ... as a first step toward concerted action at the international level."[17] Then on April 12, 2011, the UN Council on Human Rights passed Resolution 16/18, again with full support from the Obama administration. This resolution calls upon member states to impose laws against "discriminatory" speech or speech involving "defamation of religion."[18] In June 2011, Ihsanoglu said that such laws were "a matter of extreme priority" for the OIC.[19]

"Old-Fashioned Techniques of Peer Pressure and Shaming"

Secretary of State Hillary Clinton affirmed the Obama administration's support for this campaign on July 15, 2011, when she gave an address on the freedom of speech at an OIC conference on combating religious intolerance. "Together," she said, "we have begun to overcome the false divide that pits religious sensitivities against freedom of expression and we are pursuing a new approach. These are fundamental freedoms that belong to all people in all places and they are certainly essential to democracy."

But how could both be protected? Ihsanoglu offered the answer: criminalizing what he considered to be hatred and incitement to violence. "We cannot and must not ignore the implications of hate speech and incitement of discrimination and violence." At the same time, however, he claimed that the OIC did not really want to criminalize free speech: "Our cause, which stems from out genuine concerns, should not be interpreted as calls for restriction on freedom."[20] To understand how Ihsanoglu could call for restrictions on the freedom of speech while simultaneously claiming that that was not what he was doing, one had to enter his Orwellian world, in which "hate speech"—as designated by Ihsanoglu himself and his fellow Islamic supremacists—was not protected free speech.

But Clinton had a First Amendment to deal with, and so in place of legal restrictions on criticizing Islam she suggested "old-fashioned techniques of peer pressure and shaming, so that people don't feel that they have the support to do what we abhor."[21] She held a lengthy closed-door meeting with Ihsanoglu in December 2011 to facilitate the adoption of measures that would advance the OIC's anti–free speech measures. But what agreements she and Ihsanoglu made, if any, have never been disclosed.[22]

Shaming the "Islamophobes"

The American Left was already enthusiastically pursuing the "peer pressure and shaming" tactic against foes of jihad violence. In 2008, the left-wing watchdog organization Fairness and Accuracy in Reporting (FAIR) published a lengthy "report" called "Smearcasting: How Islamophobes Spread Bigotry, Fear, and Misinformation." The FAIR report focused on a list of "Islamophobia's Dirty Dozen," which began with Fox News anchors Bill O'Reilly, Sean Hannity, and Glenn Beck, and went on to include investigative reporter Steven Emerson, conservative activist and former leftist David Horowitz, author Mark Steyn, and others, including me.[23]

The FAIR "study" was entirely made up of quotes lifted out of context or misreported in the first place, presented as self-evident examples of anti-Muslim bigotry. Thus an observation by David Horowitz (described as "the Islamophobia movement's premier promoter") about public opinion surveys following the 9/11 attacks becomes a claim by Horowitz that "between 150 million and 750 million Muslims support a holy war." What Horowitz actually said was that public opinion surveys in the Muslim world after 9/11, including one conducted by the controversial Qatari television network Al Jazeera, reported that between 10 percent and 50 percent of Muslims considered Osama bin Laden a hero.

Then, in December 2010, the Huffington Post ran a lengthy diatribe by hard-Left journalist Max Blumenthal headlined "The Great Islamophobic Crusade," which began with the claim that "Nine years after 9/11, hysteria about Muslims in American life has gripped the country." According to Blumenthal, "this spasm of anti-Muslim bigotry ... [is] the fruit of an organized, long-term campaign by a tight confederation of right-wing activists and operatives who first focused on Islamophobia soon after the September 11th attacks, but only attained critical mass during the Obama era."[24] It did so, according to Blumenthal, because of conservative resentment over Obama's election and because "representatives of the Israel lobby and the Jewish-American establishment launched a campaign against pro-Palestinian campus activism that would prove a seedbed for everything to come." According to Blumenthal, Islamophobia "reflects an aggressively pro-Israel sensibility, with its key figures venerating the Jewish state as a Middle Eastern Fort Apache on the front lines of the Global War on Terror...."[25]

Not surprisingly, Blumenthal's list of conspirators included several of the "Dirty Dozen" from the FAIR document and mirrored a CAIR list of the "Worst" Islamophobes. Among those Blumenthal identified as members of the cabal were Pamela Geller, Newt Gingrich, Horowitz, Wilders, and me. Like every attack on "Islamophobia," Blumenthal's did not devote a single sentence to examining the analyses or answering the arguments laid out in the library of books written by the targets of the defamation.

Six months later, the Southern Policy Law Center published an "Intelligence Report" on "Anti-Muslim Bigotry." The SPLC had distinguished itself in a previous report by tarring establishment conservative organizations such as the American Enterprise Institute as "racist." This new report summarized the Blumenthal article and featured one of its own: "The Anti-Muslim Inner Circle" by Robert Steinback.[26] Steinback listed ten members of this inner circle (including David Horowitz and me), among them people who had never met face to face and in most cases had never even corresponded. This "circle" only existed in the minds of those who were bent on defaming its supposed members.

An event typical of the unsavory associations of the purveyors of the "Islamophobia" myth was held in October 2010, when the Center for American Progress, a George Soros–funded, Democratic Party brain trust, put on a panel called "Challenging Islamophobia."[27] The panel included an Episcopalian priest and Wajahat Ali, author of a blog that, among other complaints, bemoaned the "persecution" of the American Taliban John Walker Lindh and referred to him as "an innocent victim of America's 'war on terror.'"[28] (In 2013, Ali went to work for Al Jazeera.) A third panelist was Haris Tarin, Washington office director of the Muslim Public Affairs Council, an organization that has declared "Israelis are the worst terrorists in the world" and described Hizballah as a "liberation organization."[29]

The Center for American Progress produced the most extensive and influential of the "Islamophobia" reports in August 2011: *Fear, Inc.: The Roots of the Islamophobia Network in America*.[30] Like its earlier counterparts, it purported to show that the anti-jihad, anti-sharia movement in the United States was a sinister cabal of well-funded and dishonest hacks stirring up hate against innocent Muslims for profit. And also like its predecessors, it was highly distorted and markedly unfair, twisting the facts and cooking the data to manipulate rather than enlighten, to propagandize, not educate.

An "Anti-Muslim Misinformation Scholar"

The Center for American Progress report's charges against me are noteworthy as a case study of how the Left and its Islamic supremacist allies have set out to accomplish the "shaming" Clinton called for. The misinformation starts on the first page, where the *Fear, Inc.* authors call me "one of the anti-Muslim misinformation scholars we profile in this report."[31]

The epithet "anti-Muslim," frequently applied to foes of jihad terror, is immediate evidence of the manipulative, propagandistic nature of the CAP report and all its companion reports on "Islamophobia." My work and the work of the other scholars and activists demonized in *Fear, Inc.* has never been against Muslims in the aggregate or any people as such, but rather against an ideology that denies the freedom of speech, the freedom of conscience, and the equality of rights of all people. To call us "anti-Muslim" is tantamount to calling foes of the Nazis "anti-German."

Years ago in an exchange with an English convert to Islam at my website, Jihad Watch (www.jihadwatch.org), I said, "I would like nothing better than a flowering, a renaissance, in the Muslim world, including full equality of rights for women and non-Muslims in Islamic societies: freedom of conscience, equality in laws regarding legal testimony, equal employment opportunities, etc." Is all that "anti-Muslim"? My correspondent thought so. He responded: "So, you would like to see us ditch much of our religion and, thereby, become non-Muslims."[32]

In other words, this Muslim saw a call for equality of rights for women and non-Muslims in Islamic societies, including freedom of conscience, equality in laws regarding legal testimony, and equal employment opportunities, as a challenge to his religion. That disturbing fact has to be confronted by both Muslims and non-Muslims. But it is not "anti-Muslim" to wish freedom of conscience and equality of rights on the Islamic world—quite the contrary.

Framed for Murder

The CAP report also contained what became a regular feature of studies of "Islamophobia" in 2011 and thereafter: a lengthy excursus on Norwegian mass murderer Anders Breivik, who cited numerous foes of jihad violence in a lengthy manifesto that he published online. The CAP report said, "While these bloggers and pundits were not responsible for Breivik's deadly attacks, their writings on Islam and multiculturalism appear to have helped create a world view, held by this lone Norwegian gunman, that sees Islam as at war with the West and the West needing to be defended."[33] While granting that we are not responsible for Breivik's acts, the report also takes pains to point out that "Robert Spencer and his blog were cited 162 times in the nearly 1,500-page manifesto of Anders Breivik, the confessed Norway terrorist who claimed responsibility for killing 76 people, mostly youths."[34]

Not surprisingly, this claim is highly misleading. The CAP report doesn't mention that in all his quotations of me, Breivik never quotes me calling for or justifying violence—because I never do. In fact, Breivik even criticized me for not doing so, saying of me, historian Bat Ye'or, and other critics of jihad terror, "If these authors are to [sic] scared to propagate a conservative revolution and armed resistance then other authors will have to."[35] Nor does it note the fact that Breivik was "radicalized" by his experiences with Muslim immigrants in the early 1990s, before I had published anything about Islam.[36]

Breivik also hesitantly but unmistakably recommended making common cause with jihadists, which neither I nor any other opponent of jihad would ever do: "An alliance with the Jihadists might prove beneficial to both parties but will simply be too dangerous (and might prove to be ideologically counterproductive). We both share one common goal."[37] He even called for making common cause with Hamas in plotting jihad terror: "Approach a representative from a Jihadi Salafi group. Get in contact with a Jihadi strawman. Present your terms and have him forward them to his superiors.... Present your offer. They are asked to provide a biological compound manufactured by Muslim scientists in the Middle East. Hamas and several Jihadi groups have labs and they have the potential to provide such substances. Their problem is finding suitable martyrs who can pass 'screenings' in Western Europe. This is where we come in. We will smuggle it in to the EU and distribute it at a target of our choosing. We must give them assurances that we are not to harm any Muslims etc."[38]

These facts were not mentioned in *Fear, Inc.* because they would have interfered with its propagandistic agenda—an agenda that the mainstream media shared, as investigative journalist and author Daniel Greenfield noted:

> Jeffrey Goldberg at the *Atlantic* goes so far as to call a prominent researcher into Islamic terrorism, Robert Spencer, a jihadist. The *Washington Post* admits that Spencer and other researchers are not responsible for the shootings, but sneers nonetheless. And the *New York Times* and a number of other outlets have picked and touted the "64 times" that Spencer was quoted in the shooter's manifesto....
>
> The "64 times" cited by the *Times* and its imitators reflects lazy research since the majority of those quotes actually come from a single document, where Spencer is quoted side by side with Tony Blair and Condoleezza Rice....
>
> Many of the other Spencer quotes are actually second-hand from essays written by Fjordman that also incorporate selections of quotes on Islam and its historical background. Rather than Breivik quoting Spencer, he is actually quoting Fjordman who is quoting Spencer.
>
> Quite often, Robert Spencer is quoted providing historical background on Islam and quotes from the Koran and the Hadith. So, it's actually Fjordman quoting Spencer quoting the Koran. If the media insists that Fjordman is an extremist and Spencer is an extremist — then isn't the Koran also extremist?
>
> And if the Koran isn't extremist, then how could quoting it be extremist?
>
> The *New York Times* would have you believe that second-hand quotes like these from Spencer turned Breivik into a raging madman....
>
> Breivik was driven by fantasies of seizing power, combined with steroid abuse and escapism. He used quotes from researchers into terrorism to pad out his schizophrenic

worldview, combined with fantasies of multiple terrorist cells and an eventual rise to power.

This is not so different from lunatics who picked up a copy of *Catcher in the Rye* and then set off to kill a celebrity. A not uncommon event, for which J.D. Salinger bears no responsibility whatsoever.[39]

Indeed. Nonetheless, blame for Breivik's murders became a staple of the case against counter-jihadists and of the ongoing attempt to claim that resistance to jihad led to violence and was an exaggerated fear in any case.

In January 2014, Breivik sent a letter from prison to numerous international news outlets, including the *Wall Street Journal*, Germany's *Die Welt*, and Denmark's *Ekstra Bladet*. In it, he claimed that he had never considered himself part of the counter-jihad movement, but was actually a Nazi: an ethnic nationalist who detested counter-jihad spokesmen for denouncing jihad without embracing racism and white supremacism. He explained that he had constructed his "manifesto" so that the mainstream media would blame counter-jihadists for his murders, thereby destroying that movement and leaving neo-Nazis as the sole counterweight to European leftists and statists. With highly idiosyncratic punctuation, reproduced here as written, Breivik explained that his plan was to strengthen the ethnocentrist wing in the contra-jihad movement, by pinning the whole thing on the anti-ethnocentrist wing.... The idea was to manipulate the MSM [mainstream media] and others so that they would launch a witch-hunt and send their "media-rape-squads" against our opponents. It worked quite well.

> ... I tried to hint about this double-psychology, by quoting "war is deceit" x number of times, but I couldnt [sic] make it more obvious, as it had to be credible to the aggressive army of 2000 media psychopaths (the MSM-rape-squad). The "hug-your-opponents, kick-the-ones-you-love"-tactic is one of the oldest in the book.[40]

Elsewhere in this letter Breivik claims to have been tortured in prison; the *Wall Street Journal* reported on that, as did a few other news outlets. Every mainstream media news source in the world, however, both those that received Breivik's letter and those that did not, completely ignored his claim to have used "double-psychology" to destroy the counter-jihad movement. The media frenzy that accompanied Breivik's initial identification with that movement had served its purpose, and Breivik was no longer useful.[41]

Islam's War against the West

While claiming that Breivik committed his murders because of the worldview we had created that "sees Islam at war with the West," the Center for American Progress's *Fear, Inc.* But it is silent about the many Muslims who have declared that they are indeed at war with the West, in the name of Islam, as we shall see in greater detail in chapter twelve. Iran's former president Mahmoud Ahmadinejad has said, "Have no doubt … Allah willing, Islam will conquer what? It will conquer all the mountain tops of the world."[42] The most influential Islamic cleric in the world today, Sheikh Yusuf al-Qaradawi, has said, "Islam will return to Europe as a conqueror and victor, after being expelled from it twice."[43]

And in the United States itself, CAIR cofounder and longtime board chairman Omar Ahmad said in 1998, "Islam isn't in America to be equal to any other faith, but to become dominant. The Koran should be the highest authority in America, and Islam the only accepted religion on earth."[44] The prominent American Muslim leader Siraj Wahhaj said in 1992, "If only Muslims were clever politically, they could take over the United States and replace its constitutional government with a caliphate."[45]

True to form for these "Islamophobia" reports, *Fear, Inc.* ignores such statements and many others like them, attempting to create the impression that the ones responsible for the idea that Islam is "at war with the West" are the "Islamophobes."

"Inaccurate and Perverse"

Without offering any substantive refutation, *Fear, Inc.* simply dismisses as "inaccurate and perverse" my statement that Islam is "the only religion in the world that has a developed doctrine, theology and legal system that mandates violence against unbelievers and mandates that Muslims must wage war in order to establish the hegemony of the Islamic social order all over the world."[46] What is "inaccurate and perverse" is the report's groundless denial of this claim, since it is a matter of objective fact that all the mainstream Islamic sects and schools of Islamic jurisprudence do indeed teach that the Islamic umma must wage war against unbelievers and subjugate them under the rule of Islamic law. The report does not and cannot produce any evidence that Islam does not contain sects and schools that teach this.

Fear, Inc. says, "Spencer's views on Islam—and his credibility in discussing Islam at all—are challenged by scholars at his own alma mater. He has 'no academic training in Islamic studies whatsoever,' according to Islamic scholar Carl W. Ernst, Kenan Distinguished Professor of Islamic Studies and director of the Carolina Center for the Study of the Middle East and Muslim Civilizations at the University of North Carolina–Chapel Hill. Instead, Professor Ernst says Spencer selectively uses textual, religious evidence to mainstream the claim that 'Islam is not a religion of peace.' Indeed, Spencer gives misplaced credence to the 'Sharia threat' argument that is then mainstreamed by the Islamophobia network."[47]

Ernst's dismissal of my work on the basis of my having "no academic training in Islamic studies whatsoever" was typical of the manipulative analyses featured in these reports: besides being false, this charge is completely void of substance. The determination of whether or not one's work is accurate is not decided by the number of one's degrees, but by the nature of the work itself. But more telling is that Ernst himself flew to Tehran in December 2008 to accept an award from Iran's anti-Semitic, genocide-minded Islamic supremacist, then-president Mahmoud Ahmadinejad.[48] These are the people who have set themselves up as judges and arbiters of what constitutes acceptable public discourse about Islam and terrorism today.

Abdur-Rahman Muhammad, a former member of the Muslim Brotherhood–linked International Institute for Islamic Thought (IIIT), was present when IIIT officials decided to employ the word "Islamophobia" against critics of Islam, but now characterizes the concept of Islamophobia as a "loathsome term" that is "nothing more than a thought-terminating cliché conceived in the bowels of Muslim think tanks for the purpose of beating down critics."[49]

Endangering Innocents

To beat down those critics most effectively, however, they had to be shown not just to be engaging in impermissible speech, but to be actively endangering innocent people. Hence a major component of the campaign to silence all honest discussion of jihad terror and to discredit all those who engage in it is the claim that Muslims in America are facing an escalating barrage of "hate crimes," discrimination, and harassment—and all because of the venomous attacks of "Islamophobes," not as a reaction to jihad violence. In line with this, the OIC's Ihsanoglu claimed that Muslims were "being targeted by a campaign of defamation, denigration, stereotyping, intolerance and discrimination."[50] And according to CAIR's 2011 Islamophobia report, "in 2009 and 2010, Muslims continued to face barriers to their full and equal participation in American society."[51] Blumenthal summed up the prevailing view among his comrades with his complaint that "hysteria about Muslims in American life has gripped the country."[52]

Unprecedented Levels of Power and Influence

These attempts to portray Muslims as victims ignored the fact that Muslims had actually reached unprecedented levels of power and influence in American society at the very time when, according to media myth, they were suffering unprecedented persecution. Ihsanoglu, CAIR, Blumenthal, and others like them didn't mention amid their handwringing about "Islamophobia" that in April 2009 Barack Obama had appointed the Muslim deputy mayor of Los Angeles, Arif Alikhan, to be Assistant Secretary for Policy Development at the Department of Homeland Security.

This appointment showed how stigmatizing critics of the Islamic jihad as "Islamophobes" not only threatened freedom of speech, but also cut large holes in our security defenses against a jihad terror attack. While serving as Los Angeles's deputy mayor, Alikhan (who once called the jihad terror group Hizballah a "liberation movement") blocked a Los Angeles Police Department project to assemble data about the ethnic makeup of mosques in the Los Angeles area. This was not an attempt to conduct surveillance of the mosques or monitor them in any way. LAPD deputy chief Michael P. Downing explained that it was actually an outreach program: "We want to know where the Pakistanis, Iranians and Chechens are so we can reach out to those communities."[53] But Alikhan and other Muslim leaders claimed that the project manifested racism and "Islamophobia," and the LAPD ultimately discarded all plans to study the mosques and gain invaluable contacts in the Muslim community that might prevent terrorist attacks.

Obama rewarded Alikhan for this by appointing him to a key role at Homeland Security, the department charged with managing the defenses of the entire country. And in December 2010, the Los Angeles City Council passed a resolution condemning "Islamophobia."[54]

Alikhan is not alone. The allegedly prevailing climate of anti-Muslim hysteria did not result in a murmur of complaint from the loyal opposition when Obama appointed Kareem Shora to the Homeland Security Advisory Council, despite the fact that as executive director of the American-Arab Anti-Discrimination Committee (ADC), Shora consistently joined CAIR and other Islamic supremacist groups in lobbying against anti-terror initiatives.

Obama also created a new post, special envoy to the OIC, to which he appointed Rashad Hussain, who had distinguished himself by decrying the alleged "persecution" of convicted terrorist and Palestinian Islamic jihad leader Sami al-Arian. Nor did the supposed barriers to Muslims in American society prevent Obama from choosing Dalia Mogahed as his advisor on Muslim affairs. In October 2009, Mogahed declared on British television that most Muslim women worldwide associate Islamic law with "gender justice."

Muslim influence in the Obama administration extended even further. Obama included Islamic Society of North America (ISNA) president Ingrid Mattson, the leader of a Muslim Brotherhood front with links to Hamas, as one of the clerics offering prayers at the National Cathedral on his first Inauguration Day in 2009. Obama also sent his senior advisor Valerie Jarrett to be the keynote speaker at ISNA's national convention in 2009. Huma Abedin, who was deputy chief of staff to Secretary of State Hillary Clinton, comes from a prominent

Muslim Brotherhood family—which led to controversy in 2012, when Republican representative Michele Bachmann of Minnesota called for an investigation of Muslim Brotherhood influence in the U.S. government.

Are Obama's numerous Muslim appointments and various other forms of outreach to the Islamic world an attempt to stem the rising tide of anti-Muslim bigotry in the United States? The facts do not bear this explanation out. The idea that anti-Muslim prejudice is such an urgent problem that it needs to be aggressively addressed—even by going so far as to mute the discussion of how jihadists use the texts and teaching of Islam to justify violence and make recruits among peaceful Muslims—is not founded on any facts at all. According to the 2009 FBI report on "hate crimes," Jews, not Muslims, made up three-fourths of victims of what are classified as religiously motivated hate crimes—not a few of which were committed by Muslims against Jews. Hate crimes against Muslims made up only 8 percent of these hate crimes, or a total of 132 incidents in a nation of 300 million people.[55]

Fabricating Hate

Those statistics may help explain why CAIR has not hesitated to peddle false reports of anti-Muslim hate crimes in order to support its case that "Islamophobia" is rampant (and caused by counterterror analysis). In 2005, Daniel Pipes and Sharon Chadha published an article identifying six incidents falsely described as hate crimes in CAIR's 2004 report on such crimes. These included "the July 9, 2004 case of apparent arson at a Muslim-owned grocery store in Everett, Washington," in which "investigators quickly determined that Mirza Akram, the store's operator, staged the arson to avoid meeting his scheduled payments and to collect on an insurance policy." Although Akram's antics had already been exposed as a fraud, CAIR continued to list this case as an anti-Muslim hate crime. In another incident, a Muslim-owned market in Texas was burned down in August 2004. Although the Muslim owner was arrested the following month for having set the fire himself, CAIR included the case in its report.[56]

It was all in service of portraying Muslims in the United States as victims of pitiless scapegoating and unfounded suspicions trumped up by "Islamophobes." If those "Islamophobes" were silenced, then America's traditional welcoming of "the other" would supposedly triumph over bigotry, racism, and xenophobia. This would rule out any investigation of what role Islam itself might play in Islamic jihad terror and of the nature and goals of political Islam—which are precisely what the OIC, CAIR, and other purveyors of the "Islamophobia" myth want most desperately to obscure.

"The Future Must Not Belong to Those Who Slander the Prophet of Islam"

Barack Obama made his objectives abundantly clear in September 2012, when he said in a speech before the General Assembly of the United Nations, "The future must not belong to those who slander the prophet of Islam."[57] According to a manual of Islamic law endorsed by the foremost authority in Sunni Islam, Cairo's Al-Azhar University, slander "means to mention anything concerning a person that he would dislike"—in other words, not necessarily something untrue, but just something that a person would prefer not be known.[58] Certainly what the OIC and CAIR dislike are the airing of any criticism of Islam and jihad—and they are determined to stamp it out. Through their network of supporters in Washington, they have made significant headway toward that goal.

CHAPTER SIX

NOT JUST IN EGYPT ANYMORE

The Muslim Brotherhood in the United States

Their stated goal: "eliminating and destroying the Western civilization from within." Their methods: insinuating themselves into centers of power in the United States and Europe as "moderate" Muslims, who can exert quiet influence in the direction of eventually replacing Western culture and the U.S. Constitution with an Islamic caliphate and sharia law. Their name: the Muslim Brotherhood.

It sounds like a crazy conspiracy theory. But it only sounds that way because of the determined ignorance and downright misinformation that holds sway in our public discourse about Islam in this country. It is a cherished dogma of today's political correct elites is that Islam is no different from Christianity, Judaism, Hinduism, Buddhism, and other faiths. Playing on this blurring of the lines between very different belief systems, defenders of the Islamic supremacist project often claim that laws restricting the spread of Islamic law (sharia) in the United

States would also restrict the practice of religions with longer histories in America. But unlike other modern faiths, Islam is a political religion. Traditionally, Islam recognizes no separation between religion and state. In its canonical texts and teachings, Islam calls on believers to regard themselves as at war with those who will not submit to Allah—a call that numerous clerics regularly reinforce today in their sermons and religious instructions.

In 1990 the member states of the OIC, which as we have seen is now the largest voting bloc in the United Nations, met in Egypt and adopted the "Cairo Declaration on Human Rights in Islam." The Cairo Declaration states that "all human beings form one family whose members are united by their subordination to Allah."[1] To say that that all human beings are united in subordination to Allah has clear political implications in light of traditional and mainstream Islamic theology and law.

The Muslim Brotherhood is one of the primary organizations dedicated to Islam's political supremacy. Its vision of a liberated society is one ruled by Islamic law, which would institutionalize the oppression of women, gays, Christians, Jews, and all non-Muslims—beginning with the denial of the freedom of speech and the freedom of conscience.

The Muslim Brotherhood now generally—but not universally, as the fateful events of the summer of 2013 in Egypt made clear—eschews violence. But it has spawned two of the world's most notorious jihad terror groups. The Palestinian jihad terrorist organization Hamas identifies itself in its charter as a branch of the Brotherhood: "The Islamic Resistance Movement [Hamas] is one of the wings of the Muslim Brothers in Palestine. The Muslim Brotherhood Movement is a world organization, the largest Islamic Movement in the modern era."[2] Al Qaeda founders Abdullah Azzam and Osama bin Laden, as well as its current leader, Ayman al-Zawahiri, were all members of the Brotherhood or trained by Brotherhood members.[3]

The Brotherhood is best known today for its ill-fated stint in power in Egypt in 2012 and 2013, but it is actually an international organization with considerable influence in Western Europe and the United States. Founded in Egypt in 1928 by Hasan al-Banna, its goal is to create a unified global Islamic state in which Sharia is fully enforced. Al-Banna declared that it was "a duty incumbent on every Muslim to struggle towards the aim of making every people Muslim and the whole world Islamic, so that the banner of Islam can flutter over the earth and the call of the Muezzin can resound in all the corners of the world: God is greatest [Allahu akbar]!"[4] The motto of the Muslim Brotherhood puts its program succinctly: "Allah is our goal. The Prophet is our leader. The Qur'an is our law. Jihad is our way. Dying in the way of Allah is our highest aspiration."[5]

The Muslim Brotherhood's goals for the United States are spelled out in an internal Muslim Brotherhood document that the FBI seized in 2005 in the northern Virginia headquarters of an Islamic charity, the Holy Land Foundation. Once the largest Islamic charity in the United States, the Holy Land Foundation was shut down for sending charitable contributions to Hamas. The captured document was entitled, "An Explanatory Memorandum on the General Strategic Goal for the Group in North America."[6]

In it, Muslim Brotherhood members were told that the Brotherhood was working on presenting Islam as a "civilizational alternative" to non-Islamic forms of society and governance and supporting "the global Islamic state wherever it is."[7] In working to establish that Islamic state, Muslim Brotherhood members in the United States "must understand that their work in America is a kind of grand jihad in eliminating and destroying the Western civilization from within and 'sabotaging' its miserable house by their hands and the hands of the believers so that it is eliminated and Allah's religion is made victorious over all other religions."[8]

The Muslim Brotherhood has been active in the United States for decades and is the moving force behind virtually all of the mainstream Muslim organizations in America: the Islamic Society of North America (ISNA), the Islamic Circle of North America (ICNA), the Muslim American Society (MAS), the Muslim Students Association (MSA), the Council on American-Islamic Relations (CAIR), the International Institute for Islamic Thought (IIIT), and many others.

A Famous "Moderate"—and
Successful Brotherhood Operative

Brotherhood operatives pursued their goal—"eliminating and destroying the Western civilization from within," as you will recall—in Europe and the United States by ingratiating themselves to those in power as "moderate Muslims" and thus inserting themselves into the centers of power, from which they can exert quiet influence on events. One illustrative example is the meteoric rise and fall of the Muslim Brotherhood operative who was for a time the most well-connected and influential Muslim in the United States: Abdulrahman Alamoudi.

Alamoudi was born in Eritrea and immigrated to the United States from Yemen in 1979. In 1990, he founded the American Muslim Council, which soon became a key player in Washington politics, and the American Muslim Armed Forces and Veterans Affairs Council (AMAFVAC), which was for a considerable period one of only two Muslim groups authorized to approve Muslim chaplains for the U.S. military.

Although he was a member of the Muslim Brotherhood, Alamoudi was universally respected as a moderate Muslim and was promoted by figures in both parties, including conservative activist Grover Norquist.[9] During the presidency of Bill Clinton, Alamoudi served as a State Department "goodwill ambassador" to Muslim lands.[10] His influence did not wane when the Republicans came to power: Alamoudi attended a June 2001 White House briefing on George W. Bush's faith-based initiative program and was present with Bush at the National Cathedral in Washington for a prayer service shortly after 9/11.[11]

It was taken for granted that Alamoudi was a "moderate," but in fact he never bothered to conceal his true allegiances. In 1994, he had declared his support for the jihad terror group Hamas, claiming that "Hamas is not a terrorist group" and saying that it did "good work." In 1996, Alamoudi defended Hamas leader Mousa Abu Marzouk, who was ultimately deported because of his work with Hamas, and currently leads a branch of the terror group in Syria. "I really consider him to be from among the best people in the Islamic movement," Alamoudi said of Marzouk. "Hamas ... and I work together with him."

At a rally in October 2000, Alamoudi encouraged those in the crowd to show their support for Hamas and Hizballah. As the crowd cheered,

Alamoudi shouted, "I have been labeled by the media in New York to be a supporter of Hamas, anybody supports Hamas here?" As the crowd cheered, "Yes," Alamoudi asked the same question again and then added, "Hear that, Bill Clinton, we are all supporters of Hamas, Allahu akbar. I wish they added that I am also a supporter of Hizballah. Anybody supports Hizballah here?" The crowd again roared its approval.[12] In January 2001, the same year he was invited to the Bush White House, Alamoudi traveled to Beirut to attend a conference with leaders of al Qaeda, Hamas, Hizballah, and Islamic jihad.[13] But even that did not raise any concern among those in Washington who were confident that Alamoudi was a sterling and reliable "moderate."

But in September 2003, Alamoudi was finally and definitively unmasked. He was arrested in London's Heathrow Airport while carrying $340,000 in cash—money that, as it turned out, he had received from Libyan president Muammar Gaddafi in order to finance an al Qaeda plot to murder the Saudi crown prince, the future king Abdullah.[14] The following month he was extradited to the United States, where American officials arrested him. Indicted on numerous charges, Alamoudi was found to have funneled over a million dollars to al Qaeda; he pled guilty to being a senior al Qaeda financier and was sentenced in October 2004 to twenty-three years in prison.[15]

Even the spectacular fall of Alamoudi, however, did not raise any general concern about the goals of Muslim Brotherhood operatives in Washington. On the contrary: in the summer of 2011, the Obama administration reduced Alamoudi's sentence by six years, without making public its reasons for doing so.[16]

More Lethal Still

An even more lethal Muslim Brotherhood operative in the United States was Anwar al-Awlaki.

Born in New Mexico in 1971, al-Awlaki attended Colorado State University, where he was president of the Muslim Students Association, a Brotherhood front. While still a student, al-Awlaki began preaching at the Islamic Center of Fort Collins. One congregant later recalled, "He was very knowledgeable. He was an excellent person—very nice, dedicated to religion." Later he became imam at the Denver Islamic Society, and later still at the Dar Al-Hijrah Islamic Center, a mosque in northern Virginia, where he counseled two of the 9/11 hijackers.[17]

In the years following the September 11 attacks, al-Awlaki became one of the world's leading ideologues of jihad and abetted the plotting of numerous jihad attacks. He ultimately became internationally notorious for his role in the Christmas Day underwear bomb plot in an airplane over Detroit, the attempted Times Square car bombing, and the Fort Hood jihad massacre—after leaving the United States in 2002 because of a post-9/11 "climate of fear and intimidation," according to his friend Johari Abdul-Malik, director of outreach for the Dar Al-Hijrah mosque.[18] The Muslim Brotherhood in Yemen gave al-Awlaki shelter.[19]

Like Alamoudi, Al-Awlaki carefully cultivated a moderate image; he was so successful at this that shortly after 9/11, the *New York Times* held him up as a shining example of "a new generation of Muslim leader capable of merging East and West" and quoted him explaining how his community was now more careful to root out jihadist sentiments: "In the past we were oblivious. We didn't really care much because we never expected things to happen. Now I think things are different. What we might have tolerated in the past, we won't tolerate any more. There were some statements that were inflammatory, and were considered just talk, but now we realize that talk can be taken seriously and acted upon in a violent radical way."[20]

But that was just disinformation, as the FBI knew even at that time. They had al-Awlaki under surveillance. Nonetheless, in a precise illustration of the absurdity and incoherence of Washington's policy toward Islam and jihad, al-Awlaki's moderate credentials were so taken for granted even during the period of this surveillance that on February 5, 2002, the FBI trailed al-Awlaki as the imam traveled through Washington—all the way to the Pentagon, where he gave an address at a Defense Department luncheon on "Islam and Middle Eastern Politics and Culture."[21]

Of course, in later years, al-Awlaki emerged as one of the world's most notorious jihad terror leaders, and in 2011 was targeted and killed in Yemen by an American air strike.

Hiding in Plain Sight

Al-Awlaki is far from being the only Muslim Brotherhood activist who aided jihad terror efforts while operating within U.S. Muslim organizations that present a moderate face. Many have done so. The Center for the Study of Islam and Democracy (CSID), a Washington, D.C.–based non-profit organization, describes itself as "dedicated to studying Islamic and democratic political thought and merging them into a modern Islamic democratic discourse."[22] Serving on the board of this apparently high-minded organization is one Jamal Barzinji.

Although Barzinji condemns the 9/11 attacks as "totally against Islam and Muslim teachings," he has links to seven organizations that federal agents have raided for their involvement in the financing of jihad terrorism, including the International Institute for Islamic Thought (IIIT), yet another Muslim Brotherhood front, where he serves as vice president.[23] After 9/11, federal agents raided Barzinji's office and home. An affidavit filed in federal court in 2003 charged that "Barzinji is not only closely associated with PIJ [Palestinian Islamic Jihad] (as evidenced by ties to [Sami] al-Arian, including documents seized in Tampa), but also with Hamas."[24]

Entire organizations practice the same deception. The Muslim American Society (MAS) is the principal Muslim Brotherhood organization in the United States. Typically, MAS describes itself as "dynamic charitable, religious, social, cultural, and educational, organization."[25] It claims that it "has no affiliation with the Ikhwan al-Muslimoon (Muslim Brotherhood, also known as the Ikhwan) or with any other international organization."[26]

However, in a 2004 exposé, the *Chicago Tribune* reported that "in recent years, the U.S. Brotherhood operated under the name Muslim American Society, according to documents and interviews. One of the nation's major Islamic groups, it was incorporated in Illinois in 1993 after a contentious debate among Brotherhood members."[27] In a January 2012 prison interview with federal officials, Abdurrahman Alamoudi confirmed this, saying flatly: "Everyone knows that MAS is the Muslim Brotherhood."[28]

The MAS, like other Muslim Brotherhood groups in the United States, openly recommends Islamic law as the solution to social ills. Adjunct members of the MAS are required to read Fathi Yakun's book *To Be a Muslim*, in which Yakun declares, "Until the nations of the world have functionally Islamic governments, every individual who is careless or lazy in working for Islam is sinful." Even worse, the website of MAS's Minnesota chapter has featured these anti-Semitic, pro-jihad quotations from the Islamic prophet Muhammad:

- "If you gain victory over the men of Jews, kill them."
- "The Hour will not be established until you fight with the Jews, and the stone behind which a Jew will be hiding will say, 'O Muslim! There is a Jew hiding behind me, so kill him.'"
- "May Allah destroy the Jews, because they used the graves of their prophets as places of worship."[29]

In December 2000, MAS president Esam S. Omeish was videotaped at a rally in Washington openly endorsing the bloody Palestinian jihad against Israeli civilians: "We the Muslims of the Washington Metropolitan area are here today in sub-freezing temperatures to tell our brothers and sisters in Palestine that you have learned the way, that you have known that the jihad way is the way to liberate your land.... We are with you, we are supporting you and we will do everything that we can, insha'Allah [Allah willing], to help your cause."[30]

CAIR: Hamas's Strident U.S. Voice

But far outshining the Muslim American Society in notoriety and influence is another Muslim Brotherhood group, the Council on American-Islamic Relations (CAIR). Nihad Awad and Omar Ahmad, two officials of the Islamic Association for Palestine (IAP), which was listed as one of the Muslim Brotherhood's allied organizations in the 1991 memorandum, founded the Hamas-linked Muslim Brotherhood group CAIR in 1994.

In 2005, the federal government shut down the IAP as a Hamas front. The Immigration and Naturalization Service reported in 2001 that the IAP was so close to its parent organization that it published and distributed Hamas communiqués on its own letterhead, "as well as other written documentation to include the HAMAS charter and glory records, which are tributes to HAMAS' violent 'successes.'"[31] Oliver Revell, a former chief of the FBI's counterterrorism department, called the IAP "a front organization for Hamas that engages in propaganda for Islamic militants."[32] In 2005, the U.S. government shut down the IAP as a Hamas front. But CAIR continues to operate here and is even taken seriously as a civil rights organization, with its spokesmen courted by politicians, regularly appearing in newspaper articles and on national TV whenever either jihad attacks or effective counter-jihad raise fears of "backlash" against American Muslims.

It should come as no surprise that several CAIR officials have already been convicted of participating in violent jihad activities. Randall Todd "Ismail" Royer, CAIR's former communications specialist and civil rights coordinator, participated in the "Virginia jihad group," which was indicted on forty-one counts of "conspiracy to train for and participate in a violent jihad overseas."[33] Royer is now serving a twenty-year prison sentence after pleading guilty to lesser charges.[34]

Ghassan Elashi, the founder of CAIR's Texas chapter, is likewise now in prison for jihad activity. In 2009, he was sentenced to sixty-five years in prison for funneling over $12 million in charitable contributions to Hamas while serving as head of the Holy Land Foundation.[35] Other former CAIR officials have been convicted of jihad terror activities as well, raising the question of how this supposedly moderate group failed so abysmally to distinguish "moderates" from "extremists."

CAIR itself was named as an unindicted co-conspirator in the Holy Land case. The organization not only facilitated donations to the Holy Land Foundation, but also received money from it—no less than half a million dollars. CAIR cofounder Nihad Awad vehemently denied this fact when terror researcher Steven Emerson confronted him: "This is an outright lie. Our organization did not receive any seed money from the Holy Land Foundation. CAIR raises its own funds and we challenge Mr. Emerson to provide even a shred of evidence to support his ridiculous claim." Emerson then published an image of the canceled check.[36]

Yet despite its connections to the Muslim Brotherhood and Hamas, the terror convictions of several of its former officials, and its virtually unanimous opposition to counterterror laws, investigations, and other initiatives, CAIR remains widely respected. Nearly everyone, particularly in Washington, assumes that CAIR is exactly what it says it is: a Muslim civil rights organization, working for the rights of Muslims in the United States and deeply loyal to Constitutional principles and freedoms. The organization's website features testimonials from congressmen and senators of both parties, as well as security and military officials—all unconsciously testifying to how the organization has surpassed even Alamoudi in its deceptiveness.[37]

- "I'm glad that you have established such a strong voice in the community and that you are working to maintain a strong sense of cultural and economic identity." —former Maryland governor Robert L. Ehrlich Jr., Republican, December 2005
- "The vision of CAIR to promote 'justice and mutual understanding' is of course also an American vision, and its mission 'to enhance understating [sic!] of Islam, encourage dialogue, protect civil liberties, empower American Muslims and build coalitions that promote justice and mutual understanding' is in the best traditions of American civil rights movements, both past and present." —former New Jersey governor Jon S. Corzine, Democrat, April 2009
- "It has been a pleasure working with the Council over the years to further our mutual understanding, and I look forward to continuing our progress in the years to come." —former Michigan governor Jennifer M. Granholm, Democrat, March 2010
- "I particularly want to commend CAIR for working to educate others about Islam, a religion of more than one

billion people in the world. CAIR also has provided members of the Muslim community in the United States with an important voice in promoting social justice and mutual understanding. CAIR has 31 offices nationwide and in Canada and through your work you have helped promote a dialogue among employers, law enforcement officials, and government agencies. CAIR understands the importance of developing mutual understanding and trust." —Senator Benjamin L. Cardin, Maryland Democrat, November 2007

- "It is my understanding that CAIR seeks to enhance the understanding of Islam, encourage dialogue, protect civil liberties, empower American Muslims, and build coalitions that promote justice and mutual understanding. Seventeen years of advocacy work is a noteworthy accomplishment, and all those who have contributed to the council's success over the years should be proud of the exemplary work you have done." —Senator Carl Levin, Michigan Democrat, October 2011

- "Since its inception in 1994, CAIR has been at the forefront of enhancing understanding and building coalitions that promote justice and mutual understanding." —Senator Barbara A. Mikulski, Maryland Democrat, October 2011

- "I applaud CAIR's mission to enhance understanding and build coalitions that promote justice and mutual understanding." —former Maryland senator Paul Sarbanes, Democrat, November 2006

- "CAIR promotes a positive image of Islam and Muslims in America with the hope that this example, along with communication and grassroots activism, will eliminate any misrepresentations of Islam on the part of non-Muslims." —former senator George V. Voinovich, Ohio Republican, September 2010

- "I commend all those who work with your organization to help defend civil liberties, strengthen the dialogue between faith communities and improve the lives of others." —Senator Mark Warner, Virginia Democrat, October 2011

- "I commend the Council for their efforts promoting justice and mutual understanding." —Senator Jim Webb, Virginia Democrat, September 2011
- "CAIR has a long and distinguished history of consistent efforts that reflect a strong support for civil rights and social programs that promote the understanding and cultural heritage of the rapidly growing Muslim American community." —Representative John Conyers Jr., Michigan Democrat, September 2011
- "I thank CAIR for its advocacy and continuing to open the lines of communication to ensure that we make democracy work for everyone." —former representative Jesse L. Jackson Jr., Illinois Democrat, October 2011
- "… take great pride in recognizing CAIR. Your dedication and commitment is truly worthy of the respect, admiration and commendation of the United States Congress." —Representative Sheila Jackson Lee, Texas Democrat, October 2011
- "I applaud the Council on American-Islamic Relations for its efforts strengthening the understanding of Islam, encouraging dialogues, and building coalitions that promote justice and mutual understanding." —Representative John Lewis, Georgia Democrat, September 2011
- "CAIR does important work in defending civil rights and civil liberties and educating people about the Muslim faith in communities across the country, including Seattle, which I represent in Congress." —Representative Jim McDermott, Washington Democrat, November 2007

And on and on—so many that to reproduce them all would massively increase the size of this book. The support for CAIR cuts across all political and ideological lines. The CAIR website even carries a testimonial from Bill O'Reilly: "Number one, it's not fair of to you criticize CAIR, OK? Because CAIR isn't fostering any kind of jihad, as far as I know."[38]

The U.S. government agrees, despite the Justice Department's earlier designation of CAIR as an "unindicted co-conspirator" in the Holy Land case. In July 2010, the State Department sent the executive director of CAIR's Michigan chapter, Dawud Walid, to Bamako, Mali, to try to foster "sustained interaction" between the United States and Mali. While in Mali, instead of representing the United States in any way that could conceivably have helped earn the Muslim Malians' respect and trust, Walid sounded CAIR's familiar notes of Muslim victimhood, claiming that "American Muslims have been subjected to increased discrimination from racial and religious profiling by law enforcement."[39]

Walid was not the only operative from a Brotherhood-linked group to travel on a U.S. government junket at taxpayer expense: Zahid H. Bukhari, president of another Brotherhood group, the Islamic Circle of North America (ICNA), enjoyed a speaking tour of India, Pakistan, Portugal, Latvia, Russia, and Bosnia that cost taxpayers $60,000.[40] Meanwhile, another indication of how warmly the U.S. government regards the Muslim Brotherhood came in 2010, when Kifah Mustapha, another Muslim Brotherhood operative with links to Hamas, received an extensive tour of FBI headquarters and the National Counterterrorism Center.[41]

ISNA: Almost as Influential and Unsavory as CAIR

Just as influential as CAIR in Washington is the Islamic Society of North America (ISNA), which was founded in 1981 by operatives from the Muslim Students Association, still another Brotherhood group in the United States. One of ISNA's founders, Sami al-Arian, later pled guilty to playing a leadership role in the terror group Palestinian Islamic Jihad while holding down a job as a computer science professor at the University of South Florida.[42]

In summer 2008, federal prosecutors rejected claims that ISNA was unfairly named as an unindicted co-conspirator in the Holy Land

Foundation terror funding case.[43] ISNA has even admitted ties to the Muslim Brotherhood and Hamas, although it disingenuously insists that those ties are a thing of the past.[44]

ISNA is affiliated with still another Muslim Brotherhood group, the North American Islamic Trust (NAIT), an organization that has Saudi-government backing. NAIT reportedly holds mortgages on between 50 and 80 percent on all mosques in the United States—which means that the teaching in those mosques will inevitably favor the Wahhabi perspective on Islam, to which both the Saudi government and the Muslim Brotherhood subscribe—and which is political, authoritarian, and supremacist.[45] An Islamic writer who opposes Saudi influence on Muslims in America, Kaukab Siddique, notes, "ISNA controls most mosques in America and thus also controls who will speak at every Friday prayer, and which literature will be distributed there."[46]

According to Emerson, ISNA "is a radical group hiding under a false veneer of moderation." It "convenes annual conferences where Islamist militants have been given a platform to incite violence and promote hatred," and even held a fundraiser for the defense of Hamas leader Mousa Abu Marzook when he was arrested in 1997.[47] And the Indianapolis TV station WTHR, which is located near ISNA's headquarters, reported in 2006 that "about a dozen charities, organizations and individuals" were "under federal scrutiny for possible ties to terrorism that are in some way linked to ISNA."[48]

Nonetheless, like CAIR, ISNA enjoys widespread mainstream acceptance. In November 2007, Mohamed Magid, who was then ISNA's vice president and is now its president, went on a speaking tour of the Middle East under the auspices of the Bureau of Education and Cultural Affairs of the U.S. State Department.[49] In September 2008, Daniel Sutherland, the Department of Homeland Security Officer for Civil Rights and Civil Liberties, addressed ISNA's annual convention.[50] And that was just the beginning of ISNA's access to the highest levels of power.

ISNA in the White House

Ingrid Mattson, then president of ISNA, was invited to offer a prayer at the National Cathedral during Barack Obama's inaugural festivities on January 20, 2009. Valerie Jarrett, Obama's senior advisor for public engagement and international affairs and a longtime, close Obama aide, asked Mattson to join the White House Council on Women and Girls, which is dedicated to "advancing women's leadership in all communities and sectors—up to the U.S. presidency...."[51]

Late in January 2010, DHS secretary Janet Napolitano held a meeting with "Muslim, Arab, Sikh and South Asian American community leaders," in which Muslim leaders and others called for a relaxation of security procedures and scrutiny of the Muslim community. "Although it is not confirmed," noted the Global Muslim Brotherhood Daily Report, "the press release contains a list of media contacts including leaders from ISNA, the Muslim Public Affair Council (MPAC) and the Muslim American Society (MAS), suggesting that the Muslim 'community leaders' were in fact representatives of the U.S. Muslim Brotherhood."[52]

Just over two weeks later, ISNA officials met with John Brennan, who was then Assistant to the President on National Security for Homeland Security and Counterterrorism. At this meeting, ISNA officials downplayed the terror threat from the Muslim community in America and attempted to portray Muslims as victims of hyper-vigilant law enforcement. In response, Brennan assured them that the Obama administration would protect the civil rights of Muslims in the United States, which is all to the good—but he did not call upon them to back up their words about being opposed to jihad terror with effective action.[53]

In August 2011, President Barack Obama hosted an iftar, the nightly dinner to break the Muslim fast during the month of Ramadan, at the White House. He invited Mohamed Magid, along with several other Muslim leaders with questionable pedigrees—and, betraying his awareness of how controversial these invitations would be, left their names off the published guest list.[54] But the fact that they were there at all was an impressive display of their clout in Washington and of how little their Muslim Brotherhood ties mattered to the political elites.

Obama made sure that Muslim Brotherhood members were in the audience when he gave his Cairo speech in June 2009 and supported the Egyptian uprisings against Hosni Mubarak even though it was clear that the Brotherhood stood to be their chief beneficiary.[55] Meanwhile, domestically, according to former FBI special agent John Guandolo, "what we're seeing not just inside the White House, but inside the government entities, the national security entities, the State Department—is a strong push by the Muslim Brotherhood to get their people not just into operational positions, but policy positions—deeper, long term, bureaucratic positions."[56]

No Effective Opposition

With the Democrats so closely tied to Brotherhood interests, it is all the more imperative for the Republican Party to resist Brotherhood influence and infiltration. Unfortunately, however, the two dominant parties are not all that different in this regard. Brotherhood influence within the Republican Party may be even more extensive than in the Democrat Party, primarily because of the influence of one man: Grover Norquist, the head of Americans for Tax Reform. Norquist has so much influence within the Republican Party that virtually every 2012 Republican presidential candidate had some contact with him, and few Republican candidates in recent years have succeeded without his support. Yet for years Norquist has also been enabling Brotherhood access to the highest levels of power in Washington. Shortly after 9/11, Norquist set up a meeting for fifteen Muslim leaders with President Bush. One was Muzammil Siddiqi, then president of ISNA.[57]

Norquist was close to Alamoudi, the now-exposed and imprisoned al Qaeda financier. Alamoudi contributed $50,000 to Janus-Merritt Strategies, a lobbying group that Norquist founded.[58] Alamoudi also gave Norquist a $10,000 loan and a $10,000 gift for Norquist's organization for Muslims, the Islamic Institute.[59] Norquist also introduced Bush to Nihad Awad, CAIR's cofounder and executive director.[60]

These alliances have shown their influence in Norquist's public positions. Former Reagan administration official Frank Gaffney revealed that "Norquist was also a prime-mover behind efforts to secure one of the Islamists' top pre-9/11 agenda items: the abolition of a section of the 1996 Anti-Terrorism and Effective Death Penalty Act that permits authorities to use what critics call 'secret evidence' ... Norquist was an honoree at an event held by Sami Al-Arian's National Coalition to Protect Political Freedom in July 2001, two months before 9/11. The award was for being a 'champion of the abolishment movement against secret evidence.'"[61] Al-Arian in 2006 pleaded guilty to "conspiracy to make or receive contributions of funds to or for the benefit of Palestinian Islamic Jihad."[62]

One of Norquist's Islamic supremacist protégés, Imad "David" Ramadan, was elected to the Virginia House of Delegates by a margin of fifty votes in November 2011. Displaying a fine talent for deception, Ramadan first joined Norquist and another one of his protégés, Suhail Khan, in denouncing opposition to the proposed sixteen-story mosque at Ground Zero; then he denied having done so.[63] Only a few high-profile Republicans, including Norquist himself, registered support for the abortive Ground Zero mosque that Muslim Brotherhood–linked entities tried to begin constructing in 2011. Thanks to Norquist's sponsorship, Khan is a board member of the American Conservative Union, which holds the popular annual Conservative Political Action Conference in Washington, attended by thousands of conservatives.

Suhail Khan was a close associate of Alamoudi, the senior al Qaeda financier now in prison, who presented Khan with an award in 2001. "I'm really proud to be with Suhail Khan," Alamoudi said on that occasion. "Some of you saw him today in the White House, but inshallah [Allah willing], you will see him in better places in the White House, inshallah." Also in 2001, just before the 9/11 attacks, Khan spoke ISNA's annual convention. He was introduced there by Jamal Barzinji. Khan's father, Mahboob Khan, was one of ISNA's founders. Suhail Khan had also addressed ISNA's 1999 convention, where he declared, "The early Muslims loved death, dying for the sake of almighty Allah, more than the oppressors loved life. This must be the case when we are fighting…. What are our oppressors going to do with a people like us? We are prepared to give our lives for the cause of Islam." Khan has also collaborated with CAIR.[64]

Muslim Brotherhood influence in both parties and the U.S. government in general is not limited to these individuals; many others also have risen to positions of influence. And part of that influence involves the ability to quash any investigation of their activities and allegiances—as a small and courageous group of congressmen found out in the summer of 2012.

CHAPTER SEVEN

ISLAMIC INFILTRATION? McCARTHYISM!

In July 2012, Republican congresswoman Michele Bachmann of Minnesota and four other U.S. representatives sent letters to five U.S. defense, diplomatic, intelligence, and law enforcement agencies, calling for investigation of a "deep penetration in the halls of our United States government" by Muslim Brotherhood operatives.[1]

Immediately the focus became Bachmann herself, rather than the possible Muslim Brotherhood infiltration. Christina Warner, director of an interfaith organization known as Shoulder-to-Shoulder, said that "asking for investigations of American Muslims are cause for concern and give an undeserved and harmful platform to fringe accusations."[2] Rabbi David Saperstein of the Religious Action Center of Reform Judaism declared that the accusations "reflect a general pattern of Islamophobia that touches too many areas of our society. Allegations such as these by members of Congress add legitimacy to this distressing trend."[3]

When asked about the allegations, Counterterror Chief John Brennan, according to the online magazine Salon, "chuckled lightly, rolled his eyes, and replied, 'I would refer you to the five members of Congress who made that remark. I have no idea of what it is that they are making reference to, and I'm not even going to try to divine what it is that sometimes comes out of Congress.'"[4]

Just like Tail Gunner Joe

Others were more angry than amused. Salon excoriated Bachmann for what it called her "Muslim witch hunt," and CAIR's national executive director, Nihad Awad wrote to the congresswoman, "We remain eternally grateful that, like Sen. Joseph McCarthy before you, your power is limited, enumerated and constrained by our nation's constitution. Your letters challenging the loyalty of patriotic American Muslims based on discredited anti-Muslim conspiracy theories can only be described as devoid of a sense of decency."[5]

Awad went on to defend those Bachmann had named as possible Muslim Brotherhood operatives: "Among those you accuse, Mrs. Huma Abedin helps the Secretary of State represent the best interests of our nation overseas. The Society of Former Special Agents last year honored Mohamed Elibiary for his 'extraordinary contributions to specific cases in support of the FBI's counterterrorism mission.' Dalia Mogahed was appointed to the president's Advisory Council on Faith-Based and Neighborhood Partnerships and has advised the Department of Homeland Security. Imam Mohamed Magid enjoys widespread interfaith respect and has also advised the Department of Homeland Security. The honorable public service of these individuals deserves better treatment than political theatrics characterized by half-truths, overblown accusations and guilt by association."[6]

All of that was beside the point. None of it established that the people Awad named were not tied to the Muslim Brotherhood. The questions swirling around Elibiary, a Department of Homeland Security official, were a case in point. Bachmann's letter to the DHS's inspector general stated that Elibiary has "extensive ties to the Muslim Brotherhood" and "sympathy for Islamist causes," and accused him of "gain[ing] access to classified documents."

Napolitano Digs In

In July 2012, Congressman Louis Gohmert, Texas Republican, one of the signers of the letters asking for investigation of Muslim Brotherhood infiltration, asked Homeland Security secretary Janet Napolitano about Elibiary, "Are you saying before this Congress right now, that as Secretary of Homeland Security, that it is a lie that Mohamed Elibiary downloaded material from a classified website using the secret security clearance you gave him? Are you saying that's a lie?"

Gohmert was referring to a 2011 incident in which investigative journalist Patrick Poole reported, "Elibiary may have been given access to a sensitive database of state and local intelligence reports, and then allegedly shopped some of those materials to a media outlet." According to Poole, Elibiary approached "a left-leaning media outlet" with reports marked "For Official Use Only" that he said demonstrated rampant "Islamophobia" in the Texas Department of Public Safety (DPS). The media outlet declined to do a story, but what was Elibiary doing shopping the "Official Use Only" documents in the first place? Poole checked with Steve McCraw, director of the Texas Department of Public Safety, who "confirmed that Elibiary has access to the Homeland Security State and Local Intelligence Community of Interest (HS SLIC) database, which contains hundreds of thousands of intelligence reports and products that are intended for intelligence sharing between law enforcement agencies." Said McCraw of Elibiary, "We know that he has accessed DPS documents and downloaded them."[7]

But Napolitano responded to Gohmert's inquiry with a flat denial: "I'm saying that is inaccurate. That is correct." When Gohmert pressed her on what was inaccurate about it, Napolitano began talking about prejudice against Muslims, and then said, "I'm saying that he … as far as I know … he did not download classified documents." Gohmert saw through that immediately, responding, "One of the games that gets played by some people who come up here and testify is that they have somebody not provide them with adequate information so that they can come in here and say 'so far as I know,' 'not to my knowledge,' that kind of thing, and they obscure the truth." Then he asked Napolitano, "Has Elibiary's status on Homeland Security Advisory Council changed?" Napolitano said that it had not.[8]

Thus it was clear that Elibiary had not suffered any career difficulties because of the call for a congressional investigation into his possible ties to the Muslim Brotherhood and the report that he may have leaked classified information. Indeed, Napolitano was anxious to protect him, parrying Gohmert's questions and only reluctantly giving him straight answers. In light of the obvious favor Elibiary enjoyed within the Obama administration, it was hard to see him as a victim of the McCarthyism of which Awad had complained—unless, of course, Bachmann's allegations about him were self-evidently false and needlessly damaging to a patriot's reputation.

Elibiary's Iranian Hero

But in reality, there had been questions about Elibiary's true allegiances for years. He was one of the speakers at a December 2004 conference in Dallas titled "A Tribute to the Great Islamic Visionary." The visionary in question was none other than the founding father of the Islamic Republic of Iran, the ayatollah Khomeini.[9]

I met Elibiary several years ago, when he attended a conference at which I was speaking in Dallas, and I took the opportunity to ask him about his appearance at the Khomeini conference. Elibiary claimed that he hadn't known what kind of conference it was going to be, although he didn't explain why he went ahead and appeared there anyway, once he found out. Among those who found this explanation wanting was journalist Rod Dreher of the *Dallas Morning News*, whose skepticism angered Elibiary. The great moderate subsequently threatened Dreher, telling him, "Expect someone to put a banana in your exhaust pipe."[10]

Yet despite all this, Elibiary still got his appointment to the DHS Advisory Council, and in September 2013 was promoted to the position of senior fellow on the council.[11] There was no indication that anyone within the DHS or any other agency ever investigated Elibiary's allegiances or connections; he appears to have risen so far because government and law enforcement officials, as well as the mainstream media, have for years been so avid to find a moderate Muslim who will stand against Islamic jihad terrorism that they will accept virtually anyone's claim to be just that, no questions asked.

Mohamed Magid's position of influence was another indication of this phenomenon. Awad wrote to Bachmann, "Imam Mohamed Magid enjoys widespread interfaith respect and has also advised the Department of Homeland Security." Magid was also, however, president of the Islamic Society of North America, a group with admitted ties to Hamas and the Muslim Brotherhood.[12]

Mogahed Loves Sharia

And yet another "moderate" with less than moderate views was Dalia Mogahed, who, Awad said, "was appointed to the president's Advisory Council on Faith-Based and Neighborhood Partnerships and has advised the Department of Homeland Security." In October 2009, Mogahed appeared on British television, where she said, "Sharia is not well understood and Islam as a faith is not well understood." She asserted that non-Muslims misunderstood sharia by associating it with "maximum criminal punishments" and "laws that … to many people seem unequal to women." The Western view of sharia was "oversimplified"; most Muslim women worldwide, she said, associated it with "gender justice."

Mogahed made her defense of sharia on a TV show hosted by a member of Hizb-ut-Tahrir, an international organization that is banned as a terrorist group in many nations and which is openly dedicated to the worldwide imposition of sharia and the destruction of all governments that are constituted according to any other political philosophy—including all constitutional republics with no established state religion.

On the show with Mogahed were two Hizb-ut-Tahrir members, who repeatedly attacked "man-made law" and the "lethal cocktail of liberty and capitalism" one encounters in Western societies. They said sharia should be "the source of legislation." Not "a" source. "The" source. Mogahed offered no contradiction to any of this.[13]

In light of all this, it was not at all farfetched to ask if Mogahed, whose views of Islam clearly coincided with those of the Brotherhood and other Islamic supremacist groups, might have some affiliation with such groups. But the response from the mainstream media and government officials throughout the summer of 2012 was that Bachmann and the other representatives were in the wrong simply for raising this possibility.

The Muslim Brotherhood's Congressman

The first Muslim member of Congress, Democratic representative Keith Ellison of Minnesota, whom Bachmann had accused of having a "long record of being associated" with CAIR and the Muslim Brotherhood, suggested that Bachmann was using the accusations for political gain and demanded evidence to back her claims.[14] "Your response," he wrote in a letter to Bachmann, "simply rehashes claims that have existed for years on anti-Muslim websites and contains no reliable information that the Muslim Brotherhood has infiltrated the U.S. government."[15]

Evoking the McCarthy era by his language, Ellison declared, "I am not now, nor have I ever been, associated with the Muslim Brotherhood." He accused Bachmann of religious bigotry: "I think she has a very narrowly prescribed definition of who belongs and who doesn't. And there's a whole bloc of people she don't like. I think she thinks that we're evil because we don't understand God the way she does.... It's also about marginalizing and alienating a certain group of Americans who she does not view are American enough."[16]

Not content with that, he also accused Bachmann of petty attention-seeking: "But you have to ask yourself, you know, why did she make this so public? Why did she seem to be seeking public attention for these allegations she was making? If she really had actionable intelligence, why wouldn't she go to the agencies that investigate these things? I think the answer is clear that she wanted attention. That was her goal all along."[17]

The only problem with Ellison's wounded-martyr stance toward Bachmann's accusations is that what she said was true. Ellison really did have a "long record of being associated" with Hamas-linked CAIR and the Muslim Brotherhood.

As long ago as 2006, Ellison's closeness to CAIR's cofounder and national executive director Nihad Awad was a matter of public record.[18] Awad, who notoriously said in 1994 that he was "in support of the Hamas movement," spoke at fundraisers for Ellison, raising considerable sums for his first congressional race. Ellison has appeared frequently at CAIR events since then.[19]

Investigative journalist Patrick Poole explained that according to the "Justice Department, Awad is a longtime Hamas operative. Multiple statements made by federal prosecutors identify Awad as one of the attendees at a 1993 meeting of U.S. Muslim Brotherhood Palestine Committee leaders in Philadelphia that was wiretapped by the FBI under a Foreign Intelligence Surveillance Act (FISA) warrant. The topic of discussion during that 1993 meeting was how to help Hamas by working in the U.S. to help sabotage the Oslo Peace Accords."[20] But none of that fazed Ellison. Nor did he ever express any concern over the fact that CAIR is also linked to the Muslim Brotherhood through its parent group, the Islamic Association for Palestine (IAP).

But Ellison's ties to the Muslim Brotherhood were even more direct. In 2008, Ellison accepted $13,350 from the Muslim American Society (MAS) to go on a pilgrimage to Mecca.[21] As we have seen, the Muslim American Society is the principal arm of the Muslim Brotherhood in the United States.

Mahdi Bray, executive director of the Muslim American Society Freedom Foundation, denied that MAS had funded Ellison's hajj: "Keith Ellison is a member of Congress who knows that congressmen don't take trips sponsored by nonprofits. That would be a breach of congressional ethics." Bray apparently failed to check with Ellison's office before issuing this statement, as the congressman's office issued its own statement saying, "The trip, funded by the Muslim American Society of Minnesota, was fully reviewed and approved in advance by the House Ethics Committee."[22]

Ellison has also retailed the concept of "Islamophobia," which is designed to intimidate Americans into being ashamed to resist jihad terror and Islamic supremacism.[23] And in March 2011, Ellison famously began weeping during the first hearings on Islamic jihad terrorism chaired by Peter King, Republican congressman from New York, as Ellison read what turned about to be a false report about a Muslim who went missing on 9/11 and was suspected of terror ties until he turned out to have been killed in the jihad attacks of that day.[24] Ellison's crocodile tears stole the show, successfully diverting media attention from what should have been the focus of the hearing: Islamic jihad activity in the United States.

The Real Witch Hunt

Consistent with the Left's ongoing advocacy for Islamic suprema-cists, in January 2013 the leftist advocacy group People for the American Way (PFAW) launched an all-out war against Bachmann, presenting House speaker John Boehner (R-OH) with a petition bearing 178,000 signatures demanding that Bachmann not be reappointed to the House Permanent Select Committee on Intelligence.[25]

Michael Keegan, president of PFAW, explained Bachmann's crime: "Michele Bachmann has used her position on the Intelligence Committee to spread baseless conspiracy theories and smear the reputations of honorable public servants. Speaker Boehner himself called her actions 'dangerous.' It's mysterious, then, why he has chosen to reward her reckless extremism with continued access to sensitive national security information and a powerful platform for her agenda."[26]

Since Boehner had previously criticized Bachmann over her call for investigation of Muslim Brotherhood infiltration, he might have been expected to be susceptible to this appeal; he did not, however, heed PFAW's call and remove Bachmann from the committee.

Corroboration?

Boehner may have felt less pressure to remove Bachmann from the committee after corroboration of some of her allegations came from an unlikely quarter—Egypt's *Rose El-Youssef* magazine, which asserted in a December 2012 article that six highly placed Muslim Brotherhood infiltrators within the Obama administration had transformed the United States "from a position hostile to Islamic groups and organizations in the world to the largest and most important supporter of the Muslim Brotherhood."[27]

The article said that "the six named people include: Arif Alikhan, Assistant Secretary of Homeland Security for policy development; Mohammed Elibiary, a member of the Homeland Security Advisory Council; Rashad Hussain, the U.S. special envoy to the Organization of the Islamic Conference; Salam al-Marayati, co-founder of the Muslim

Public Affairs Council (MPAC); Imam Mohamed Magid, president of the Islamic Society of North America (ISNA); and Eboo Patel, a member of President Obama's Advisory Council on Faith-Based Neighborhood Partnerships."[28]

Besides Elibiary and Magid, Bachmann had also raised concerns about the OIC, to which Hussain was Barack Obama's ambassador. And so the Egyptian article vindicated her concerns, and showed that her request that an investigation of Muslim Brotherhood infiltration be opened was entirely reasonable and not a manifestation of "bigotry," "racism," or "McCarthyism" at all—contrary to the hysterical (and formulaic) claims of her leftist detractors.

Of course, the Egyptian article had to be taken with a grain of salt. It could have been the product of a Muslim Brotherhood advocate in Egypt, exaggerating out of eagerness to bolster perceptions of his movement's clout and credibility. But it was equally possible that the article represented a genuine indication that Bachmann's concerns were entirely justified, and that the Muslim Brotherhood had indeed penetrated to the highest levels of the U.S. government.

That there was infiltration in American institutions was undeniable. Louay Safi, a Muslim activist with ties to two Muslim Brotherhood entities, the Islamic Society of North America and the International Institute of Islamic Thought, as well as to convicted jihad leader Sami al-Arian, was still training troops and even meeting with the families of victims at Fort Hood in December 2009, the month after Nidal Hasan's massacre.[29] Safi later became a leader of the Syrian opposition to Bashar Assad that was dominated by al Qaeda and other pro-sharia Islamic supremacist groups.[30]

And Gehad el-Hadded, a top Muslim Brotherhood official in Egypt, was for five years employed with the William J. Clinton Foundation.[31] The Clinton Foundation, of course, is not a government agency, but el-Hadded's involvement with it afforded him access to a former president of the United States and his associates, including present and former government officials. In September 2013, Egypt's military government arrested el-Hadded for his Muslim Brotherhood activities.[32]

Safi and el-Hadded were able to attain positions of influence; why was it prima facie impossible that other Islamic supremacists with ties to the Muslim Brotherhood did so as well, inside Washington itself? We will never know for sure without a careful investigation—which was exactly what Michele Bachmann had called for.

Huma and Hillary

For all the furor over Bachmann's call for an investigation of Muslim Brotherhood influence in Washington, nothing caused as much controversy as her naming Huma Abedin, then-Secretary of State Hillary Clinton's closest personal assistant and advisor. Abedin is an observant Muslim who lived in Saudi Arabia as a child; her brother Hassan works "as a fellow and partner with a number of Muslim Brotherhood members." Her mother, Saleha Mahmoud Abedin, is a professor in Saudi Arabia and a member of the Brotherhood's woman's division, the Muslim Sisterhood.[33] Her father, Syed Z. Abedin, was a professor in Saudi Arabia who founded the Institute for Muslim Minority Affairs, an organization supported by the Muslim World League, a Brotherhood organization.[34] Despite these facts, Senator John McCain, Arizona Republican, upbraided Bachmann on the Senate floor: "Recently, it has been alleged that Huma, a Muslim American, is part of a nefarious conspiracy to harm the United States by unduly influencing U.S. foreign policy at the Department of State in favor of the Muslim Brotherhood and other Islamist causes."[35]

He explained that the letter Bachmann and the other representatives sent asking for an investigation into Muslim Brotherhood influence in the government "alleges that three members of Huma's family are 'connected to Muslim Brotherhood operatives and/or organizations.' Never mind that one of those individuals, Huma's father, passed away two decades ago."[36]

However, in a letter to Keith Ellison, Bachmann had explained exactly why it was reasonable to be concerned about Abedin's family members' Brotherhood ties: "The concerns about the foreign influence of immediate family members is such a concern to the U.S. Government that it includes these factors as potentially disqualifying conditions for obtaining a security clearance, which undoubtedly Ms. Abedin has had to obtain to function in her position. For us to raise issues about a highly-based U.S. Government official with known immediate family connections to foreign extremist organizations is not a question of singling out Ms. Abedin. In fact, these questions are raised by the U.S. Government of anyone seeking a security clearance."[37] That reasoning apparently left McCain unmoved.

Family Ties

Oddly, McCain seemed to expect Bachmann to produce the outcome of an investigation before any investigation had even taken place: "the letter and the report offer not one instance of an action, a decision, or a public position that Huma has taken while at the State Department that would lend credence to the charge that she is promoting anti-American activities within our government. Nor does either document offer any evidence of a direct impact that Huma may have had on one of the U.S. policies with which the authors of the letter and the producers of the report find fault."[38]

As Bachmann noted, questions about foreign influence on family members "are raised by the U.S. Government of anyone seeking a security clearance." Former *New York Post* columnist Arnold Ahlert observed, "It remains impossible to understand how Abedin received security clearance to work at the State Department, which allows her access to top-secret documents."[39] Why should Huma Abedin have been exempt? Would an official who had family connections with the Ku Klux Klan or the Aryan Nations have been similarly exempt from scrutiny? If not, why should someone with familial connections to a group dedicated to "eliminating and destroying Western civilization from within"?

As Bachmann pointed out in her letter to Ellison, the Muslim Brotherhood ties of Abedin's mother, father, and brother, long noted in the international press, had never been a secret. Abedin herself had never publicly distanced herself from the Brotherhood or explained how her worldview or her vision of Islam differed from that of her parents or brother. By what moral calculus could it possibly have been "sinister," as McCain put it, to ask that Abedin be subjected to the same scrutiny that would have been focused upon anyone seeking a security clearance that would allow access to sensitive material comparable to that which she enjoyed?

In Abedin's defense, McCain recounted, "Some years ago, I had the pleasure, along with my friend, the Senator from South Carolina, Senator Lindsey Graham, of traveling overseas with our colleague, then-Senator Hillary Clinton. By her side, as always, was Huma, and I had the pleasure of seeing firsthand her hard work and dedicated service on behalf of the former Senator from New York—a service that continues to this day at the Department of State, and bears with it significant personal sacrifice for Huma."[40]

If he really meant what he said, McCain was demonstrating an astonishing naïveté. That Abedin has worked hard and served Clinton with dedication was never in dispute. The lingering question was: To what end? It may be true that she is just as patriotic and loyal to American principles and American freedoms as McCain implied. It may also be true that her familial loyalties have led her to take a stance that is positive toward the Muslim Brotherhood and ultimately inimical to the interests of the United States.

Brotherhood: Jump. State Department: How High?

Although the Representatives' letter and report didn't list any actions by the State Department showing any undue influence by the Muslim Brotherhood, they could easily have done so. In an article about Abedin and her influence, former U.S. prosecutor Andrew C. McCarthy listed a great many strange collaborations between Hillary Clinton's State Department and Muslim Brotherhood organizations, including the following:

- The State Department announced that the Obama administration would be "satisfied" with the election of a Muslim Brotherhood–dominated government in Egypt.
- Secretary Clinton personally intervened to reverse a Bush administration ruling that barred Tariq Ramadan, grandson of the Brotherhood's founder and son of one of its most influential early leaders, from entering the United States.
- The State Department collaborated with the Organization of Islamic Cooperation, a bloc of governments heavily

influenced by the Brotherhood, in seeking to restrict American free-speech rights in deference to sharia proscriptions against negative criticism of Islam.

- The State Department excluded Israel, the world's leading target of terrorism, from its "Global Counterterrorism Forum," a group that brings the United States together with several Islamist governments, prominently including its co-chair, Turkey—which now finances Hamas and avidly supports the flotillas that seek to break Israel's blockade of Hamas. At the forum's kickoff, Secretary Clinton decried various terrorist attacks and groups; but she did not mention Hamas or attacks against Israel—in transparent deference to the Islamist governments, which echo the Brotherhood's position that Hamas is not a terrorist organization and that attacks against Israel are not terrorism.

- The State Department and the Obama administration waived congressional restrictions in order to transfer $1.5 billion dollars in aid to Egypt after the Muslim Brotherhood's victory in the parliamentary elections.

- The State Department and the Obama administration waived congressional restrictions in order to transfer millions of dollars in aid to the Palestinian territories notwithstanding that Gaza is ruled by the terrorist organization Hamas, the Muslim Brotherhood's Palestinian branch.

- The State Department and the administration hosted a contingent from Egypt's newly elected parliament that included not only Muslim Brotherhood members, but a member of the Islamic Group (Gamaa al-Islamiyya), which is formally designated as a foreign terrorist organization. The State Department refused to provide Americans with information about the process by which it issued a visa to a member of a designated terrorist organization, about how the members of the Egyptian delegation were selected, or about what security procedures

were followed before the delegation was allowed to enter
our country.[41]

McCain's outrage at Bachmann epitomized how it had become
socially and politically unacceptable even to raise questions about
Muslim Brotherhood influence, or to express any skepticism about the
politically correct dogmas regarding Islam and jihad. For in Abedin's
case, the evidence was not lacking. The politically correct elites had
simply forbidden any examination or discussion of it. Even to question
whether Abedin had any connections with the Brotherhood and
whether those connections had any influence over Hillary Clinton's
decisions as secretary of state was to demonstrate that one was a bigot,
a racist, an Islamophobe, and a hatemonger, as well as a hysterical
paranoiac.

Indeed, one infallible way to determine a stranger's political positions on just about anything in the middle of Barack Obama's second
term was to ask whether or not he or she thought Huma Abedin had
ties to the Muslim Brotherhood. If the stranger responded with righteous outrage, one was almost certainly face to face with a doctrinaire
mainstream liberal. If, on the other hand, the response was, "Yes, that
is something that should be investigated," the person answering was
likely to be a Tea Partier.

The New Alger Hiss

That's how Huma Abedin became the new Alger Hiss. For decades,
ever since the former State Department official and advisor to President
Franklin Delano Roosevelt was outed as a Soviet spy in the most celebrated espionage case of the nation's history, the leftist establishment
stoutly insisted that Hiss was innocent. Even today, some refuse to
acknowledge the "present-day consensus among historians ... that
Alger Hiss was in fact a Soviet spy."[42]

But the controversy over whether or not Hiss was a Communist and
a spy for the Soviets was (and is) not just a dispute over the evidence.
It was, for the Left, a measure of whether or not one was a decent
human being. Anna Roosevelt Halsted, the daughter of Eleanor and

Franklin, said in 1956 that Hiss's accuser, Whittaker Chambers, was "contemptible" and clearly "out to get" Hiss. Her mother said at a 1961 dinner party that Chambers was "utterly contemptible and probably a psychopathic liar." Adlai Stevenson, present at the same gathering of liberal glitterati, agreed that the prosecution of Hiss was "one of the darker chapters in U.S. history."[43]

Such views were universal on the Left in those days and thereafter, despite the fact that it was abundantly clear from the beginning that Hiss was exactly what Chambers said he was. But the denials began immediately, and with Hiss himself: when Chambers produced classified State Department documents that Hiss had given him when they were both Communist spies and the documents were proven to have been typed on Hiss's typewriter, Hiss accused Chambers of "forgery by typewriter."

Even today, some claim that military intelligence agents fabricated a typewriter identical to Hiss's in order to frame him, although they lack a motive. Chambers is supposed to have falsely accused Hiss out of rage at Hiss's rejection of his homosexual advances, but how this Communist spy and rejected homosexual convinced military intelligence operatives to forge documents to frame the object of his spurned affections has never been explained.

Nonetheless, right up to the moment when material from the Soviet archives revealed that Hiss was indeed a Soviet spy, and even after that, if you didn't love Hiss, you weren't just wrong: you were a bad person. McCain's defense of Huma Abedin was reminiscent of the moral preening surrounding the Hiss case. He upbraided Bachmann for what he called an "an unwarranted and unfounded attack on an honorable woman, a dedicated American, and a loyal public servant." He accused the members of the House of Representatives who had asked for an investigation of Abedin's Brotherhood ties of launching "specious and degrading attacks against fellow Americans on the basis of nothing more than fear of who they are and ignorance of what they stand for."

Brimming with righteous indignation, McCain thundered, "These sinister accusations rest solely on a few unspecified and unsubstantiated associations of members of Huma's family, none of which have been shown to harm or threaten the United States in any way. These attacks on Huma have no logic, no basis, and no merit. And they need to stop now."[44]

McCain: Soft on the Brotherhood

McCain's indignation over these charges against Abedin was ironic, since he himself apparently didn't have much of a problem with the Muslim Brotherhood, given the fact that in 2013 he cheerfully and unapologetically posed for photos with Syrian jihad terrorists, insisting all the while that they were "moderates."[45] In the same way, the people who were angriest at the charges against Hiss were hard leftists who wouldn't have been all that upset with the idea of working for the Soviets in the first place. And "homosexual" was a pejorative term for leftists only when used of Whittaker Chambers.[46]

Also ironic was the wholesale assumption that it was absolutely preposterous that the Muslim Brotherhood could have infiltrated the Obama administration.

In fact, whether or not it had actually happened, that possibility could make sense of events that were otherwise difficult to explain. The Obama administration's support for the Muslim Brotherhood in Egypt was so obvious that when Hillary Clinton visited Egypt, demonstrators against the Muslim Brotherhood Morsi regime pelted her motorcade with tomatoes and shoes for delivering that country up to the rule of the Brotherhood. Protestors held signs reading "Message to Hillary: Egypt will never be Pakistan"; "To Hillary: Hamas will never rule Egypt"; and "If you like the Ikhwan [Brotherhood], take them with you!"[47] Later, when the Brotherhood was toppled from power, numerous anti-Brotherhood protesters held signs accusing Obama of supporting terrorists. One foe of the Brotherhood made a music video including the lyrics, "Hey Obama, support the terrorism / Traitor like the Brotherhood members / Obama say it's a coup / That's not your business dirty man."[48]

Did Huma Abedin have any influence over the Obama administration's warm support for the Brotherhood? No one knew. Michele Bachmann didn't know and didn't claim otherwise. John McCain, for that matter, didn't know that Abedin didn't have this kind of influence. That is precisely why an investigation should have been conducted.

But it has become increasingly common for the Left (and its reliable water boys in the loyal opposition, like McCain) to demonize its opponents. In Hiss's day it wasn't so common, but his case was the first big instance of it. It is now generally accepted among leftists that those who dare to stand against any aspect of the politically correct agenda are not only wrong. They are evil, morally bankrupt, and stupid to boot—except for the diabolical ingenuity they employed to frame their pure-as-the-driven-snow victims.

Yet even if all her accusers were indeed terrible people who kicked their Shih Tzus and didn't recycle, that would not in itself have told us anything about Huma Abedin's ties to the Muslim Brotherhood. She could still have been a Muslim Brotherhood operative even if her accusers had been Jeffrey Dahmer and John Wayne Gacy. And to hear the Left and the mainstream media tell it, that's exactly who they were. Alger Hiss and Huma Abedin were innocent, and those who didn't believe that, or even dared to think that the question was worthy of investigation, were condemned to be bound hand and foot and cast into the outer darkness by an increasingly authoritarian and thuggish Left.

CHAPTER EIGHT

MARGINALIZING
FREEDOM FIGHTERS

O n August 19, 2013, the *Chicago Sun-Times* reported that "a state
law-enforcement board and Lombard officials canceled plans for
anti-terrorism trainer Sam Kharoba to teach a class Monday after
a Muslim advocacy group labeled him a 'Muslim bigot' and claimed he
would be 'promoting hate.'"[1] The paper meant that Kharoba had been
called an "anti-Muslim bigot"—the error was typical of the carelessness
of its coverage.

Kharoba, a Jordanian Christian, is president of the Counter Terrorism Operations Center (CTOC) in Cape Coral, Florida. The story quoted
Kevin McClain, executive director of the Illinois Law Enforcement
Training and Standards Board, saying that the law enforcement board
was "looking into his credentials and the content of the course to see
whether it is inappropriate."[2] McClain explained that in bowing to
demands to cancel the class, "I would rather err on the side of caution."[3]

Lombard Village president Keith Giagnorio suggested that the class was canceled so as to avoid offending local Muslims: "Once I learned of the content in past training sessions that this particular trainer had given, I was extremely uncomfortable with it. In Lombard, we have a really diversified community and a growing Muslim population. They are very involved in the community and getting more involved, and we felt like we couldn't support something like this being held in the village of Lombard."[4]

An indication that any local Muslims' feelings of offense were unlikely to be justified: the "Muslim advocacy group" that labeled Kharoba a bigot was the Chicago chapter of the Council on American-Islamic Relations, which claimed that "Kharoba's training materials on Islam are riddled with inaccuracies, sweeping generalizations and stereotypes."[5] And Ahmed Rehab, executive director of CAIR-Chicago, wanted more than just the cancellation of the class. He said that CAIR wanted to work with Illinois state government officials "to ensure that there are standards in place to scrutinize the qualification and expertise of trainers on the subject matter. We are willing to work with NEMRT [North East Multi-Regional Training] to suggest qualified experts on Islam who enjoy credibility within the American Muslim community."[6]

Rehab had made a similar demand in an earlier press release calling for the cancellation of Kharoba's training session: "Counterterrorism training is too important to be left to those who promote a bigoted political or religious agenda. Our state's law enforcement agencies should work with credible leaders of the Muslim community to address any issues related to Islam."[7]

Journalistic Omissions

While the *Sun-Times* reported all that, the paper did not mention CAIR's Hamas ties or its record of opposing any and all counterterror efforts. Nor did it specify exactly what was bigoted or hateful about Kharoba's presentation. CAIR, however, did so in its press release, which quoted Kharoba as saying, "Most of us have heard statements similar to 'Islam is a religion of peace' and that 'Muslim radicals hijacked, twisted and altered Islam to justify their Jihad against non-Muslims.'

This book will provide definitive proof contradicting these statements and allegations."[8]

CAIR's press release fastidiously left out the details, but an AP story also quoted Kharoba criticizing Muhammad: "When I look at the life of Muhammad, I get a very nasty image ... I am talking about a pedophile, a serial killer, a rapist."[9] Kharoba also pointed out that Muhammad's Qur'anic revelations were "initially peaceful and tolerant but later became radical and militant."[10] However, so far from being evidence of anti-Muslim hate, all these statements could easily be justified not from the rantings of anti-Muslim "bigots" but from core Islamic texts—as we shall see later in this book.

Kharoba stood his ground, telling AP that CAIR's complaints were "manufactured distractions designed to shift blame onto the law enforcement agencies that are protecting the American people."[11] He said that around one hundred Muslim law enforcement officers had attended his classes, and that none had complained. "I have an in-depth knowledge of Islam," said Kharoba, "to the extent that Muslims themselves are not able to debate me. I extend an invitation to any critics to debate me on any subject matter related to Islam and terrorism."[12]

CAIR was in no mood to debate; the August 2013 cancellation was just the latest skirmish in a long battle they had waged against Kharoba. In July 2012, CAIR-Tampa's Hassan Shibly characterized Kharoba's class in lurid terms, as "troubling, un-American and frankly, quite possibly illegal training. It makes us less safe and less free."[13] The AP reported this wild accusation, but like the *Sun-Times* it did not note—in this story or any other one filed on the controversies over Kharoba—CAIR's troubling associations and record.

Why a group like CAIR should have any say over who trains law enforcement personnel about the jihad terror threat was a question never asked by any media outlet reporting on the cancellations of Kharoba's talks or on similar stories.

Inciting Violence?

And there were many similar stories. CAIR, well funded and well staffed, was ready to pounce on anyone who dared say a critical word about jihad terror. Another target was Jonathan Matusitz, a tenured professor at the University of Central Florida (UCF). When Florida's Brevard County allowed ACT! For America, a counter-jihad advocacy group, space in a county commission meeting room for an August 2013 talk by Matusitz, CAIR swung into action again. Ibrahim Hooper, CAIR's national communications director, fumed, "It creates the perception of endorsement and approval by the Brevard County government of this group's hateful views." Hassan Shibly's rhetoric was once again heated; he said of Matusitz, "This individual makes statements to incite violence against the Muslim community, so I think that the line has been crossed. ACT! is an extremist group no different than the KKK. And if the KKK wanted to use that room, there would be a protest."

This comparison was absurd and defamatory. Matusitz never incited violence against Muslims. He is dedicated to resisting jihad terror and the spread of Islamic law in the United States, not to committing acts of violence against innocent Muslims in some emulation of the Ku Klux Klan. But officials with little knowledge of CAIR, ACT!, or Matusitz were at a disadvantage, and so they did their best to remain neutral. Brevard commission chairman Andy Anderson explained cautiously that ACT!'s use of the room "would be like a group renting out a room at the library to hold a meeting. The room is owned by the people and is open to anyone who wants to use it. Unless there was a reason for us to stop a group from using it because of some kind of issue that would be outside the protection of the First Amendment."[14]

The *Orlando Sentinel's* coverage of this controversy, true to typical mainstream media practice, didn't mention CAIR's unsavory connections or its advice to Muslims not to cooperate with law enforcement. The organization's own claims that it is merely a civil rights organization were repeated uncritically and without examination. Since targeted local officials are unlikely to know about CAIR, they are generally blindsided and put on the defensive by its attacks, and usually give the "civil rights group" what it wants: the cancellation and marginalization of every speaker who is remotely critical of Islam.

CAIR had previously complained to UCF about Matusitz's classes, and they took issue with some statements in a YouTube video of a talk he gave outside the classroom. Matusitz stresses the link between terrorism and Islamic culture. In the video, Matusitz asks, "Why do so many Muslims, relative to other religions, want to kill us? The answer is easy, very easy. It is seven letters: culture." One would think that CAIR would have been happy about this, since Matusitz blamed Islamic culture rather than the religion of Islam itself. But they were upset about another statement in the video: "How can you change a movement in which you have 1.5 billion members? It's impossible. We just have to resist it and just elect people who are willing just to resist it and just be true American. That's the only answer. We're not going to change Islam."[15]

Since CAIR leaders are believing Muslims who think Allah delivered the Qur'an in perfect form to Muhammad and then preserved it miraculously through all the centuries, it's unlikely that they took issue with Matusitz's saying that Islam was not going to change: one does not change the eternal and perfect word of Allah, or what the Qur'an calls the perfect religion (5:3). What angered them was doubtless his saying that Americans should "resist" Islam.

In light of the ongoing jihad terror threat, was this really an unreasonable thing to say? CAIR thought so and tried to take Matusitz's job for it. University officials, however, were cautious. UCF spokesman Grant Heston said, "Dr. Matusitz is expressing his opinion, which is his right. He is not speaking on behalf of the university, and we do not endorse his views."[16] That Heston had to assure the public that the university didn't endorse Matusitz's views was evidence of how effective CAIR's campaigns were. University officials were not in a position to evaluate the truth or falsehood of what Matusitz was teaching, or what CAIR was claiming, so they gingerly distanced themselves from Matusitz. It is good that they didn't cave in to the pressure altogether and dismiss him outright, but the noncommittal position they took demonstrates that by merely voicing a complaint CAIR and other Islamic supremacists can compel people in positions of power to at the very least partially disavow the figures they target—and they can leverage such disavowals to their advantage in the future. For example, once I was dropped from speaking at a Catholic conference and banned from Britain—both as a result of smear campaigns in which I was given no opportunity to respond to charges made against me—both incidents became a staple of subsequent attempts to get me canceled from speaking in other venues: a bishop banned him from speaking! He was barred from entering Britain! He is far too controversial for decent audiences!

Claiming Peaceful Islam Has Been Hijacked Will Not Spare You

No one is immune. In June 2013, Republican congressman Mike Pompeo of Kansas took U.S. Muslim leaders to task on the floor of the House of Representatives, saying that their silence on jihad terrorism had been deafening. (In fact, American Muslim advocacy groups have issued only vague and pro-forma condemnations of terrorism, and they have not taken any effective or serious action against the spread of jihadist and Islamic supremacist beliefs in the Muslim community.)

Representative Pompeo added that Muslim leaders in the United States must teach that it is wrong to kill innocents. Apparently he did not realize that some Muslim scholars maintain that no non-Muslim can ever be innocent. Nor did he appear to be aware of the details of Muhammad's career, according to Islamic tradition, that Islamic jihadists point to today in order to justify jihad terror attacks: his massacres of the Jewish Qurayza tribe and of poets who offended him, his exhortations to wage war against non-Muslims, the expedition to make an unprovoked attack on the Christians of Tabuk, his declaration "I have been made victorious through terror," his statement "I have been commanded to fight against people until they confess that there is no god but Allah and I am his messenger," and more.

In fact, Pompeo was one of a long, long line of politicians who have assumed—in the teeth of all the evidence—that the core texts of Islam teach peace, and that jihad terrorists are transgressing against the meaning of those texts as clearly as Fred Phelps of the Westboro Baptist Church is transgressing against the teachings of Christianity. Nonetheless, even Pompeo's mild criticism was too much for CAIR. Corey Saylor, the director of CAIR's Department to Monitor and Combat Islamophobia, wrote to the congressman that his remarks were "false and irresponsible" and listed various condemnations of terrorism by Muslim groups.[17]

What was most noteworthy about CAIR's outrage over his remarks was that Pompeo had taken pains to assure the House that jihad terrorists had "hijacked" Islam and that Muhammad would condemn modern Islamic jihad terrorism. The fact that he genuflected to these politically correct fictions—with which CAIR supposedly agrees as well—didn't stop CAIR from going after him.

Every Critic Is Out of Bounds

This incident demonstrated yet again that there is *no one* who opposes jihad terror who is acceptable to CAIR and its allies. When CAIR targets so-called "Islamophobes" and details all their alleged enormities, some have thought that they could avoid this demonization and defamation by highlighting the work of "moderate Muslims" and talking, as Pompeo did, about how the true Islam is peaceful. But CAIR's attack on Pompeo showed that that approach would not spare critics of jihad terror from charges of "Islamophobia."

A 2011 report on Islamophobia in the United States, which CAIR produced in conjunction with the Center for Race & Gender at the University of California, Berkeley, states, "It is not appropriate to label all, or even the majority of those, who question Islam and Muslims as Islamophobes. Equally, it is not Islamophobic to denounce crimes committed by individual Muslims or those claiming Islam as a motivation for their actions. 'A critical study of Islam or Muslims is not Islamophobic,' former CAIR Research Director Mohamed Nimer wrote in 2007. 'Likewise, a disapproving analysis of American history and government is not anti-American…. One can disagree with Islam or with what some Muslims do without having to be hateful.'"[18]

Similarly, at an "International Conference on Islamophobia" held in Istanbul in September 2013, Turkey's director general of press and information (BYEGM) and OIC official Murat Karakaya asked, "How does one identify and describe legitimate criticisms or anxieties on the one hand and hate-filled or irrational criticisms and anxieties on the other, in the media, law, politics?"[19]

But this was all empty rhetoric. Neither CAIR's report nor the "International Conference on Islamophobia" offered any examples of what they considered to be acceptable and legitimate criticism of Islam and jihad. Neither CAIR, nor the Islamophobia conference participants, nor the University of California Center for Race & Gender has ever done so anywhere else. Nor has any other leftist or Muslim group. In reality, anyone and everyone who dares to oppose jihad and Islamic supremacism will become a target for a CAIR smear campaign. The real agenda of Islamic supremacist groups in the United States is clearly not to distinguish legitimate resistance to jihad from bigotry and hatred, but to stigmatize all resistance to jihad as bigotry and hatred—clearing away all obstacles to the advance of that jihad.

Stigmatizing the Resistance

This agenda has made great headway. Resistance to jihad has been stigmatized as "bigotry" in the eyes of large segments of the general public, and even of government and law enforcement officials. In May 2013, my colleague the author and human rights activist Pamela Geller, was scheduled to speak at a synagogue in Toronto—until Inspector Ricky Veerappan of the York Regional Police Force's "diversity, equity and inclusion bureau" pressured the rabbi of the synagogue to cancel the event. (Geller spoke anyway, at a different location.) Questioned about why he had done this, Veerappan replied, "Some of the stuff that Ms. Geller speaks about runs contrary to the values of York Regional Police and the work we do in engaging our communities."[20]

To that, Geller replied with bitter irony, "Let me understand this. The 'stuff' that I speak about—gender apartheid, creed apartheid, Islamic Jew-hatred, honor killing—runs contrary to their values? What exactly are their values? Imposing Sharia? Because that's exactly what they're doing. My value is life. What's theirs?"[21]

And that was the rub. While it became generally accepted that standing up to jihad terror was "bigotry," no one could clearly explain why. CAIR objected to statements from Kharoba, Matusitz, Geller, and others like them that were demonstrably true—while the public was kept uninformed by a media that approved of this effort and so usually did not even report what the targeted speakers were actually saying—and never told their audience that it was, in fact, true. When Geller and I both spoke at an event in Toronto in September 2013, the mainstream media thronged to cover a press conference of the National Conference of Canadian Muslims protesting our appearance—but not a single reporter bothered to show up to hear what either of us actually had to say.

A highly tendentious and politically manipulative perspective has been foisted upon the American people as accepted wisdom. Opponents of jihad terror were cast as bigots; efforts increased to rule their perspective altogether out of the realm of acceptable public discourse.

Acceptable Vandalism

Even outright thuggery became acceptable. In September 2012, the internationally noted and highly respected Egyptian-American journalist Mona Eltahawy took a can of spray paint and began spray-painting over an ad that she didn't like in the Times Square subway station. Eltahawy vandalized the ad until a supporter of its message got in between her and it; shortly thereafter, Eltahawy was arrested and charged with criminal mischief, and spent the night in jail.[22]

That a prominent journalist would stoop to this crude act of vandalism was noteworthy in itself, but even more striking was the fact that so many on the Left and in the mainstream media applauded her for it.

The ad that enraged Eltahawy read, "In any war between the civilized man and the savage, support the civilized man. Support Israel. Defeat jihad." It was created by Pamela Geller and sponsored by the American Freedom Defense Initiative (AFDI), of which I am associate director. The mainstream media widely circulated the claim that this ad was somehow referring to and demeaning all Muslims, even though the words "Muslim" and "Islam" never appear in it, and it quite clearly referred to those jihad terrorists who committed acts of savagery against Israeli civilians and then celebrated those acts.

Nonetheless, whether as part of their ongoing efforts to demonize and marginalize all those who speak out against jihad, or out of visceral hatred for Israel, or both, leftist and putatively "moderate" Muslim writers enthusiastically praised Eltahawy's vandalism and called for more ads to be defaced. Cyrus McGoldrick, at that time an official of

CAIR's New York chapter, tweeted exultantly about Eltahawy's vandalism: "THIS is GOLD."[23]

Christina Abraham, the "civil rights director" of CAIR's Chicago chapter, went even further, tweeting that "what some might call hate ads," Eltahawy "sees as a blank canvas. Everyone should do the same." Ironically, Abraham described herself in her Twitter profile as a "human rights enthusiast."[24]

Likewise, the Muslim writer Reza Aslan, who enjoys a widespread reputation as a "moderate Muslim" despite being a board member of the National Iranian American Council, which, it was established in federal court, is a lobbying group for the Islamic Republic of Iran, was enthusiastic about the vandalism and wanted more.[25] "Hey New York!," he tweeted. "How many racist ads are left unscathed? Get busy."[26]

Despite (or perhaps because of) this enthusiastic and unapologetic thirst for violent suppression of the free speech of others, Aslan is a frequent speaker on college campuses and in other prominent liberal fora. He is the epitome of the new leftist spokesman who no longer has a problem with forcibly suppressing the free speech of his opponents and cheerfully owns up to wanting to do so.

Hatred of the Truth

Contempt for the freedom of speech is rapidly becoming commonplace on the Left. *Washington Square News* is the student newspaper of New York University, but it is editorially and financially independent from the university and has a circulation of about sixty thousand in lower Manhattan—one of the epicenters of the Far Left in the United States. An indication of how the restriction of the freedom of speech has become a fashionable opinion among the leftist intelligentsia at universities and elsewhere came in September of 2012, when the *News* ran a piece calling for restrictions on the First Amendment.

Referring to the AFDI ads in a *Washington Square News* piece headlined "Have we taken free speech too far?," Faria Mardhani wrote, "The decision that the United States must now make is whether hate speech like this should be legal. Do values of free speech override the values of equality and of preventing profound personal offense to any singular group? Was the First Amendment passed with the intention of grouping very diverse people into one entity and then vilifying them?"[27]

In the 1930s, when the Nazis were taking power in Germany, brown-shirted storm troopers regularly terrorized Hitler's foes, shouting them down when they spoke, vandalizing their messages, and even physically threatening them. We are rapidly approaching the same situation—not because of a resurgence in "right-wing extremism," but because of the Left's increasingly positive attitude toward thuggery. Hundreds of people have hailed Eltahawy as a hero on Twitter and elsewhere, and many have echoed the calls from Aslan and Abraham to imitate her vandalism. When Geller or I or any other speaker who opposes jihad terror and Islamic supremacism does manage to avoid getting canceled and speak on a college campus, it's a scene that could easily have taken place in 1934 in Berlin or Munich: we have to go with bodyguards and prepare to be shouted down by self-righteous thugs.

Left fascism like that displayed by Mona Eltahawy and her supporters increasingly threatens the freedom of all Americans. If their cavalier (at best) attitude toward the freedom of speech is any indication of their respect for human rights in general, and if they do succeed in forcibly silencing all their foes and come to a point where they are able to exert their will unchallenged, the result will be tyranny on a scale that Americans have never before experienced.

The efforts of CAIR to get speaking engagements of people like Kharoba, Matusitz, and Geller (and many others) canceled are part of the same effort as Mona Eltahawy with her spray paint. The ultimate goal of both is to shut down all dissent from the establishment line about the nature of jihad terror, its causes, and the proper response to it. And this effort has achieved great success—all the way up to the highest levels of the U.S. government.

CHAPTER NINE

BANNED IN THE LAND OF HOPE AND CHANGE

The Administration Suppresses the Truth about the Jihad

The crowning victory in the effort to stigmatize resistance to jihad terror and Islamic supremacism came in February 2012, when the Obama administration purged more than one thousand documents and presentations from counterterror training material for the FBI and other agencies. This material was discarded at the demand of Muslim groups, which had deemed it inaccurate or offensive to Muslims.[1]

This triumph was several years in the making. The movement toward it began in earnest in August 2010, when I gave a talk on Islam and jihad to the FBI's Joint Terrorism Task Force—one of many such talks I gave to government agencies and military groups in those years. While some had counseled me to keep these talks quiet so as to avoid attracting the ire of CAIR, the possibility of that pressure seemed to me to make it all the more important to announce my appearances publicly, so as to show that the U.S. government was not going to take dictation from a group linked to Hamas and the Muslim Brotherhood.

Those who had urged silence were proven correct, however, for the government was indeed disposed to take dictation from CAIR. CAIR sent a series of letters to FBI director Robert Mueller and others demanding that I be dropped as a counterterror trainer; the organization even started a "coalition" echoing this demand, and Jesse Jackson and other leftist luminaries joined it.[2]

Andrew C. McCarthy pointed out in *National Review* that CAIR was seeking total control over counterterror training material: "According to this thinking, Islamist groups like CAIR have a monopoly on what Americans—including American law-enforcement and intelligence agents—are permitted to hear about Islam from academic, media, and government sources. No dissenting views are permitted, no matter how steeped the dissenters may be in Islamic doctrine and no matter how much these dissents accord with what your lyin' eyes are seeing."[3]

At PJ Media, Roger L. Simon added, "Frankly, I was pleased to hear the FBI was welcoming the likes of Spencer, especially since our Department of Justice ... has gone out of its way to *ignore* radical Islam as a motivation for terrorism even when it couldn't be more obviously so. From Ft. Hood to Times Square, it hasn't been just the thousand pound gorilla in the room, it has been every gorilla in every room from here to Beijing and back."[4]

At the FBI, Mueller made no public comment on CAIR's demand, and so it initially appeared that CAIR's effort had failed. But I was never again invited to provide counterterror training for any government agency, after having done so fairly regularly for the previous five years.

CAIR's campaign to keep me from taking part in counter-terror training was, of course, not personal. They targeted me simply because I told the truth, just as they would target anyone else who dared do so.

Counterterrorism Offends Muslims and Leftists

Although Mueller was publicly silent, the Islamic supremacists and their leftist allies didn't give up. In the summer and fall of 2011, the online tech journal Wired published several "exposés" by Far-Left journalist Spencer Ackerman, who took the FBI to task for training material that spoke forthrightly and truthfully about the nature and magnitude of the jihad threat.

In a typical sally from one of these exposés, Ackerman reported that "the FBI is teaching its counterterrorism agents that 'main stream' [sic] American Muslims are likely to be terrorist sympathizers; that the Prophet Mohammed was a 'cult leader'; and that the Islamic practice of giving charity is no more than a 'funding mechanism for combat.' At the Bureau's training ground in Quantico, Virginia, agents are shown a chart contending that the more 'devout' a Muslim, the more likely he is to be 'violent.' Those destructive tendencies cannot be reversed, an FBI instructional presentation adds: 'Any war against non-believers is justified' under Muslim law; a 'moderating process cannot happen if the Koran continues to be regarded as the unalterable word of Allah.'"[5]

Like virtually all leftist and Islamic supremacist critiques of anti-jihad and anti-terror material, Ackerman's piece took for granted that such assertions are false—without bothering to explain how or why he knew better. Apparently Ackerman believed that their falsity was so self-evident as to require no demonstration; unfortunately, there is considerable evidence that the assertions in this FBI training material are true.

Ackerman condemned the training material for intimating that mainstream American Muslims were "likely to be terrorist sympathizers." Certainly all the mainstream Muslim organizations condemn al Qaeda and 9/11; however, as we have seen, some of the foremost of those organizations, such as ISNA, MAS, ICNA, the MSA, CAIR, and others, have links of various kinds to Hamas and the Muslim Brotherhood. A mainstream Muslim spokesman in the United States, Ground Zero Mosque imam Faisal Abdul Rauf, refused to condemn Hamas until it became too politically damaging for him not to do so; another, CAIR's Nihad Awad, openly declared his support for Hamas in 1994.[6] Another mainstream Muslim spokesman in this country, Reza Aslan, has praised another jihad terrorist group, Hizballah, and called on the United States to negotiate with Hamas.[7] Other mainstream Muslim spokesmen in the United States, such as Rashad Hussain, Obama's ambassador to the Organization of Islamic Cooperation, and media gadfly Hussein Ibish, have praised and defended Sami al-Arian, the confessed leader of another jihad terror group, Palestinian Islamic Jihad.[8]

Do these men and organizations represent a tiny minority of extremists that actually does not express the opinions of the broad mainstream

of Muslims in this country? Maybe, but there simply are no counterparts—no individuals of comparable influence or groups of comparable
size—that have not expressed sympathy for some Islamic terror group.

Were the Training Materials Accurate?

Ackerman also claimed that the training materials called Muhammad a "cult leader." One definition of a cult is a group whose members
are not free to opt out if they choose to do so—and it was Muhammad
who enunciated Islam's notorious death penalty for apostasy: "Whoever
changes his Islamic religion, then kill him."[9] Also, there are several
celebrated incidents in which Muhammad lashed out violently against
his opponents, ordering the murders of several people for the crime of
making fun of him—including the poet Abu 'Afak, who was over one
hundred years old, and the poetess 'Asma bint Marwan. Abu 'Afak was
killed in his sleep by assassins inspired by Muhammad's question, "Who
will avenge me on this scoundrel?" Similarly, stung by the poetess's
verses ridiculing him, Muhammad cried out, "Will no one rid me of this
daughter of Marwan?" One of his followers, 'Umayr ibn 'Adi, went to
her house that night, where he found her sleeping next to her children.
The youngest, a nursing babe, was in her arms. But that didn't stop
'Umayr from murdering her and the baby as well. Muhammad com-
mended him: "You have done a great service to Allah and His Messenger, 'Umayr!"[10]

Ackerman scored the training material for asserting that the
"Islamic practice of giving charity" was no more than a "'funding mechanism for combat.'"[11] If this was really self-evidently false, one wonders
why so many Islamic charities in the United States and around the
world—including what was once the largest Islamic charity in the
United States, the Holy Land Foundation for Relief and Development
(HLF), as well as the Global Relief Foundation (GRF), the Benevolence
International Foundation (BIF), and many others—have been shut
down for funding terrorism.

Also assuming that the claim was self-evidently false, Ackerman
noted that the material claimed that "the more 'devout' a Muslim, the
more likely he is to be 'violent,'" and that the "moderating process cannot happen if the Koran continues to be regarded as the unalterable

word of Allah."[12] Yet while certainly not all devout Muslims are terrorists, virtually all Islamic terrorists are devout Muslims, and they often cite the Qur'an and the words and deeds of Muhammad to justify their actions. It should not be controversial to state these readily demonstrable facts.

Finally, Ackerman criticized the materials for claiming that "any war against non-believers" can be "'justified' under Muslim law."[13] While not any war against non-Muslims can really be justified under Islamic law, certainly sharia delineates particular circumstances under which warfare against unbelievers can indeed be justified. It is hard to see how the statement was all that far off the mark.

Capitulation

Nonetheless, in the face of Ackerman's reports, the FBI went into full retreat. In September 2011, it announced that it was dropping one of the programs that Ackerman had zeroed in on.[14]

The Islamic supremacists didn't rest on their laurels. On October 19, 2011, Salam al-Marayati of the Muslim Public Affairs Council (MPAC) took this campaign to the mainstream media, writing in the *Los Angeles Times* that "a disturbing string of training material used by the FBI and a U.S. attorney's office came to light beginning in late July that reveals a deep anti-Muslim sentiment within the U.S. government." Al-Marayati warned that "if this matter is not immediately addressed, it will undermine the relationship between law enforcement and the Muslim American community—another example of the ineptitude and/or apathy undermining bridges built with care over decades." He also noted that the FBI was beginning to move on these demands, although as far as al-Marayati was concerned, much more was needed: "It is not enough to just call it a 'very valid concern,' as FBI director Robert Mueller told a congressional committee this month."[15]

It was a coordinated full-court press. The same day that al-Marayati's op-ed was published, Farhana Khera of Muslim Advocates, who had complained for years about supposed Muslim profiling and entrapment, wrote a letter to John Brennan, who was then the Assistant to the President on National Security for Homeland Security and Counterterrorism. The letter was signed not just by Khera, but by the leaders of virtually all the significant Islamic groups in the United States: fifty-seven Muslim, Arab, and South Asian organizations, many with ties to Hamas and the Muslim Brotherhood, including the CAIR, ISNA, MAS, the Islamic Circle of North America (ICNA), Islamic Relief USA, and al-Marayati's MPAC.[16]

Moving In for the Kill

The letter denounced what it characterized as U.S. government agencies' "use of biased, false and highly offensive training materials about Muslims and Islam," and emphasized that this was an issue of the utmost importance: "The seriousness of this issue cannot be overstated, and we request that the White House immediately create an interagency task force to address this problem, with a fair and transparent mechanism for input from the Muslim, Arab, and South Asian communities, including civil rights lawyers, religious leaders, and law enforcement experts."[17]

The task force was needed because "while recent news reports have highlighted the FBI's use of biased experts and training materials, we have learned that this problem extends far beyond the FBI and has infected other government agencies, including the U.S. Attorney's Anti-Terrorism Advisory Councils, the U.S. Department of Homeland Security, and the U.S. Army. Furthermore, by the FBI's own admission, the use of bigoted and distorted materials in its trainings has not been an isolated occurrence. Since last year, reports have surfaced that the FBI, and other federal agencies, are using or supporting the use of biased trainers and materials in presentations to law enforcement officials."[18]

Khera complained that my books could be found in "the FBI's library at the FBI training academy in Quantico, Virginia"; that a reading list accompanying a PowerPoint presentation by the FBI's Law Enforcement Communications Unit recommended my book *The Truth About Muhammad*; and that in July 2010, I "presented a two-hour seminar on 'the belief system of Islamic jihadists' to the Joint Terrorism Task Force (JTTF) in Tidewater, Virginia," and "presented a similar lecture to the U.S. Attorney's Anti-Terrorism Advisory Council, which is co-hosted by the FBI's Norfolk Field Office."[19]

These were supposed to be terrible things because I was bigoted and hateful. But many of the examples Khera adduced of "bigoted and distorted materials" involved statements that were not actually bigoted and distorted at all, but simply accurate. What was distorted was Khera's representation of them. For instance, Khera stated,

> A 2006 FBI intelligence report stating that individuals who convert to Islam are on the path to becoming "Homegrown Islamic Extremists," if they exhibit any of the following behavior:
>
> - "Wearing traditional Muslim attire"
> - "Growing facial hair"
> - "Frequent attendance at a mosque or a prayer group"
> - "Travel to a Muslim country"
> - "Increased activity in a pro-Muslim social group or political cause"[20]

But the FBI intelligence report that Khera purported to be describing didn't actually say that converts to Islam were necessarily "on the path" to becoming "extremists" if they wore traditional Muslim attire, grew facial hair, and frequently attended a mosque; it simply included these behaviors among a list of fourteen indicators to "identify an individual going through the radicalization process." Others included "travel without obvious source of funds"; "suspicious purchases of bomb making paraphernalia or weapons"; "large transfer of funds, from or to overseas"; and "formation of operational cells."[21] Khera selectively quoted and misrepresented the list to give the impression that the FBI was saying that devout observance of Islam led inevitably and in every case to "extremism."

Khera's letter also stated that "in 2007, William Gawthrop, a [sic] FBI intelligence analyst who has stated that the Prophet 'Muhammad's mindset is a source for terrorism' taught a class at the National Defense Intelligence College, the professional education institution run by the Defense Intelligence Agency."[22]

Protesting against the Truth

Khera left it to the reader to assume that Gawthrop's statement was self-evidently false. In fact, numerous terrorists have invoked Muhammad as their model and his teachings as their inspiration. In December 2003, an Iraqi jihadist invoked Muhammad to explain why he was fighting against America's presence in Iraq: "The religious principle is that we cannot accept to live with infidels. The Prophet Muhammad, peace be on him, said, 'Hit the infidels wherever you find them.'"[23] The "mindset" expressed in these words of the prophet Muhammad does seem pretty clearly to have been "a source for terrorism" in this case.

Fawwaz bin Muhammad al-Nashami, leader of the jihadists in the Khobar Towers attack on American military personnel in 2004, which killed twenty-two people, also invoked Muhammad: "We are Mujahideen, and we want the Americans. We have not come to aim a weapon at the Muslims, but to purge the Arabian Peninsula, according to the will of our Prophet Muhammad, of the infidels and the polytheists who are killing our brothers in Afghanistan and Iraq."[24] And al Qaeda sheikh Aamer Bin Abdallah al-Aamer wrote in the al Qaeda online journal Sawt al-Jihad: "Perform the Jihad against your enemies with your hands, sacrifice your souls and your property in fighting your enemy, as an imitation of your Prophet [Muhammad] in the month of Ramadan, enrage your enemies."[25]

Despite the factual accuracy of the material about which they were complaining, the Muslim groups signing the letter demanded that the task force "purge all federal government training materials of biased materials"; "implement a mandatory re-training program for FBI agents, U.S. Army officers, and all federal, state and local law enforcement who have been subjected to biased training"; and more—to ensure that all that law enforcement officials would learn about Islam and jihad would be what the signatories wanted them to learn.[26]

Brennan Folds

Brennan seemed amenable to that. He took Khera's complaints as his marching orders. In a November 3, 2011, letter to Khera, that—significantly—was written on White House stationery, Brennan made no attempt to defend counterterror materials and procedures but instead accepted Khera's criticisms without a murmur of protest and assured her of his readiness to comply. "Please allow me to share with you the specific steps we are taking," Brennan wrote to Khera, "to ensure that federal officials and state, local and tribal partners receive accurate, evidence-based information in these crucial areas."[27]

"I am aware," Brennan went on, "of recent unfortunate incidents that have highlighted substandard and offensive training that some United States Government elements have either sponsored or delivered. Any and all such training runs completely counter to our values, our commitment to strong partnerships with communities across the country, our specific approach to countering violent extremist recruitment and radicalization, and our broader counterterrorism (CT) efforts. Our National Strategy for Empowering Local Partners to Prevent Violent Extremism in the United States highlights competent training as an area of primary focus and states that 'misinformation about the threat and dynamics of radicalization to violence can harm our security by sending local stakeholders in the wrong direction and unnecessarily creating tensions with potential community partners.' It also emphasizes that our security is 'inextricably linked to our values,' including 'the promotion of an inclusive society.'"[28]

Brennan assured Khera that all her demands would be met: "Your letter requests that 'the White House immediately create an interagency task force to address this problem,' and we agree that this is necessary." He then detailed other specific actions being undertaken, including "collecting all training materials that contain cultural or religious content, including information related to Islam or Muslims."[29] In reality, this material wouldn't just be "collected"; it would be purged of anything that Farhana Khera and others like her found offensive—that is, any honest discussion of how Islamic jihadists use Islamic teachings to justify violence. Brennan assured Khera that he saw the problem just as she did, and that remedies were being implemented quickly: "We share your concern over these recent unfortunate incidents, and are moving forward to ensure problems are addressed with a keen sense of urgency. They do not reflect the vision that the President has put forward, nor do they represent the kind of approach that builds the partnerships that are necessary to counter violent extremism, and to protect our young people and our homeland. America's greatest strength is its values, and we are committed to pursuing policies and approaches that draw strength from our values and our people irrespective of their race, religion or ethnic background."[30]

The letter concludes with Brennan again assuring Khera that her "concerns" would be soon assuaged: "While much work remains, I am confident that concrete actions are being taken to address the valid concerns you raised. Thank you again for your letter and for your leadership in addressing an issue that is critical to ensuring the security of the United States."[31]

Disastrous Alacrity

The alacrity with which Brennan complied was unfortunate on many levels. Numerous books and presentations that gave a perfectly accurate view of Islam and jihad were purged—and the Assistant to the President on National Security for Homeland Security and Counter Terrorism was complying with demands from quarters that could hardly be considered authentically moderate.

But his letter was no real surprise. Brennan's complacency regarding the jihad threat and eagerness to enable jihadists had manifested itself as early as May 2010, when he expressed a desire to encourage "moderate elements" of the jihad terror group Hizballah.[32] He did not explain where such elements could be found, how they could be identified, or what separated them from Hizballah "extremists." At least Brennan has been consistent: in a controversial 2008 article, he called on U.S. officials to "cease public Iran-bashing" and recommended that the United States "tolerate, and even ... encourage, greater assimilation of Hezbollah into Lebanon's political system, a process that is subject to Iranian influence."[33]

In "The Conundrum of Iran: Strengthening Moderates without Acquiescing to Belligerence," published in the *Annals of the American Academy of Political and Social Science* in July 2008, Brennan naïvely claimed that Hizballah's participation in Lebanese politics was evidence that it was leaving behind its terrorist roots:

Hezbollah is already represented in the Lebanese parliament and its members have previously served in the Lebanese cabinet, reflections of Hezbollah's interest in shaping Lebanon's political future from within government institutions. This political involvement is a far cry from Hezbollah's genesis as solely a terrorist organization dedicated to murder, kidnapping, and violence. Not coincidentally, the evolution of Hezbollah into a fully vested player in the Lebanese political system has been accompanied by a marked reduction in terrorist attacks carried out by the organization. The best hope for maintaining this trend and for reducing the influence of violent extremists within the organization—as well as the influence of extremist Iranian officials who view Hezbollah primarily as a pawn of Tehran—is to increase Hezbollah's stake in Lebanon's struggling democratic processes.[34]

Brennan was recommending that the United States encourage the mainstreaming and assimilation of a group about which the Under Secretary of the Treasury for Terrorism and Financial Intelligence, David Cohen, once noted that "before al Qaeda's attack on the U.S. on September 11, 2001, Hezbollah was responsible for killing more Americans in terrorist attacks than any other terrorist group."[35] Brennan's remarks suggesting the mainstreaming of Hizballah were disturbingly similar to those of MPAC's Salam al-Marayati, who called the terror group's actions "legitimate resistance." But ultimately, granting Hizbollah legitimacy means legitimizing their terror attacks. According to al-Marayati, "If the Lebanese people are resisting Israeli intransigence on Lebanese soil, then that is the right of resistance and they have the right to target Israeli soldiers in this conflict. That is not terrorism. That is a legitimate resistance. That could be called liberation movement, that could be called anything, but it's not terrorism."[36]

Brennan was acting as if participation in the political process and jihad terror activity were mutually exclusive—as if Lebanon's involvement in parliamentary politics by definition made it less of a terror

group. But a presence in the Lebanese parliament did not make Hizballah moderate—any more than a presence in the Reichstag moderated
the Nazis.

Praising Jihad

Brennan had attempted to distance contemporary Islamic terrorism
from Islam itself, and even from the concept of jihad, long before he
told Farhana Khera that he would give her virtually everything she
wanted. In August 2009, Brennan noted that Barack Obama did not see
the struggle against al Qaeda "as a fight against jihadists. Describing
terrorists in this way, using the legitimate term 'jihad,' which means to
purify oneself or to wage a holy struggle for a moral goal, risks giving
these murderers the religious legitimacy they desperately seek but in
no way deserve."[37]

At New York University Law School in February 2010, Brennan
declared,

> As Muslims you have seen a small fringe of fanatics who
> cloak themselves in religion, try to distort your faith, though
> they are clearly ignorant of the most fundamental teachings
> of Islam. Instead of finding the inherent dignity and decency
> in other human beings, they practice a medieval brand of
> intolerance. Instead of saving human lives, as the Quran
> instructs, they take innocent life. Instead of creating, they
> destroy—bombing mosques, schools and hospitals. They are
> not jihadists, for jihad is a holy struggle, an effort to purify
> for a legitimate purpose, and there is nothing, absolutely
> nothing holy or pure or legitimate or Islamic about murder-
> ing innocent men, women and children.[38]

Going even further, on May 26, 2010, in an address at the Center for
Strategic and International Studies, he said, "Nor do we describe our
enemies as jihadists or Islamists because jihad is a holy struggle, a
legitimate tenet of Islam meaning to purify oneself or one's community."[39] Brennan added, "And there is nothing holy or legitimate or

Islamic about murdering innocent men, women and children. Indeed, characterizing our adversaries this way would actually be counterproductive. It would play into the false perception that they are religious leaders defending a holy cause when in fact, they are nothing more than murderers, including the murder of thousands upon thousands of Muslims."[40] In a press release the next day, CAIR "expressed appreciation" for Brennan's remarks.[41]

Brennan had not even attempted to address, however, the actual Islamic theological claims of jihad terrorists—in particular, the fact that some imams justify the actions of those terrorists by contending that non-Muslims cannot be considered innocent, so that Islam's prohibition on killing the innocent does not apply to them.[42] Brennan simply assumed that violent jihad was not a legitimate tenet of Islam—blithely ignoring the extensive evidence to the contrary within Islamic theology and law.

Given these glaring omissions in his account of jihad, Brennan has understandably had trouble defending his flat denial that America's enemies can rightly be dubbed "jihadists." In 2010, he stormed out of an interview with the *Washington Times* when the interviewer pressed Brennan on his idiosyncratic understanding of jihad, which would seem to define it out of existence: "Can you give me an example of a jihad in history? Like, has there ever been a jihad ... an armed jihad anywhere in history? Has it ever existed for real, or is it just a concept?"[43]

When Brennan responded, "I'm not going to go into this sort of history discussion here," the interviewer explained, "But it's important to frame the concept, because we want to say that what al-Qaeda is doing is not jihad. They say it is." The interviewer then paraphrased for Brennan the jihadist claim, as repeated by al Qaeda cofounder Abdullah Azzam, that the idea that the spiritual jihad was the "greater jihad" had no basis in Islamic theology: "Abdul Azzam has said, in fact, 'there's not even a greater jihad.' [Azzam has said] that that's just a myth—that hadith didn't even really happen."[44]

A hadith is a tradition of Muhammad's words and deeds; the interviewer is pointing out Azzam's insistence that the story in which Muhammad referred to the spiritual jihad as the "greater jihad" was inauthentic. Azzam, the interviewer continued, claimed "that there's only armed jihad. Ayatollah Khomeini said 'there is only armed jihad....'"[45]

But instead of explaining on what grounds he dismissed actual Muslim authorities' equation of jihad with armed struggle to be illegitimate, and on what basis he justified his own contrasting understanding, Brennan said abruptly, "I think we've finished. I have to get going," and left.[46]

Engaging with the Enemy

It's not surprising that Brennan has been instrumental in the Obama administration's recasting of America's defense against Islamic terror as a localized struggle against al Qaeda. Not only has he denied that America's enemies can be called jihadists; he has also repeatedly denied that the United States is engaged in a war on terrorism.

In his August 6, 2009, address at the Center for Strategic and International Studies in Washington, D.C., "A New Approach for Safeguarding Americans," Brennan explained that the Obama administration was putting the resistance to al Qaeda in its rightful place: "the fight against terrorists and violent extremists has been returned to its right and proper place, no longer defining, indeed distorting, our entire national security and foreign policy, but rather serving as a vital part of those larger policies." This reordering, he said, involved "committing the United States to a new partnership with Muslims around the world, a partnership based on mutual interest and mutual respect."[47]

This "new partnership with Muslims" and keeping the fight against terrorists in its "right and proper place" apparently meant turning a blind eye to the unsavory ties of many Muslim leaders in the United States. On February 16, 2010, ISNA boasted in a press release that it had "facilitated a meeting" on February 13 between Brennan and "Muslim American leaders to explore issues of national security, including the important role the Muslim American community plays to thwart security threats and improve the deteriorating relationships with Muslim countries." The press release stated that the White House had organized the meeting and that it was cosponsored by a White House office, along with Muslim groups: "The meeting, organized by the White

House under the title 'A Dialogue on Our Nation's Security,' was co-sponsored by the Islamic Center at New York University, the Islamic Law Students Association at NYU, and the White House Office of Public Engagement."[48]

At this meeting Brennan praised ISNA's then president Ingrid Mattson as "an academic whose research continues the rich tradition of Islamic scholarship and as the President of the Islamic Society of North America, where you have been a voice for the tolerance and diversity that defines Islam." [49] Brennan did not mention ISNA's admitted ties to Hamas and the Muslim Brotherhood; apparently they were of little concern to the White House.[50]

Brennan did, however, praise relief efforts in Haiti by Islamic Relief and the Zakat Foundation—Islamic charities with ties to jihad terror. In 2006, Israeli authorities had arrested Ayaz Ali, program manager for Islamic Relief Worldwide's activities in Gaza.[51] According to the Israeli prime minister's office, Ali provided material support to Hamas institutions and worked with Hamas operatives in Jordan.[52]

Yet in his NYU address, Brennan's focus was on Muslims as victims of counterterror efforts: "Over the years the actions of our own government have at times perpetuated those attitudes—violations of the Patriot Act, surveillance that has been excessive, policies perceived as profiling, over-inclusive no-fly lists subjecting law abiding individuals to unnecessary searches and inconvenience."[53]

Promoted for Incompetence and Denial

Brennan's record was littered with dangerous revisionism, appeasement of jihadists and Islamic supremacists, and naïve acceptance of Muslim Brotherhood groups' propaganda recasting jihad to make it more palatable to the American public and of their sanitizing interpretations of Islam and denials of the very existence of radical Islam—all of which enable terrorism. So Barack Obama appointed him head of the Central Intelligence Agency.

How can an intelligence chief do his job properly when he is willfully blind to politically inconvenient realities? Unfortunately, Brennan was just one of many such Obama administration diplomatic, military, and intelligence officials.

"Lysenkoism" was the name for the ideologically biased junk science regarding biology and agriculture that was adopted as official policy by the Soviet Union under Stalin. The real scientists who told the truth were sent to the gulag.

Naturally, in an environment in which officials refuse to speak about "Islam" and "terrorism" in the same sentence—a policy that must involve quite a lot of mental and verbal gymnastics when jihad terrorists start quoting Qur'an and other Islamic sources—the truth about Islam is going to come under fire whenever it appears as part of counterterrorism studies. Officials who insist, against all the evidence, that the Muslim Brotherhood is "largely secular" and that jihad is a wholly positive interior spiritual struggle, are going to get nervous at revelations that somewhere the truth about Islam and jihad are still getting through.

As Lysenkoism grows more entrenched, and heads at the FBI and the CIA are planted ever more firmly in the sand, the likelihood of another catastrophic jihad attack in the United States grows apace.

CHAPTER TEN

TAKING AIM AT THE *REAL* DANGER

"Right-Wing Extremists"

The removal of all mention of Islam and jihad from government training materials on terrorism left a void. And it soon became clear with what the Obama administration was going to fill it. Fox News reported in April 2013 that "the U.S. Army listed Evangelical Christianity and Catholicism as examples of religious extremism along with Al Qaeda and Hamas during a briefing with an Army Reserve unit based in Pennsylvania.... The incident occurred during an Army Reserve Equal Opportunity training brief on extremism."[1]

The list was headed "Religious Extremism"; topping it was "Evangelical Christianity (U.S./Christian)," followed by "Ikhwan or Muslim Brotherhood (Egypt/Muslim)" and then "Ultra-Orthodox (Israel/Judaism)"—making for a politically correct trifecta of the three main monotheistic religions. Also on the list were "Al Quaeda [sic] (Transnational/Islam)"; "Hamas (Palestinian/Islamist)"; "Abu Sayyah [sic] (Philippines/

Islam)"; "Ku Klux Klan (U.S/Christian)"; and "Catholicism (U.S./Christian)," among others.[2]

The list also included "Islamophobia" as a form of "religious extremism"—apparently on the basis of the by-then mainstream assumption that those who opposed the global jihad and Islamic supremacism were Christian fanatics motivated by some kind of religious one-upmanship.

The idea that there was *any* factor unifying these disparate groups was howlingly absurd, and the list would have been a joke—if it had not come from the U.S. Army. Apparently this politically manipulative and ridiculous nonsense was what replaced the truthful information about Islam and jihad that had been removed from counterterror training material.

Throughout his presidency, Obama repeated many, many times that we are not at war with Islam, and the mainstream media consistently took the line that to suggest otherwise would be evidence of "hatred" and "bigotry." But apparently it was not "hatred" and "bigotry" for the United States to declare that Catholicism is the same sort of thing as al Qaeda. The list did also include "Sunni Muslims," but specified those in Iraq—no way was the Obama administration going to classify all Sunni Muslims as "extremists."

According to the list, Catholicism was a form of "religious extremism," though apparently only in the United States That was bad enough. But the larger implications of the U.S. Army's "Religious Extremism" list were quite ominous. If Evangelical Christianity (in the United States), Catholicism (in the United States) and "Islamophobia" were forms of "Religious Extremism" on par with al Qaeda and Hamas, then would the Obama administration go to war against them, as it had repeatedly declared that it was at war with al Qaeda?

The Proliferation of "Hate Groups"

For this list was not an isolated case of the administration lumping law-abiding Americans—and particularly its domestic critics—in with Islamic terrorists. Investigative reporter Matthew Vadum reported in September 2013 that "conservative organizations are 'hate groups' and Tea Party supporters are potentially dangerous extremists, according to educational materials the Obama administration is using to indoctrinate members of the nation's armed forces."

Vadum noted that a Defense Department diversity training center guide entitled "Extremism," published in January 2013, warned that "instead of 'dressing in sheets,' radicals today 'will talk of individual liberties, states' rights, and how to make the world a better place.'" It even identified the Founding Fathers as "extremists": "In U.S. history, there are many examples of extremist ideologies and movements. The colonists who sought to free themselves from British rule and the Confederate states who sought to secede from the Northern states are just two examples."

Meanwhile, reported Vadum, "the DoD teaching guide treats Islamic terrorism as insignificant, ignoring, for example, the murder spree committed by self-described 'soldier of Allah,' U.S. Army Major Nidal Malik Hasan, at Fort Hood in 2009. The guide references Islamic extremism only in passing and doesn't provide a precise definition for extremism. '[W]hile not all extremist groups are hate groups, all hate groups are extremist groups,' it states."[3]

This extraordinary denial of the reality of Islamic jihad and fearmongering about an imaginary Christian terror threat has taken place even at Fort Hood itself. Investigative reporter Todd Starnes reported in October 2013 that "soldiers attending a pre-deployment briefing at Fort Hood say they were told that evangelical Christians and members of the Tea Party were a threat to the nation and that any soldier donating to those groups would be subjected to punishment under the Uniform Code of Military Justice." The briefing paid only glancing attention to the Islamic jihad threat.

According to a soldier who attended the briefing, a counterintelligence agent went on at length about how evangelical Christian groups were "tearing the country apart." The soldier asked not to be identified in Starnes's article, as he feared reprisals from Obama-era military brass. He told Starnes, "My first concern was if I was going to be in trouble going to church. Can I tithe? Can I donate to Christian charities? What if I donate to a politician who is a part of the Tea Party movement?"

Another soldier at the briefing recounted, "I was very shocked and couldn't believe what I was hearing. I felt like my religious liberties, that I risk my life and sacrifice time away from family to fight for, were being taken away. Our community is still healing from the act of terrorism brought on by Nidal Hasan—who really is a terrorist. This is a slap in the face. The military is supposed to defend freedom and to classify the vast majority of the military that claim to be Christian as terrorists is sick."

The briefing raised the specter of Christian terrorist attacks. "They said," according to one of the soldiers present, "that evangelical Christians protesting abortions are the mobilization stage and that leads to the bombing of abortion clinics."

A Pentagon spokesman disclaimed any responsibility on the part of the army: "None of these slides [shown at the briefing] were produced by the Army, but by soldiers who included information found during an Internet search."

For its part, Fort Hood denied the soldiers' allegations outright. Tom Rheinlander, the base's public affairs director, issued a statement saying that while "a [sic] inquiry is occurring," there was no truth to the claims: "At this time, initial information gathered about the training and what you claim occurred is not substantiated by unit leadership and soldiers present at this training venue."[4]

Yet the fact that this was not an isolated incident cast doubt on Fort Hood's denial. The Pennsylvania briefing and the Defense Department diversity training center guide were telling indications of an attempt to demonize Christianity much farther-reaching than just the briefing at Fort Hood.

And in April 2013, Starnes published "an email written by a lieutenant colonel at Fort Campbell in Kentucky—advising three dozen subordinates to be on the lookout for soldiers who might be members of 'domestic hate groups.'"

This lieutenant colonel was unlikely to have been acting solely on his own initiative on such a hot-button issue, especially given the exhaustive list he then supplied of these alleged "domestic hate groups." His language suggested that he was passing on material he had received from his superiors, as he explained that he wanted to "ensure everyone is somewhat educated on some of the groups out there that do not share our Army Values." Army values are a matter of concern for the entire army, not just one lieutenant colonel in Kentucky.

"When we see behaviors that are inconsistent with Army Values," the email continued, "don't just walk by—do the right thing and address the concern before it becomes a problem." The lieutenant colonel then included an extensive list of "Domestic Hate Groups," including groups classified as "Anti-Gay, Anti-Immigrant, Anti-Muslim, Black Separatist, Christian Identity, Ku Klux Klan, Neo-Confederate, Neo-Nazi, Patriot Movement, Racist Skinhead, Sovereign Citizens Movement, and White Nationalist."

No Islamic groups were on the list, and it was likewise telling that "anti-Muslim" groups would be lumped together with neo-Nazis, skinheads, and the KKK. The section on anti-Muslim groups explained that these groups "exhibit extreme hostility toward Muslims. The organizations portray those who worship Islam as fundamentally alien and attribute to its followers an inherent set of negative traits."

That the lieutenant colonel spoke of Muslims as people who "worship Islam" was just one indication of the deep wellspring of ignorance from which this list originated. "Muslims," his email continued, "are depicted as irrational, intolerant and violent, and their faith is frequently depicted as sanctioning pedophilia, marital rape and child marriage." The email made no attempt to refute claims that Islam sanctioned pedophilia, marital rape, and child marriage; it simply took it as self-evident.

Also held up as self-evident proof of anti-Muslim bigotry was any idea that Islamic supremacists might have plans to subvert U.S. Constitutional government: "These groups also typically hold conspiratorial views regarding the inherent danger to America posed by its Muslim-American community. Muslims are depicted as a fifth column intent on undermining and eventually replacing American democracy and Western civilization with Islamic despotism. Anti-Muslim hate groups allege that Muslims are trying to subvert the rule of law by imposing on Americans their own Islamic legal system, Shariah law."

Needless to say, the lieutenant colonel did not see fit to mention the captured internal document of the Muslim Brotherhood, in which it explained its goal in the United States of "eliminating and destroying Western civilization from within."

Included on the list of "Anti-Muslim Groups" were "groups" that were actually no more than websites, such as Pamela Geller's AtlasShrugs.com and TheReligionofPeace.com, which keeps a running tally of Islamic jihad attacks worldwide. Included among these were very obscure groups such as "Christian Phalange" and "Aggressive Christianity," whose inclusion suggested that concerns about jihad terror were primarily the province of Christian "extremists" and neofascists.[5]

Then in early October 2013, Starnes reported, "several dozen active duty troops at Camp Shelby in Mississippi, were told the American Family Association, a well-respected Christian ministry, should be classified as a domestic hate group because it advocates for traditional family values."

"Again," Starnes noted, "the military called it an isolated incident with a trainer using material that was not sanctioned by the military." To that, attorney Michael Berry of the Liberty Institute responded, "How much longer can the Army claim no knowledge or responsibility for these things? These repeated incidents show either that this training was directed from Army leadership at the Pentagon, or else the Army has a real discipline and leadership problem on its hands because a bunch of rogue soldiers are teaching this nonsense."[6]

The Threat of "Right-Wing Extremism"

In the age of Barack Obama, it was much more likely that this training was directed from high levels. This was, after all, the administration that, just three months after taking office, had issued a report entitled *Right-wing Extremism: Current Economic and Political Climate Fueling Resurgence in Radicalization and Recruitment*, produced by the Department of Homeland Security in conjunction with the FBI.

The report said that while there was "no specific information that domestic right-wing terrorists are currently planning acts of violence," nonetheless, economic hard times "could create a fertile recruiting environment for right-wing extremists and even result in confrontations between such groups and government authorities similar to those in the past." It warned that "the threat posed by lone wolves and small terrorist cells is more pronounced than in past years."

These small terrorist cells, the report warned, could be populated by military veterans: "The willingness of a small percentage of military personnel to join extremist groups during the 1990s because they were disgruntled, disillusioned or suffering from the psychological effects of war is being replicated today."

Islamic jihad groups, meanwhile, actually were planning acts of violence at that time, but Obama's Homeland Security Department appeared to be much less concerned about them than about these "right-wingers."

When challenged about this outlandish demonization of American military veterans and willful blindness to the Islamic jihad threat, Homeland Security secretary Janet Napolitano responded piously: "Let me be very clear: We monitor the risks of violent extremism taking root here in the United States. We don't have the luxury of focusing our efforts on one group; we must protect the country from terrorism whether foreign or homegrown and regardless of the ideology that motivates its violence."[7]

The High Cost

There is a cost to all this. Ironically, the Boston Marathon jihad bombings took place less than two weeks after the list labeling Evangelical Christianity and Catholicism as extremist came to light. In the aftermath of that attack, Obama promised that he would be taking lessons from the Boston Marathon jihad bombings: "When an event like this happens, we want to review every step that was taken, we want to leave no stone unturned, we want to see if there is in fact additional protocols and procedures [sic] that could be put in place that would further improve and enhance our ability to detect a potential attack."[8]

This sounded impressive, but ultimately all Obama offered were words—words that were unlikely to be backed up by real action. The one thing that needed to be done—an official acknowledgement of the reality and magnitude of the global jihad, and the commitment of U.S. intelligence to understanding and combating it—was the one thing that would not be done.

Learning All the Wrong Lessons

The administration official whom Obama charged with ferreting out the lessons of Boston was his director of national intelligence, James Clapper, who had been widely ridiculed for claiming in 2011 that the Muslim Brotherhood was "largely secular"—a claim that seemed to sum up the administration's willful ignorance about the jihad terror threat.[9] Nonetheless, in his post–Boston jihad bombing remarks, Obama explained, "Part of what Director Clapper is doing is to see if we can determine lessons learned from what happened" in Boston.[10] He didn't explain how Clapper was going to be able to do this within an administration that denied him and all its other officials the use of the only frame of reference that made sense of the Boston attack.

Indeed, one of the foremost lessons of the Boston bombings was that the denial of the nature and magnitude of the jihad threat, which the Obama administration (as well as the mainstream media) had pursued so assiduously, was wrongheaded and dangerous—and that people as blind to that threat as James Clapper should never have been entrusted with the nation's intelligence-gathering apparatus. The Russians, as we have seen, had Boston jihad bomber Tamerlan Tsarnaev under surveillance, were deeply concerned about his contacts with jihad terrorists, and shared those concerns with the FBI.[11] Yet President Obama said it was "not right" to criticize the way the FBI handled that intelligence: "not right, although I am sure it generated some headlines. It's not as if the FBI did nothing. They not only investigated the older brother, they interviewed the older brother, they concluded that there were no signs he was engaging in extremist activity."

Obama concluded from this that "the question then is, is there something that happened that triggered radicalization and an actual decision by the older brother to engage in the tragic attack we actually saw in Boston, and are there additional things that could have been done in the interim that might have prevented it?"

But that is hardly the only conclusion that can be drawn from the fact that the FBI interviewed Tamerlan Tsarnaev and found no signs that he was "engaging in extremist activity." The conclusion that leaps to mind, in fact, is that the FBI had no idea how to tell whether or not

Tamerlan Tsarnaev was "engaging in extremist activity" or not because the "extremist activity" he was engaging in was Islamic jihad, a subject that Obama's FBI has been forbidden to study. And so the politically correct FBI ignored Tamerlan Tsarnaev despite repeated warnings from Russian authorities. Insofar as they did investigate him, they didn't know what to look for or how to understand what they were seeing.

The leftist journalists and Islamic supremacist groups who pressured Obama—(as well as Obama and his administration officials themselves)—ought to be held accountable for the law enforcement and intelligence failures connected to the Boston jihad bombings. For this state of affairs was their doing.

Going after the Freedom of Speech

Right after the Benghazi massacre, the father of one of those slain there recounted that Secretary of State Hillary Clinton spoke to him about the Muhammad filmmaker at a memorial service, saying, "We're going to have that person arrested and prosecuted."[12] And she did. The filmmaker Nakoula Basseley Nakoula, aka "Sam Bacile," had a record full of run-ins with the law and at the time of the Benghazi attacks was out on parole. A condition of his parole, however, was that he not go on the internet—which he apparently did in order to upload the notorious video to YouTube.

For that, he was arrested and imprisoned for several months, thereby becoming the first political prisoner in the United States in Obama's war on free speech and enforcement of sharia blasphemy laws. In reality he was imprisoned not for the technicality of the probation violation, but for insulting Muhammad. His arrest was a symbol of America's capitulation to the sharia. He was nothing more than the fall guy who became the first offender against the new de facto federal crime of blasphemy against Islam.

The effort to make that de facto crime a de jure one got a boost in June 2013 in rural Tennessee, of all places, when Bill Killian, the Obama-appointed U.S. attorney for the eastern district of Tennessee, held a public meeting about his intention, as reported by Politico, to "use federal civil rights statutes to clamp down on offensive and inflammatory speech about Islam." Said Killian, "We need to educate people about Muslims and their civil rights, and as long as we're here, they're going to be protected."[13]

Killian, along with FBI special agent Kenneth Moore and Zak Mohyuddin of the American Muslim Advisory Council, hosted an event called "Public Disclosure in a Diverse Society" in the town of Manchester, Tennessee. "This is an educational effort with civil rights laws," Killian explained, "as they play into freedom of religion and exercising freedom of religion. This is also to inform the public what federal laws are in effect and what the consequences are."[14]

Killian offered an example: "A recent controversy where a local Tennessee politician posted a photo of a man aiming a shotgun at the camera with the caption 'How to wink at a Muslim.'" He asked the rhetorical question, "If a Muslim had posted 'How to Wink at a Christian,' could you imagine what would have happened?"[15]

Nothing much, most likely. To have acted would have been "Islamophobic." The larger problem, however, was that neither the Obama administration nor Islamic supremacist groups that have campaigned against the freedom of speech for years have ever drawn any distinction between genuinely threatening speech (which the shotgun photo may arguably have been) and honest analysis of how jihadists used the texts and teachings of Islam to justify violence and supremacism.

On the contrary, they conflate the two, smearing as "hateful" all examination of the motives and goals of the jihad terrorists who have vowed to destroy the United States and conquer the free world. Writing about the Tennessee meeting, Byron Tau of Politico reported that the Justice Department did not respond to "a question about what guidelines it draws concerning offensive speech and Islam, or whether the department believes that civil rights statutes could be used to stifle criticism of Islam."[16]

It wasn't the first time the question had come up. In July 2012, then-Assistant Attorney General Tom Perez of the Department of Justice's civil rights division was asked by Republican representative Trent Franks of Arizona, "Will you tell us here today that this Administration's Department of Justice will never entertain or advance a proposal that criminalizes speech against any religion?" Perez, who has now been nominated by President Obama to be Secretary of Labor, refused to rule out that possibility—strongly suggesting, by his refusal to answer, that the Obama administration is indeed contemplating ways to circumvent the First Amendment and outlaw criticism of Islam.

The Tennessee meeting did not go as Killian, Moore, and Mohyuddin had probably expected. My American Freedom Defense Initiative colleague Pamela Geller and I called for a protest of what was clearly an event designed to intimidate Americans into being afraid to criticize the elements of Islam that give rise to violence and supremacism, and nearly two thousand protesters assembled at the Manchester Convention Center to register their disapproval of this latest Obama administration attempt to silence criticism of Islam and jihad.

Predictably, Killian, Moore, and Mohyuddin spoke extensively about hate crimes, hate speech, and how Tennesseans needed to be more inclusive and welcoming of the increasing numbers of Muslims in their midst. They all spoke to the crowd with extraordinary condescension, as if it could be taken for granted that their only reason for being suspicious of Muslims was the color of their skin (Killian said exactly that) and cultural differences. The audience, however, was having none of it, and frequently shouted responses to the various (and numerous) disingenuous and manipulative assertions coming from the speakers.

That gave the mainstream media their take on the event; their reporting on the event uniformly portrayed the pro–free speech protesters as a gang of racist, bigoted thugs, shouting down the valiant paladins of tolerance. Reporters completely ignored the genuine concern that people have about jihad and Islamic supremacist activity and the fact that Muslim groups (aided and abetted by Barack Obama) use claims of "hate" and "bigotry" to shut down honest discussion of how jihadists use the texts and teachings of Islam to justify violence and supremacism.

And so while the large number of protesters was heartening, the mainstream media and government narrative did not budge. The drive toward laws restricting free speech regarding Islam and jihad rolled along.

If the United States ultimately does adopt any kind of law criminalizing criticism of Islam, that would be the end of any effective resistance to jihad, as we will be rendered mute and thus defenseless against its advance. And while this possibility still seems wildly farfetched to most people, it must be borne in mind that the First Amendment is not automatically self-enforcing. If those charged with guarding and protecting it are determined to do away with it, they can hedge it around with nuances and exceptions that will render it as toothless and essentially void as the Second Amendment already is in many major cities.

In the meantime, while we still can, we must state the truths about Islam and jihad that the Obama administration and the media establishment would prefer you didn't know.

CHAPTER ELEVEN

DO THE JIHADIS
HAVE A CASE?

arack Obama is right. Islam really does teach justice, tolerance, and the dignity of all human beings, as he said in Cairo. And on this assumption, of course, rests the entire Obama policy of downplaying Islamic terrorism and focusing on other threats.

Every one of the points Obama touched on in his infamous Cairo speech is indeed emphasized in the Qur'an. The Muslim holy book certainly does teach that believers should be just: "O you who have believed, be persistently standing firm in justice, witnesses for Allah, even if it be against yourselves or parents and relatives. Whether one is rich or poor, Allah is more worthy of both. So follow not (personal) inclination, lest you not be just. And if you distort (your testimony) or refuse (to give it), then indeed Allah is ever, with what you do, acquainted" (4:135; words in parentheses are added by the translator for clarity and do not appear in the original Arabic).

There are many such verses: "O you who have believed, be persistently standing firm for Allah, witnesses in justice, and do not let the hatred of a people prevent you from being just. Be just; that is nearer to righteousness" (5:8). "And if you judge, judge between them with justice. Indeed, Allah loves those who act justly" (5:42).

As for progress, the Qur'an asks, "Are those who know equal to those who do not know?" (39:9), a verse that has been used to extol the value and importance of education.[1] Tolerance is the message of sura 109, which directs the prophet on what to say to non-Muslims: "Say, 'O disbelievers, I do not worship what you worship. Nor are you worshippers of what I worship. Nor will I be a worshipper of what you worship. Nor will you be worshippers of what I worship. For you is your religion, and for me is my religion'" (109:1–6).

The dignity of all human beings appears in a verse that says, "O mankind, indeed We have created you from male and female and made you peoples and tribes that you may know one another" (49:13). Another verse says, "O mankind, fear your Lord, who created you from one soul and created from it its mate and dispersed from both of them many men and women" (4:1).

Same Words, Different Meanings

However, in Islamic theology and law all these concepts have quite different meanings from those that generally prevail in non-Muslim societies.

Justice in the Qur'an does not mean equal treatment for all—because the Qur'an doesn't teach that all people are equal in dignity. On the contrary, it tells Muslims that they are "the best nation produced (as an example) for mankind" (3:110) but says that "they who disbelieved among the People of the Scripture and the polytheists" are "the worst of creatures" (98:6). The Qur'an directs Muslims not to treat each group equally, but rather to be "forceful against the disbelievers" while being "merciful among themselves" (48:29).

In line with this unequal justice, the Islamic law of retaliation (qisas) for murder establishes as a point of law that the life of a non-Muslim does not have the same value as that of a Muslim—and that a woman's life is not as valuable as a man's. A sharia manual certified by the most respected authority in Sunni Islam, Al-Azhar University in Cairo, as conforming to the "practice and faith of the orthodox Sunni community," stipulates that the payment for taking a woman's life is half of that to be paid for taking a man's, and that there is also a sliding scale based on religious belief: if one kills a Jew or Christian, one need only pay one-third of that which must be paid for killing an adult male Muslim.[2]

An Iranian Sufi Muslim cleric, Sheikh Sultanhussein Tabandeh, who was instrumental in formulating the legal code of the Islamic Republic of Iran after the Islamic revolution of 1979, justified this inequality in a commentary on the United Nations' Universal Declaration of Human Rights. "If a Muslim deliberately murders another Muslim," he explains, "he falls under the law of retaliation and must by law be put to death by the next of kin. But if a non-Muslim who dies at the hand of a Muslim has by lifelong habit been a non-Muslim, the penalty of death is not valid. Instead the Muslim murderer must pay a fine and be punished with the lash." Why? Because "Islam regards non-Muslims as on a lower level of belief and conviction." Therefore, "if a Muslim kills a non-Muslim ... then his punishment must not be the retaliatory death, since the faith and conviction he possesses is [sic] loftier than that of the man slain." Tabandeh concludes, "Islam and its peoples must be above the infidels, and never permit non-Muslims to acquire lordship over them."[3]

Warfare against Non-Muslims: Taught in the Qur'an

But what about the tolerance that Muslims are supposed to show to non-Muslims—"For you is your religion, and for me is my religion" (Qur'an 109:6)? According to the Tafsir al-Jalalayn, a venerable and mainstream commentary on the Qur'an, this passage of the Qur'an was revealed to Muhammad before he received "the command to fight" against non-Muslims.[4]

But ultimately, that command to fight did come: "Permission (to fight) has been given to those who are being fought, because they were wronged. And indeed, Allah is competent to give them victory (Qur'an 22:39). Osama bin Laden quoted this verse in his October 6, 2002, letter to the American people, situating his war against the United States within the Qur'an's command to Muslims to defend themselves and their communities from aggressors.

Allah commands the Muslims to fight against the unbelievers, promising angelic aid: "(Remember) when your Lord inspired to the angels, 'I am with you, so strengthen those who have believed. I will cast terror into the hearts of those who disbelieved, so strike (them) upon the necks and strike from them every fingertip'" (8:12). This is specifically a religious war: "That is because they opposed Allah and His Messenger. And whoever opposes Allah and His Messenger—indeed, Allah is severe in penalty. 'That (is yours), so taste it.' And indeed for the disbelievers is the punishment of the Fire" (8:13-14).

These passages appear to endorse only a defensive war against unbelievers who are attacking the Muslims: "O you who have believed, when you meet those who disbelieve advancing (for battle), do not turn to them your backs (in flight). And whoever turns his back to them on such a day, unless swerving (as a strategy)for war or joining (another) company, has certainly returned with anger (upon him) from Allah, and his refuge is Hell—and wretched is the destination." (8:15–16). As another passage puts it: "So whoever has assaulted you, then assault him in the same way that he has assaulted you" (2:194).

However, this immediately follows a passage that tells Muslims, "Fight them until there is no (more) fitnah and (until) worship is (acknowledged to be) for Allah. But if they cease, then there is to be no aggression except against the oppressors" (2:193). Fitna is a key sin in Islam; the word is variously translated as disturbance, upheaval, chaos, and sedition. If Muslims are to fight until there is no more fitna and worship is for Allah, non-Muslims will have to have all become Muslims, thereby eradicating the fitna caused by unbelief, and ensuring that worship is all rightly directed toward Allah.

This idea is reinforced by other passages of the Qur'an, which establish the Islamic doctrine of not just defensive jihad, but offensive jihad as well: a religious war to establish the supremacy and hegemony of Islam. Islamic tradition attributes these words to Muhammad: "I have been commanded to fight against people, till they testify to the fact that there is no god but Allah, and believe in me (that) I am the messenger (from the Lord) and in all that I have brought. And when they do it, their blood and riches are guaranteed protection on my behalf except where it is justified by law, and their affairs rest with Allah."[5]

Other verses of the Qur'an echo that call. Allah tells Muhammad, "O Prophet, fight [jahidi, a verbal form of the noun jihad] against the disbelievers and the hypocrites and be harsh upon them. And their refuge is Hell, and wretched is the destination" (9:73). Muslims are to do the same: "O you who have believed, fight those adjacent to you of the disbelievers and let them find in you harshness. And know that Allah is with the righteous" (9:123).

These statements, coupled with the Qur'an's statements about Muslims having to fight until religion is all for Allah, constitute an open-ended license to wage war against and plunder non-Muslims. This is expressed in chillingly direct fashion in the Qur'an's famous "Verse of the Sword," which directs Muslims to kill polytheists until they adopt Muslim practices of prayer and almsgiving—that is, until they convert to Islam: "And when the sacred months have passed, then kill the polytheists wherever you find them and capture them and besiege them and sit in wait for them at every place of ambush. But if they should repent, establish prayer, and give zakah, let them (go) on their way. Indeed, Allah is Forgiving and Merciful" (9:5).

While non-Muslims' "blood and riches" are fair game unless they convert, this war and plunder are not to be for the sake of material gain or for any selfish purpose, but only for the sake of weakening the infidel party and strengthening that of the worshippers of the true God. Muhammad's first biographer, Ibn Ishaq, explained that Qur'an 2:193 meant that Muslims must fight against non-Muslims "until God alone is worshipped."[6] Ibn Kathir, another mainstream and respected Qur'an commentator whose works are still widely read among Muslims today, glossed the verse as meaning that Muslims must fight "so that the religion of Allah becomes dominant above all other religions."[7]

A twentieth-century Islamic scholar, Maulana Bulandshahri, explains why in detail: "The worst of sins are Infidelity (Kufr) and

Polytheism (shirk) which constitute rebellion against Allah, The Creator. To eradicate these, Muslims are required to wage war until there exists none of it in the world, and the only religion is that of Allah."[8]

Another Qur'anic passage reinforces this, saying, "And fight them until there is no fitnah and (until) the religion, all of it, is for Allah. And if they cease—then indeed, Allah is seeing of what they do." (8:39). The venerable Qur'an commentary *Tafsir al-Jalalayn* explains, "Fight them until there is no more fitna (shirk) and the din [religion] is Allah's alone—meaning that only He is worshipped."[9]

Also Taught in the Qur'an: Subjugating Non-Muslims

Those who refuse to become Muslims must be made subject to Muslim rule: "Fight those who do not believe in Allah or in the Last Day and who do not consider unlawful what Allah and His Messenger have made unlawful and who do not adopt the religion of truth from those who were given the Scripture—(fight) until they give the jizyah [the special tax levied only on non-Muslims] willingly while they are humbled" (9:29).

A hadith has Muhammad expanding on this verse: "Fight in the name of Allah and in the way of Allah. Fight against those who disbelieve in Allah. Make a holy war.... When you meet your enemies who are polytheists, invite them to three courses of action. If they respond to any one of these, you also accept it and withhold yourself from doing them any harm. Invite them to (accept) Islam; if they respond to you, accept it from them and desist from fighting against them.... If they refuse to accept Islam, demand from them the Jizya. If they agree to pay, accept it from them and hold off your hands. If they refuse to pay the tax, seek Allah's help and fight them."[10]

The Qur'an commentator Ibn Juzayy explains that Qur'an 9:29 is "a command to fight the People of the Book"—in Qur'anic parlance, primarily Jews and Christians. Muslims must fight them because of their false beliefs—on the Jews' part, that Ezra is the Son of God, and on the Christians' part, that Jesus is. This odd statement, false as regarding the Jews, none of whom ever claimed that Ezra was God's Son, and true regarding the Christians, is found in the immediately subsequent Qur'anic verse: "The Jews say, 'Ezra is the son of Allah'; and

the Christians say, 'The Messiah is the son of Allah.' That is their statement from their mouths; they imitate the saying of those who disbelieved [before them]. May Allah destroy them; how are they deluded?"
(9:30). Ibn Juzayy says that Muslims must also fight Jews and Christians
because they consider "as lawful carrion, blood, pork, etc." and because
"they do not enter Islam." He says that the collection of the jizya signifies "submission and obedience."[11] Another venerable Qur'an scholar,
As-Sawi, explains that when Jews and Christians pay the jizya, it demonstrates that they are "humble and obedient to the judgements of
Islam."[12]

In the modern age, Bulandshahri says regretfully that "in today's
times, the system of Atonement (Jizya) is not practised at all by the
Muslims. It is indeed unfortunate that not only are the Muslim States
afraid to impose Atonement (Jizya) on the disbelievers (kuffar) living
in their countries, but they grant them more rights than they grant the
Muslims and respect them more. They fail to understand that Allah
desires that the Muslims show no respect to any disbeliever (kafir) and
that they should not accord any special rights to them."[13]

Bulandshahri's language of "special rights" intimates that the practice of jizya makes a political statement as well as a religious one.
Islamic law (sharia), as envisioned by all the traditional schools of
Islamic jurisprudence, doesn't govern solely matters of ritual and worship; indeed, it is not an exaggeration to say that it covers every aspect
of life. This comprehensiveness is often a matter for boasting among
Islamic apologists, who compare Christianity's set of vague moral pre-
cepts with Islam's rules for everything a human being could conceivably
do. But this comprehensiveness also means that Islam is political as
well as religious. If the "People of the Book" are to live in "submission
and obedience" to the Muslims, obviously they are not to be placed in
charge of the affairs of state.

Accordingly, the twentieth-century Pakistani political leader and
Islamic scholar Syed Abul A'la Maududi understood that the idea that
Muslims must fight until fitna was eradicated and religion was all for
Allah meant that non-Muslims must not be entrusted with the respon-
sibilities of governing a state—any state. He declared that non-Muslims
have "absolutely no right to seize the reins of power in any part of God's

earth nor to direct the collective affairs of human beings according to their own misconceived doctrines. For if they are given such an opportunity, corruption and mischief will ensue. In such a situation the believers would be under an obligation to do their utmost to dislodge them from political power and to make them live in subservience to the Islamic way of life."[14]

Writing about Qur'an 9:29, which contains the order for Muslims to wage war against the "People of the Book," Maududi states that Muslims are not to fight in order to force non-Muslims to convert to Islam—after all, "There is no compulsion in religion" (Qur'an 2:256): "the purpose for which the Muslims are required to fight is not, as one might to think, to compel the unbelievers into embracing Islam." On the contrary, "its purpose is to put an end to the suzerainty of the unbelievers so that the latter are unable to rule over people. The authority to rule should only be vested in those who follow the True Faith; unbelievers who do not follow this True Faith should live in a state of subordination. Anybody who becomes convinced of the Truth of Islam may accept the faith of his/her own volition. The unbelievers are required to pay jizyah (poll tax) in return for the security provided to them as the dhimmis ("Protected People") of an Islamic state. Jizyah symbolizes the submission of the unbelievers to the suzerainty of Islam."[15]

Justice, tolerance, and the dignity of all human beings are seen through this prism. These laws are just because they come from Allah. Non-Muslims, or at least the "People of the Book," are tolerated as long as they submit to Muslim rule and pay the jizya. The dignity of all human beings is respected, as long as the "worst of creatures" submits to the "best of people."

Jihad Trumps Tolerance

We have seen that Major Nidal Hasan, the Fort Hood shooter, argued in his PowerPoint presentation on grand rounds that Muslims must not fight against other Muslims (it's forbidden by Qur'an 4:92), explained that the Qur'an also mandates both defensive and offensive jihad against unbelievers, and even quoted Qur'an 9:29, the verse calling for war against the "People of the Book" until they pay the jizya and submit.

In making these claims, clearly Hasan could rely upon a broad tradition within Islamic teaching. It is not the only understanding of Islam, true. Islamic spokesmen in the West insist that it is an understanding held by no Muslims except a tiny minority of extremists. Yet it has numerous proponents, and the even larger number of Muslims who do not adhere to it have failed to work in any effective way to rein it in. Instead, Muslim organizations in the United States and Europe are far more concerned with branding any discussion of these questions at all as "Islamophobic."

What of Mujaahid Abu Hamza, the Woolwich murderer, and David Cameron's claim that his beheading of Lee Rigby was a "betrayal of Islam"? Abu Hamza killed a British soldier on a London street. The Qur'an says, "Fight in the way of Allah those who fight you but do not transgress. Indeed. Allah does not like transgressors" (2:190). The phrase "do not transgress" has often been interpreted by Islamic scholars as meaning "do not begin hostilities." But in this case, as the killer himself made clear, he believed that the soldier was already participating in the fight against Muslims in Islamic lands—Iraq and Afghanistan. Because the soldier was already fighting Muslims, the killer, in his own mind, was not "transgressing" by fighting "in the way of Allah those who fight you."

How is one to fight them? Abu Hamza explicitly referred to Surat at-Tawba, the Qur'an's ninth chapter, or "sura," which contains the "Verse of the Sword": "kill the polytheists wherever you find them" (9:5)—even on, say, a street in Woolwich.

Many Muslims in the United State today assert that the bloody prescriptions of sura 9 no longer apply in our present day of pluralism, and that the Qur'an's verses of tolerance, such as sura 109, are the only ones with which non-Muslims need be concerned. Unfortunately, however, a mainstream view widely subscribed to by Muslims around the world, including some in the United States, holds that the passages enjoining tolerance were superseded by verses enjoining warfare against and subjugation of unbelievers.

Muhammad's first biographer, the pious eighth-century Muslim Ibn Ishaq, explains that at first Muhammad "had not been given permission to fight or allowed to shed blood.... He had simply been ordered to call men to God and to endure insult and forgive the ignorant." This was true even though the Muslims were being persecuted: "The Quraysh had persecuted his followers, seducing some from their religion, and exiling others from their country. They had to choose whether to give up their religion, be maltreated at home, or to flee the country, some to Abyssinia, others to Medina."

However, Ibn Ishaq continues, "when Quraysh became insolent towards God and rejected His gracious purpose, accused His prophet of lying, and ill treated and exiled those who served Him and pro-claimed His unity, believed in His prophet, and held fast to His religion, He gave permission to His apostle to fight and to protect himself against those who wronged them and treated them badly."[16]

In connection with Qur'an 22:39, which grants the Muslims "per-mission to fight," Ibn Ishaq explains that Allah gave this permission "only because they have been unjustly treated while their sole offence against men has been that they worship God. When they are in the ascendant they will establish prayer, pay the poor-tax, enjoin kindness, and forbid iniquity, i.e. the Prophet and his companions all of them."[17] "When they are in the ascendant"—in other words, they will establish the observance of Islamic prayer and almsgiving and institute Islamic laws ("forbid iniquity").

After that came further revelations. "Then God sent down to him: 'Fight them so that there be no more seduction,' i.e. until no believer is seduced from his religion. 'And the religion is God's, i.e. Until God alone is worshipped.'"[18] This is Qur'an 2:193, which commands Muslims to fight until "the religion is God's."

This view of the stages of the Qur'an's development regarding the doctrine of jihad, culminating with offensive jihad as the crowning and final stage, has persisted to the present day. According to a twentieth-century chief justice of Saudi Arabia, Sheikh 'Abdullah bin Muhammad ibn Humaid, "at first 'the fighting' was forbidden, then it was permitted and after that it was made obligatory."[19] He cites several of the Qur'an verses quoted above, notably 9:5 and 9:29, in support of that interpreta-tion.

Muslim Brotherhood theorist Sayyid Qutb (1906–1966) held the same view of the Qur'an. In *Milestones*, his influential and succinct summation of the Muslims' responsibility to wage jihad, Qutb quotes the medieval Islamic scholar Ibn Qayyim (1292–1350), who he says has "summed up the nature of Islamic Jihaad." The quotation from Ibn Qayyim outlines the same three stages of Qur'anic teaching on jihad: "For thirteen years after the beginning of his messengership, he called people to God through preaching, without fighting or Jizyah, and was commanded to restrain himself and to practice patience and forbearance. Then he was commanded to migrate, and later permission was given to fight. Then he was commanded to fight those who fought him, and to restrain himself from those who did not make war with him. Later he was commanded to fight the polytheists until God's religion was fully established."[20] Thus, according to Qutb, if anyone rejects Islam, "then it is the duty of Islam to fight him until either he is killed or until he declares his submission."[21]

The Pakistani brigadier S. K. Malik's 1979 book *The Qur'anic Concept of War*—which Pakistan's then future president, Muhammad Zia-ul-Haq, praised as explaining "the ONLY pattern of war" that a Muslim country should rightly wage and which was found in the library of the American jihadists Jeffrey Leon Battle and October Martinique Lewis, part of the "Portland Seven," who plotted to assist the Taliban in Afghanistan after 9/11—delineates the same stages in the Qur'anic teaching about jihad: "The Muslim migration to Medina brought in its wake events and decisions of far-reaching significance and consequence for them. While in Mecca, they had neither been proclaimed an Ummah [community] nor were they granted the permission to take up arms against their oppressors. In Medina, a divine revelation proclaimed them an 'Ummah' and granted them the permission to take up arms against their oppressors. The permission was soon afterwards converted into a divine command making war a religious obligation for the faithful."[22]

This idea of stages of Qur'anic development stems from the doctrine of abrogation: that Allah may change his commands for Muslims: "We do not abrogate a verse or cause it to be forgotten except that We bring forth (one) better than it or similar to it. Do you not know that Allah is over all things competent?" (Qur'an 2:106). In line with this, some Islamic scholars throughout the ages have made the case that sura 9's violent exhortations actually abrogate the Qur'an's peaceful passages. Respected Qur'anic commentators have claimed that the "Verse of the Sword" abrogated as many as 124 Qur'an verses enjoining tolerance.[23] The *Tafsir al-Jalalayn* asserts that the Qur'an's ninth sura "was sent down when security was removed by the sword."[24] Ibn Kathir declares that sura 9:5 "abrogated every agreement of peace between the Prophet and any idolater, every treaty, and every term.... No idolater had any more treaty or promise of safety ever since Surah Bara'ah [the ninth sura] was revealed."[25] Ibn Juzayy says that the "Verse of the Sword's" purpose is "abrogating every peace treaty in the Qur'an."[26]

Authorities Agree

In his 1955 book *War and Peace in the Law of Islam*, Majid Khadduri, an internationally renowned scholar of Islamic law, wrote, "The Islamic state, whose principal function was to put God's law into practice, sought to establish Islam as the dominant reigning ideology over the entire world.... The jihad was therefore employed as an instrument for both the universalization of religion and the establishment of an imperial world state."[27]

In a book about Islamic law, Imran Ahsan Khan Nyazee, Assistant Professor on the Faculty of Sharia and Law of the International Islamic University in Islamabad, quotes the twelfth-century Maliki jurist Ibn Rushd: "Muslim jurists agreed that the purpose of fighting with the People of the Book ... is one of two things: it is either their conversion to Islam or the payment of jizyah." Nyazee makes it clear that this idea is not a relic of history, but an ongoing imperative that modern Muslims must take up: "This leaves no doubt that the primary goal of the Muslim community, in the eyes of its jurists, is to spread the word of Allah through jihad, and the option of poll-tax [jizya] is to be exercised only after subjugation" of non-Muslims.[28]

Minhaj al-Muslim: A Book of Creed, Manners, Character, Acts of Worship and Other Deeds, published in 2001 by Abu Bakr Jabir al-Jaza'iri, a lecturer in the Noble Prophetic Mosque in Mecca, says the same thing: jihad is "fighting against the disbelievers and those who wage war against Islam."[29] Subjugated non-Muslims will "respond to the Muslims by paying the Jizyah tax. It is a pact in which they promise the Muslims to adhere to the laws of Islamic Shari'ah related to the prescribed laws of punishment, such as for murder, stealing and breach of honor."[30] They are forbidden to work at "constructing Churches or Synagogues, or renovating the demolished ones," or "erecting the residence of non-Muslims above the homes of the Muslims." They're also forbidden to drink alcohol or eat pork in public or to eat or drink anything at all in public during the daytime in Ramadan.[31]

A manual of Islamic law certified by Cairo's Al-Azhar University, the foremost authority in Sunni Islam, as conforming "to the practice and faith of the orthodox Sunni community," defines the "lesser jihad" (the greater jihad being a spiritual struggle) as "war against non-Muslims."[32] It elaborates by specifying that "the caliph makes war upon Jews, Christians, and Zoroastrians ... until they become Muslim or pay the non-Muslim poll tax." It adds a comment by a Jordanian jurist explaining that the caliph must fight these unbelievers "provided that he has first invited [Jews, Christians, and Zoroastrians] to enter Islam in faith and practice, and if they will not, then invited them to enter the social order of Islam by paying the non-Muslim poll tax (jizya) ... while remaining in their ancestral religions."[33] This is one of the reasons why Islamic jihad groups worldwide want to reestablish the caliphate. But the manual also says that if there is no caliph, Muslims must still wage jihad to defend Islam.[34]

Enthusiastic Admiration by "Extremists" ...

It should have come as no surprise, then, that a Muslim cleric linked to al Qaeda praised Tamerlan and Dzhokhar Tsarnaev's jihad in Boston. Abu Dhar 'Azzam, who frequently appears in al Qaeda videos, in the summer of 2013 published an article in *Turkestan Al-Islamiyya*, the journal of the Turkestan Islamic Party, in which he said that the umma, the worldwide Muslim community, was "in dire need of children [who will be] slaughterers and fighters of the infidels and the devils—children who will be ascetics by night and knights by day, children who will fight the infidels and the leaders of polytheism."

In the Tsarnaev brothers, Abu Dhar found two just such children:

In the very house of unbelief, two Chechen brothers destroyed the infidels' fortresses on April 16, 2013. During the [ensuing] search [by the authorities for the perpetrators], the elder brother died as a martyr in the field of glory and honor, Allah willing. The younger brother, Dzokhar, remained, and told his dear nation: "We did this operation as revenge for what America does in Palestine, Iraq, and Afghanistan." He didn't mention his homeland Chechnya, since this jihad is a jihad of [an entire] nation, not [a campaign] for the liberation of a single land.... The Muslims' lands are one and their honor is one.

Perhaps after perusing *Rolling Stone*, Abu Dhar called Dzokhar Tsarnaev "a handsome young man in the prime of his youth." He said approvingly that "his older brother raised him on jihad and martyrdom-seeking. So, years later, he grew up to be a lion who demolished the fortresses of the infidels and massacred them, rocking the throne of the greatest tyrant on earth."

Abu Dhar called on other Muslims to imitate the Tsarnaevs:

"Yes, this should be our model. In the very house of unbelief and misguidedness, in the city of Boston, the city of American universities that spread poison around the world—this is where Dzokhar was raised; in an environment that ridicules and denies faith, Dzokhar and his brother carried out an attack that pleases the believers and makes us content. By his act, he said to us: This is what you should do, oh pearls [the name Dzokhar is derived from the Arabic jawhar, meaning pearl] of Muhammad, and weep not. Weeping is unbefitting for men. This is but one pearl, oh infidels. Our sacrificing nation will offer many more pearls, until glory and honor is restored to their rightful people—the Muslims.... Peace on Dzokhar and his brother, and on anyone who follows their example—an example from the pearls of an immortal nation."[35]

But of course, this is an al Qaeda cleric. Over the years since 9/11, as I have explained the relationship between terror attacks and the teachings of Islam and quoted these Qur'an verses, I have invariably been accused of ignoring "moderate" voices and bestowing legitimacy upon "extremists," anointing their view of the Qur'an and Islam as the only true one. Indeed, there are other voices within Islam, including some that downplay the Qur'an's exhortations to violence. Unfortunately, the existence of these other interpretations has done nothing to mitigate the spread of the violent jihad ideology all over the world today—and that spread has proceeded in great part because of the claims of authenticity that those who hold this view of Islam make. Al Qaeda and groups like it make recruits among peaceful Muslims by representing themselves as the exponents of true and authentic Islam; whether or not the claim is true, it makes great headway among Muslims, and moderates have not been able to blunt its effectiveness.

... and Toothless, Ambiguous Condemnation by "Moderates"

What's more, the distinction between "extremist" and "moderate" Muslims can be a lot less clear than most non-Muslims assume. For example, in May 2009, four Muslims were arrested for plotting to blow up two Bronx synagogues and bring down an airplane. The plot demonstrated anew the virulence and ugliness of Islamic anti-Semitism. Said one plotter, "If Jews were killed in this attack ... that would be all right." And plotter James "Abdul Rahman" Cromitie, a jailhouse convert to Islam, said, "I hate those mother------, those f----- Jewish b-----.... I would like to get [destroy] a synagogue."

Muslim groups were quick to issue statements condemning the plot. Condemnations came from CAIR, ISNA, MPAC, and New York Muslim leaders. MPAC (the Muslim Public Affairs Council) said it was "outraged over the alleged plan of four men to carry out attacks against Jewish houses of worship in New York City." MPAC executive director Salam al-Marayati wrote to Jewish leaders of his "shock and dismay over reports that four Muslims planned to bomb synagogues in the New York City area. This criminal attitude is reprehensible and wretched." In its statement MPAC reaffirmed "the position of condemning acts of violence against any faith group in the name of Islam."

MPAC has been saying this sort of thing for years—making it even odder that, as we have seen, their "counterterror" guidelines appear to be more concerned about misbehavior by non-Muslim law enforcement officials in mosques than about the possibility of terrorist activity in those mosques. And MPAC, like the other groups, has no program to teach Muslims to reject anti-Semitism.

Fozia Khan of the American Muslim Women's Association said, "We believe that violence has no place in our community and is in no way a part of the tenets of Islam. Unfortunately, incidents of this kind hamper our efforts to create harmonious relationships with other religious organizations within our community."

Since Fozia Khan's holy book calls for warfare against Jews and Christians until they submit as inferiors to Islamic rule (Qur'an 9:29), and mandates the beheading of unbelievers (47:4), among many other belligerent passages, her assertion that violence "is in no way a part of the tenets of Islam" could bear some elucidation. None, however, was forthcoming from her.

So why not teach those who are "misguided and confused and ignorant or unaware"—to quote Khan's own words—about peaceful, tolerant Islam? One might wonder why Muslim groups don't become more proactive and institute programs in mosques and Islamic schools in the West (as well as in the Islamic world) to teach Muslims why the views of Osama bin Laden et al. are wrong, and how the true Islam eschews violence against and hatred of unbelievers. Yet CAIR, ISNA, MPAC, and the rest have never instituted or even called for such a program. They are ready with the condemnations after arrests or explosions, but why wait passively? Why not act to head off jihadist activity by Muslims?

ISNA's statement, meanwhile, complained that "several media reports referred to the suspects as Muslim. ISNA rejects the association of Islam with such criminality, hatred and bigotry."

This was a tried and true tactic. When Islamic preachers preach hate and bloodshed in mosques, these groups say nothing. But when non-Muslims note that this preaching is going on, it's … "Islamophobia"! And the whole world pretends that it was the non-Muslims, not the preachers—or the bombers—who associated Islam with violence.

CAIR was also concerned that the media not link Islam to these plots, requesting "that media outlets and public officials refrain from linking this case to mainstream Islam and to challenge those who will inevitably exploit this disturbing incident to promote anti-Muslim fear and stereotypes."

But who really linked these plots to Islam? Media outlets and public officials, or the plotters themselves? As always, CAIR deftly glossed over that question.

A group of Muslim and Jewish leaders met to condemn the plots. Imam Muhammad Shamsi Ali of the Islamic Cultural Center of New York said rather cryptically, "We call upon Muslim leaders to stand firm against the forces of evil." For his part, Rabbi Marc Schneier, president of the Foundation for Ethnic Understanding and founding rabbi of the New York Synagogue, said, "It is reassuring to hear the voices of Muslim leaders speaking out in solidarity with the Jewish community and unequivocally condemning acts of terrorism and violence."

It would have been more reassuring if the Muslim leaders had unequivocally condemned attempts to impose sharia, whether by terrorism or other means, onto non-Muslim countries and declared their willingness to live with non-believers as equals in a secular society on an indefinite basis. But they did not—and they generally have not done so, in innumerable similar instances. That in itself reveals a great deal about the relationship between "extremists" and the "moderate" Muslims who ineffectually condemn their actions.

These condemnations were not necessarily insincere. But their high words have all too often been cryptic and evasive, like Ali's statement, avoiding unequivocal and unmistakable language. And even the more straightforward condemnations of terrorism have not been backed up with deeds.

Apparently, it is too much to ask that Muslim groups stand against the jihad doctrine and Islamic supremacism clearly and openly in both deed and word. But if it is too much to ask, then it is a mystery why these groups are still so widely regarded as "moderate."

And while "moderate" Muslims issue toothless statements and dither, Muslims whose hearts' desire is to restore the caliphate are working to achieve their goal.

CHAPTER TWELVE

FREE SOCIETY OR CALIPHATE?

n recent years, Islamic jihadists have repeatedly stated their desire to restore the caliphate. From the beginnings of Islam until the early twentieth century, at least among Sunnis (who constitute 85 to 90 percent of Muslims worldwide), the caliphate (khilafa) was the center of the supranational unity of the global Muslim community (umma). The caliph, theoretically chosen from among the most pious and capable men of the community, was considered to be the political, military, and religious successor of Muhammad as the leader of the Muslim community. He ruled according to the dictates of the sharia (Islamic law), implementing Allah's decrees of justice on Earth.

The State of Their Dreams

The caliphate was abolished by the secular Turkish government in 1924. It is the foremost aspiration of jihad groups worldwide to restore it. The Muslim Brotherhood was founded in Egypt in 1928 partly as a reaction to the end of the caliphate, and from the beginning a central part of the Brotherhood's program has been to work toward restoring it and then recovering lands that have been lost to Islam. Brotherhood founder Hasan al-Banna explained,

> We want the Islamic flag to be hoisted once again on high, fluttering in the wind, in all those lands that have had the good fortune to harbor Islam for a certain period of time and where the muzzein's call sounded in the takbirs and the tahlis. Then fate decreed that the light of Islam be extinguished in these lands that returned to unbelief. Thus Andalusia, Sicily, the Balkans, the Italian coast, as well as the islands of the Mediterranean, are all of them Muslim Mediterranean colonies and they must return to the Islamic fold. The Mediterranean Sea and the Red Sea must once again become Muslim seas, as they once were.[1]

Not Quite Democracy

The government of a restored caliphate would not be a pluralistic democracy by any stretch of the imagination. Hamza Tzortzis of the Britain-based Islamic Education and Research Academy has stated this plainly: "We as Muslims reject the idea of freedom of speech, and even the idea of freedom. We see under the Khilafa [caliphate], when people used to engage in a positive way, this idea of freedom was redundant, it was unnecessary, because the society understood under the education system of the Khilafa state, and under the political framework of Islam, that people must engage with each other in a positive and productive way to produce results."[2]

The desired results, obviously, have nothing to do with freedom as it is understood in Western societies. Abu Mohammad al-Julani, leader of the Syrian jihad group Jabhat Al-Nusra (Al-Nusra Front), who has expressed a desire to establish a caliphate in Syria, explains, "Being Muslims, we do not believe in political parties or parliamentary elections, but rather in an Islamic regime based on the Shura (advisory council) and which implements justice.... Our heading towards the establishment of Islamic law is jihad in Allah's way."[3]

Ahmad 'Issa, commander of another Syrian jihad group, the Suqur Al-Sham Brigades, interviewed on Al Jazeera network on June 12, 2013, joined Barack Obama in praising Islam's imperative for justice, which 'Issa said the caliphate had always manifested: "We have been providing the minorities with their rights ever since the establishment of the state of Islam, since the beginning of the Caliphate in the days of the Prophet Muhammad, and in the days of the Righteous Caliphs, and to this day. Throughout history, nobody has suffered injustice under the state of Islam—the state of truth and justice." Nobody!

However, 'Issa's idea of justice did not involve non-Muslims having the right to equal participation in the nation's political life. "Islam," he said, "must be the single source of authority of the state.... We demand that the president and parliament speaker be Sunni Muslims, and that the state's sole source of authority be Islam." He said that his group would "not accept" a Christian as the head of the Syrian state. This would not be a democracy, but a state ruled by Islamic law: "We are talking about a state of justice and truth. We want the people to be ruled by an infallible law—the law of Allah. We do not want people to be ruled by man-made laws...."[4]

On June 21, 2013, Al Jazeera aired a speech of Professor Mohammed Malkawi, the founder of the Chicago-based organization Hizb ut-Tahrir (Party of Liberation) America, which is dedicated to non-violent implementation of sharia in the United States and around the world. The speech illuminated the Islamic supremacist perspective on the 1924 abolition of the caliphate and the necessity for its restoration. Malkawi blamed non-Muslims for Islam's decline and the fall of the caliphate: "After Islam had reached the peak of glory and the Muslims were masters of the world, there came a time when the infidels conspired against the Muslims, who were in a deep slumber. Britain conspired against them, along with Arab and Turkish collaborators and traitors, and ended the Islamic Caliphate and its glory."

This was, he said, a great tragedy, for also like Barack Obama in his Cairo speech, Malkawi says he believes that a state based on Islamic law embodies justice: "Ever since the Caliphate was destroyed, the world has lost an exemplar of justice, a model for humanity in its entirety. Since then, the world has been held hostage by wolves, who do not respect the honor of a man or a believer. Two world wars cost the lives of over 70 million people, yet they accuse us of terrorism. They killed over 70 million people, and dropped atomic bombs on Japan, yet they level accusations against us."

In contrast, Malkawi said, "We demand a state ruled by the Koran," and led the crowd in chanting that phrase. Another speaker added: "We reject secularist rule. We reject the rule of Satan."

Malkawi asserted that the United States, and Barack Obama in particular (despite the American president's publicly expressed enthusiasm for Islam) had made people "terrified of the word 'caliphate.'" He continued, "They say to you: 'You can say anything except that you want Islamic law.' For them, Islamic law is something unimaginably harsh. For them, Islamic law prevents usury. It prevents them from exploiting the peoples. Islamic law and the caliphate bring about the rule of justice, which will make all those rulers face piles of garbage—for garbage is all that they are worth."

This is hardly the real reason that people think Islamic law is harsh. People think Islamic law is harsh because of the stonings, the amputations, the institutionalized oppression of women and non-Muslims, the denial of the freedom of speech, the death penalty for apostasy, and so much more. But as far as Malkawi is concerned, those things and the other elements of sharia constitute justice:

> All these other rulers are dwarfs—from Obama, the master of the White House, to the rulers of those palaces in the lands of the Muslims. They are all dwarfed by the Islamic caliphate and law, and that is why they try to make us scared of it. They scare the Muslims. They say to the rebels in Syria: "Do not demand a caliphate out loud, because the US will deny you equipment and aid." They say to the Egyptian people: "Do not demand to instate Islamic law, because America will not be happy about that."
>
> They say that the caliphate makes the infidels angry. Don't we want to make the infidels angry? Isn't this Islam?

Let America and Britain hate the caliphate. Let Britain, America, and the entire West go to hell, because the caliphate is coming, Allah willing.[5]

Ready to Take Up Arms

In early June 2013, thousands of Muslims in the Palestinian Authority held a mass rally, sponsored by the local chapter of Malkawi's organization, Hizb ut-Tahrir, calling for the restoration of the caliphate. Speakers called for the worldwide imposition of Islamic law, "liberation of Palestine from the hated Jews," and the "freeing of mankind from the chains of capitalism."[6]

Also in the summer of 2013, there was demonstration for ousted Egyptian president Mohamed Morsi, a member of the Muslim Brotherhood, at the Al-Aqsa Mosque on the Temple Mount in Jerusalem. Muslim clerics led the crowd in chanting for the caliphate: "O Obama, listen up ... The Caliphate shall return ... The Caliphate is the solution ... We are the nation of the best men." That was a reference to the Qur'an: "You are the best nation produced for mankind. You enjoin what is right and forbid what is wrong and believe in Allah" (3:110). The demonstrators apparently subscribed to the idea that the caliphate could only be restored through jihad, as they also chanted: "Down with peaceful solutions."

They also chanted, "Allahu akbar. May America be destroyed," "Allahu akbar. May France be destroyed," "Allahu akbar. May Britain be destroyed," and "Allahu akbar. May Rome be conquered." And also: "Khaybar, Khaybar, oh Jews, the army of Muhammad will return." According to Islamic tradition, Muhammad carried out a surprise attack against the Jews who lived at the Khaybar oasis in Arabia, massacring many and exiling the survivors.[7]

Likewise in January 2013, a group of British Muslims held a demonstration outside the French Embassy in London against France's intervention in Mali, which toppled the fledgling sharia state that Islamic supremacists had established there. One demonstrator declared, "The Muslims reached the gates of Vienna ... our eyes are on Paris, our eyes are on Brussels, our eyes are on London. We will not stop, as Muslims, until the whole world is governed by Islam.... The Islamic movement will become a system of life under your nose. Your wife, French women, the people of France, will live under the Islamic movement, even if you don't like it. We will collect the jizya poll tax."[8]

At that rally, jihadist leader Anjem Chaudary declared, "A caliphate for Mali, Somalia, Sudan, Afghanistan, Iraq.... The Islamic nation is boiling. We got rid of some of our dictators—Ben Ali, Mubarak, and Al-Qadhafi. Now it's time for the dictators in Mali, in Pakistan, in Bangladesh, and all over the Muslim lands to be removed and replaced by the shari'a, by Islam."[9]

Another demonstrator led the crowd in chanting, "Sharia for France ... Sharia for Paris ... Sharia for the world in its entirety."[10]

After pleading guilty to trying to set off a car bomb in Times Square in 2010, jihadist Faisal Shahzad warned the courtroom that the caliphate was coming, and by violence: "This time it's the war against people who believe in the book of Allah and follow the commandments, so this is a war against Allah. So let's see how you can defeat your Creator, which you can never do. Therefore, the defeat of U.S. is imminent and will happen in the near future, inshallah, which will only give rise to much awaited Muslim caliphate, which is the only true world order."[11]

Australian Islamic leader Musa Cerantonio also warned of a coming war and exhorted Muslims to fight it, in a 2012 lecture. "Reestablishing the Islamic state," he said, "is eventually going to be a military matter, and it is a matter that concerns a large part of the Islamic nation."

Cerantonio praised the Taliban as "the heroes of the Islamic nation these days" and claimed that America was "so determined to defeat them" solely in order "to stop them from ruling by the Book of Allah." And he summarized Islamic eschatology, which envisions a savior figure ("the Imam Mahdi") returning at the end of the world with Jesus (envisioned as a Muslim prophet, not the Christian Son of God and Savior) to subdue the infidels and Islamize the world:

> The advent of Imam Mahdi and the return of the Caliphate
> is going to be a time of great warfare and tribulation. Every
> single prophet, from Adam until Muhammad, warned their

nation about this time. The greatest strife is going to be at the time that the Antichrist appears on the earth. This is when Imam Mahdi comes. This is going to be when the Caliphate is going to be established. There are going to be caliphs who are going to exist before him, then he will also rule over the Muslims, and Jesus will come. This strife is going to be massive. These are, no doubt, times that are coming upon us. We have to be prepared for this. We have to see what the reality is—that we are going to be fought.

Referring to the Israeli/Palestinian conflict, Cerantonio invoked the Qur'an: "The answer to Palestine is not by holding hands with the Infidels. It's not by pleading to the U.N. to accept Palestine as a nation. The answer is, as the Prophet said, to fight the infidels until the religion belongs to Allah." This was a reference to Qur'an 8:39 (even though the Qur'an is, in the Muslim view, the words of Allah, not of Muhammad): "And fight them until there is no fitnah and (until) the religion, all of it, is for Allah."

Cerantonio was adamant that this goal would be achieved only through armed conflict: "The primary goal or strength that we are going to have is in physical warfare. For me and you today, this is not our utmost concern, being in Australia, but no doubt, as a nation, this is what we have to focus on. This is what we have to focus on. Now we have to know our religion, be prepared for these times, educate ourselves, and prepare, as Allah says: 'Prepare against them all you can from strength.' Every strength—unity is strength, knowledge is strength, and steel is strength. 'Prepare what you can against them.' This is what we have to do in this nation."[12]

Cerantonio was referring again to the Qur'an: "And prepare against them whatever you are able of power and of steeds of war by which you may terrify the enemy of Allah and your enemy and others besides them whom you do not know (but) whom Allah knows. And whatever you spend in the cause of Allah will be fully repaid to you, and you will not be wronged" (8:60).

He concluded, "This isn't going to come cheap. It's not going to come easy. It is going to come with our effort, our life, our sweat, and our blood. I ask Allah to grant victory to all of those mujahideen who fight for His cause, to uphold the banner of 'There is no god but Allah, and Muhammad is His Messenger.'"[13]

Demonstrators against Syrian dictator Bashar Assad in Damascus in September 2012 were ready to give their blood for this cause—as they implied when they chanted a demand for weapons—and made it clear that they envisioned the Islamic caliphate as incompatible with Western notions of freedom. They chanted, "We want to instate the Qur'an.... To hell with freedom.... We want an Islamic caliphate.... To hell with being peaceful.... We want weapons and AK-47s."[14]

A previously unknown jihad group that murdered an Israeli construction worker on the Israel-Egypt border posted a video online in June 2012, in which a masked man states, "We announce the formation of the Shura Council of the Mujahideen of Jerusalem as the foundation of a blessed Jihadi operation, with a clear path and features to be a brick in the global project of bringing back the caliphate. To the foes of God—the Jews—we say, you infidels must know that what is coming is different than what has preceded and we shall make you drink from the same poisonous glass you gave to the people of Islam in Jerusalem."[15]

And in Indonesia, a young man named Bayu Setiono was part of a jihad cell that murdered a police officer and attacked two police stations in August 2012. In the ten-minute video released at police headquarters, Setiono explained, "We planned to kill policemen and create a situation like Ambon and Poso, for the sake of upholding Islamic Shariah and the establishment of a caliphate in Indonesia. Our targets, since 2007 until now, are infidels and policemen."[16] Ambon and Poso were two principal sites in Indonesia where Muslims killed Christians on a large scale in the 1990s and 2000s; some estimate the death toll among Indonesian Christians to be as high as ten thousand, with countless thousands more left homeless.[17]

Mainstream Caliphate Dreams

But the desires to restore the caliphate are not restricted solely to jihad terrorists, frenzied imams, and chanting mobs. Muslim Brotherhood cleric Safwat Higazi said in the summer of 2012, "If you read the literature of the Muslim Brotherhood, you will find in the literature of the Brotherhood, that which they can never abandon: The Islamic Caliphate and mastership of the world. Yes, we will be masters of the world, one of these days."[18]

Indeed, before it was toppled, Egypt's Muslim Brotherhood government was working toward transforming Egypt into a sharia state and making it the center of a reemergent caliphate. IPT News reported in June 2012 that "according to an Arabic-language report last Tuesday of a closed-door senior-level Brotherhood confab, the Islamist group intends to get rid of film and 'artistic heritage,' replace police uniforms with 'Islamic garb,' and make memorization of Islam's holy book a precondition for advancement in school.... The first step in the plan is to 'replace the national anthem with the so-called anthem of the Islamic Caliphate,' soon after followed by 'the abolition of the Ministry of Information and replacing it with an Islamic media organization' whose sole aim would be to 'publish Islamic heritage only.'"[19]

Because the Morsi government was ousted, the Brotherhood wasn't able to do what it wanted to do in Egypt. But the dream of the caliphate has not died. Turkish foreign minister Ahmet Davutoglu spoke in March 2013 about how the Turks were going to restore the Ottoman Empire, the seat of the last caliphate, and the caliphate itself. He was dismissive of the Turkish secular state: "Last century was only a parenthesis for us." The days of the secular state were over: "We will close that parenthesis. We will do so without going to war, or calling anyone an enemy, without being disrespectful to any border, we will again tie Sarajevo to Damascus, Benghazi to Erzurum to Batumi."

Davutoglu explained, "This is the core of our power. These may look like all different countries to you, but Yemen and Skopje were part of the same country 110 years ago, or Erzurum and Benghazi. When we say this, they call it 'new Ottomanism.' The ones who united the whole Europe don't become new Romans, but the ones who unite the Middle East geography are called as new Ottomanists. It's an honor to be reminded with the names of Ottomans, Seljuks, Artuklu or Eyyubi, but we have never or will ever have our eye on anyone's land based on a historic background."[20] Apparently the great reunion will, in Davutoglu's view, take place freely and spontaneously.

Muslim leaders have called for the United States also to be conquered by Islam and become an Islamic state. In 2008, Hamas parliamentarian and Muslim cleric Yunis al-Astal declared, "Very soon, Allah willing, Rome will be conquered, just like Constantinople was, as was prophesized by our Prophet Muhammad. Today, Rome is the capital of the Catholics, or the Crusader capital.... This capital of theirs will be an advanced post for the Islamic conquests, which will spread through Europe in its entirety, and then will turn to the two Americas."[21]

And when he became leader of the Muslim Brotherhood in 2004, Muhammad Mahdi Othman 'Akef said, "I have complete faith that Islam will invade Europe and America, because Islam has logic and a mission."[22] He explained that "the Europeans and the Americans will come into the bosom of Islam out of conviction."[23]

Hankering for an American Caliphate

It is an entrenched dogma of the government and media establishment in the United States that no Muslims in America harbor any such aspirations. Popular Muslim writer Reza Aslan has said, "No American Muslim, zero, absolutely none, not a single one has ever, ever called for the imposition of Shariah in America."[24] But that is simply not true. For example, scholar Daniel Pipes noted that Imam Siraj Wahhaj, an American convert to Islam and sought-after speaker in mosques and Islamic centers nationwide, advocated for a caliphate in a 1992 speech to a U.S. Muslim audience, "If only Muslims were clever politically," he told his New Jersey listeners, "they could take over the United States and replace its constitutional government with a caliphate." Said Wahhaj, "If we were united and strong, we'd elect our own emir [leader] and give allegiance to him.... [T]ake my word, if six to eight million Muslims unite in America, the country will come to us."[25]

And in 2003, Muhammad Faheed, a speaker at a Muslim Students Association meeting at Queensborough Community College in New York, declared that Muslims "must not recognize any government authority, or any authority at all besides Allah." Working himself into a frenzy, he shouted, "We are not Americans. We are Muslims. [The U.S.] is going to deport and attack us! It is us vs. them! Truth against falsehood! The colonizers and masters against the oppressed, and we will burn down the master's house! We reject the U.N., reject America, reject all law and order. Don't lobby Congress or protest because we don't recognize Congress. The only relationship you should have with America is to topple it.... Eventually there will be a Muslim in the White House dictating the laws of Shariah."[26]

And as we have seen, Omar Ahmad, CAIR's cofounder and longtime board chairman, told a Muslim crowd in California in 1998 that "Islam isn't in America to be equal to any other faith, but to become dominant. The Koran ... should be the highest authority in America, and Islam the only accepted religion on Earth."[27]

After he received negative publicity, however, Ahmad denied saying these things, several years after the fact. But the original reporter, Lisa Gardiner of the *Fremont Argus*, stands by her story. Art Moore of World Net Daily asked Gardiner in December 2006 about Ahmad's statement, and reported that Gardiner was "100-percent sure Ahmad was the speaker and that he made those statements, pointing out nobody challenged the story at the time it was published eight years ago."[28] Ahmad reacted sharply: "She's lying. Absolutely, she's lying. How could you remember something from so long ago? I don't even remember her in the audience." But he didn't explain why Gardiner would have wanted to make such an outrageously false claim. And CAIR's spokesman Ibrahim Hooper has made a similar statement: "I wouldn't want to create the impression that I wouldn't like the government of the United States to be Islamic sometime in the future."[29]

In 2007, As-Sabiqun, a Muslim group based in Washington, D.C., announced on its website its intention to establish an Islamic state in America by midcentury: "As-Sabiqun is an Islamic movement that believes in the Islamic State of North America no later than 2050. Those who engage in this great effort require a high level of commitment and determination. We are sending out a call to the believers: Join with us in this great struggle to change the world!"[30]

Tareq al-Suwaidan, a Kuwaiti Muslim Brotherhood leader, lived in the United States for seventeen years and frequently speaks to Muslim groups in Britain, Canada, and Australia. An extremely popular speaker, al-Suweidan earns over a million dollars a year from giving talks on Islam.[31] In 2000, al-Suwaidan addressed an Islamic Circle of North

America conference, where he said that Muslims should issue a warning to non-Muslims in the West: "We must tell the West that we are extending a hand of peace now, but it will not be so for long. Even if a civilization is ready to crumble—like the West, with all the characteristics of deterioration of past fallen empires—it will not fall until we, the Muslims, strive to give it that last push, the last straw that will break the camel's back."[32]

Al-Suwaidan is affiliated with the Muslim Brotherhood. But Siraj Wahhaj, the imam who predicted that Muslims "could take over the United States and replace its constitutional government with a caliphate" if they were only "clever politically" (in Daniel Pipes's summation), is no "extremist." He regularly speaks at mainstream Muslim gatherings around the United States. But he generally doesn't talk about his desire to establish a caliphate in the United States—at least not in his public addresses. One group that does, however, is Hizb ut-Tahrir (Party of Liberation), an international organization dedicated to restoring the caliphate and imposing Islamic law.

Hizb ut-Tahrir is banned in many countries for its open calls to subvert the established order and replace it with Islamic government. Although it claims that it "does not work in the West to change the system of government, but works to project a positive image of Islam to Western society and engages in dialogue with Western thinkers, policymakers and academics," the organization makes no secret of its desire for the caliphate in the United States.

Hizb ut-Tahrir holds an annual "Khilafah Conference" in the Chicago area. Its announcement for its 2013 conference identified the caliphate (khilafah) as the "Islamic System of Mercy & Justice" and stated that the conference would be held on June 9, "the anniversary of the abolishment of the Islamic System of Mercy & Justice (Khilafah) sent to us by Allah through His Messenger Mohammad."[33] It explained that "the objective of the conference is to present the current condition of the Muslim Ummah in the absence of the Islamic System of Mercy & Justice and how today we should once again seek guidance and inspiration from Mohammad as a Messenger, Leader & Statesman and work practically and tirelessly to once again bring the Mercy & Justice of Islam back for all of humanity."[34]

At its website, Hizb ut-Tahrir America directly contrasts the caliphate with republican rule and democracy:

> The republican system is based on democracy, where sovereignty is given to the people. Thus, the people have the right of ruling and legislation. They reserve the right to lay down a constitution and enact laws and to abolish, alter or modify both the constitution and the law. This bares [sic] no resemblance to the Islamic system, which is based solely on the Islamic Aqeedah [faith] and the Islamic legislation. Sovereignty is to the legislation of Allah and not to the ummah. So the ummah has no right to legislate nor does the Khaleefah. The sole legislator is Allah, and the Khaleefah has the right only to adopt rulings for the constitution that is derived from the Book of Allah and the Sunnah Prophet Muhammad (Peace be upon him).[35]

Hizb ut-Tahrir is a small group among Muslims in America; only a few hundred people generally attend the annual Khilafah Conference. The correspondence of its goals, however, with those of much larger and more influential organizations worldwide, most notably the Muslim Brotherhood, ensures that the United States has not had its last encounter with those who dream of a restored caliphate, and are ready to do violence to further their goal.

CHAPTER THIRTEEN

LIFE UNDER SHARIA

The Grim Reality and the Indifference of the Enlightened

Non-Muslims can see what the perfectly just society of sharia and the caliphate would look like by exploring the growing Islamic enclaves in Europe. In May 2013, the Dutch newspaper Trouw visited one such enclave, the Schilderswijk district in The Hague, which is known as the "small caliphate." It found that "more orthodox Muslims are living together here than anywhere else in the city, and they want to apply their rules on the street." This means sharia police admonishing non-Muslim passersby "on matters that do not please the orthodox majority, such as smoking on the street and the use of alcohol and pork meat." Also, "girls are addressed by veiled women who express their disapproval about 'skirts above the knee' and 'dresses with spaghetti straps.'"[1]

And in late 2012, a group calling itself the Muslim Patrol attempted to enforce sharia in what it designated "Muslim areas" of London. Young Muslims tore down advertising depicting women they considered to be immodestly dressed and harassed female non-Muslim passersby for the same offense. A video the group posted to YouTube showed them also accosting people carrying alcohol, telling them, "Alcohol banned. This is a Muslim area. Muslims patrol the area."[2]

After their videos drew negative attention, the group posted another, in which a spokesman declared, "Those people attacking Muslim Patrol because of our activities against Western society are clearly misguided away from the understanding of worship of Allah.... Islam is here in London, Mr. David Cameron, Mr. police officer, whether you like it or not. We are commanding good and forbidding evil on this Saturday night, while the police, they try to get us through the media." Another added, "The kuffar [unbelievers], you can go to hell; this is not a Christian country. Christianity, you can go to hell. We are in East London, we are in South London, we are in North London ... the police cannot stop us, the kuffar cannot stop us. We are coming to implement Islam immediately.... Anyone who tries to stop us, we will take their alcohol, we will tell the women to cover up, and we will implement Islam upon your own necks, David Cameron."[3]

Members of the Muslim Patrol were duly arrested, however, and surely such thuggish sharia supremacism couldn't manifest itself among the moderate and prosperous Muslims in America, could it? Maybe not, but in the first minutes of January 1, 2014, as a New Year's party was in full swing at the gay nightclub Neighbours in Seattle, someone poured gasoline on a flight of stairs in the club and set it on fire. The partygoers escaped unhurt, but a man named Musab Mohamed Masmari was arrested a month later as he was preparing to leave the country.

Was Masmari a spurned lover out for revenge? Perhaps. But in Pakistan, Afghanistan, Indonesia, Iraq, Egypt, and many other places in recent years, Islamic supremacists have on numerous occasions implemented their moral vision by force, torching bars, liquor stores, music stores, and other sites they deem immoral. Was this case of arson the first manifestation of violent Sharia morals enforcement in the U.S.? True to form, mainstream media sources gave no hint that that could have been what happened, but the involvement of the Joint Terrorism

Task Force in the investigation of the arson at Neighbours certainly made it a possibility.[4]

Sharia? What's That?

Prominent Muslim spokesmen in the United States, however, say that there's nothing to be concerned about because mainstream Muslims don't have any interest in bringing sharia to Britain or the United States, and the elements of sharia that clash most sharply with Western principles of human rights are not intrinsic to it, anyway. Ground Zero Mosque imam Faisal Abdul Rauf said in 2011 that "the only truly clashing area" between sharia and U.S. law "is the penal code, and no Muslim has the intention of introducing that to America. The penal code is the area that people in the Western world are worried about—but these are things that aren't even observed today in most of the Muslim world. Apart from the Taliban and a few places like that, where do you see this happening?"[5]

Rauf thus tacitly admitted that the Taliban's draconian Islam was simply an implementation of the sharia penal code; he didn't say that the Taliban had gotten sharia wrong. All he said was that the Taliban's strictness was not seen elsewhere in the Islamic world. But this left open the question of whether, if that penal code was part of the sharia, Muslims outside of Afghanistan could enforce it if they decided to do so. And indeed, since Rauf's statement, Muslims in parts of Egypt and Syria, as well as in the short-lived sharia state of Mali, have been accused of implementing "Taliban-like" strictures on behavior they deemed un-Islamic. In their own defense, they insisted they were simply imposing sharia.

And so other prominent Muslims in the United States have tried to distance sharia from the denial of basic rights and freedoms that is in fact integral to it by claiming that sharia is so amorphous as to defy characterization. Muslim author Reza Aslan, who shot to the top of the bestseller lists in the summer of 2013 with a book challenging the historicity of the New Testament's accounts of Jesus, denied on an Australian television show in 2010 that sharia had any particular character at all:

There's really no such thing as just Sharia, it's not one mono-lithic Continuum—Sharia is understood in thousands of different ways over the 1,500 years in which multiple and competing schools of law have tried to construct some kind of civic penal and family law code that would abide by Islamic values and principles, it's understood in many dif-ferent ways, there are three foundational issues or three divisions that I should say that Sharia fits into, one is penal law of course and that is what gets all the attention, there's two countries in the world right now that actually have a Federal mandate to enact penal law according to the Sharia, that's Saudi Arabia, and Iran.

Then there's financial law, obviously, which has become quite popular, actually in the US and in the west, ever since the global economic meltdown, and then there is something about family law, and that involves marriage, divorce, inher-itance, these kinds of issues. So when you say Sharia, even to a Muslim, it's understood in vastly different ways, in many ways it's part of an identity and most Muslims when they talk about wanting Sharia to play a role in their lives really mean it in so far as it talks about family law, you know, issues like, as I said marriage, divorce.

Also on the show with Aslan was Nonie Darwish, an ex-Muslim and author of *Cruel and Usual Punishment*, a book about sharia. Darwish challenged Aslan's claims with specifics about the human rights abuses that sharia engenders but got no help from the show's host, Jenny Brockie, who seemed determined not to allow her to finish making a point:

JENNY BROCKIE: How comfortably do those values in Sharia law sit with democratic values?

REZA ASLAN: There's no such thing as values in Sharia law, that is what I was trying to explain, it's understood in thousands of different ways by tens of thousands of different institutions, who really disagree with each other far more than they disagree with people of other religions, the values that you bring to Sharia are whatever values you yourself have, if you are a bigot, misogynist and a violent person, your interpretation of Sharia will be bigoted, violent and misogynistic, if you are a democrat and a pluralist and someone who is peace loving, that's how you'll see the Sharia.

JENNY BROCKIE: Nonie, a response from you?

NONIE DARWISH: This is very evasive—Sharia law is a malignant law, it's totally based on the interpretation of the Qur'an and the Hadith, and the way Islam and the prophet [sic] lived. I don't know understand why he's whitewashing the meaning of Sharia—Sharia is a set of laws....

REZA ASLAN: I'm a scholar of Sharia, that's why.

NONIE DARWISH: Excuse me.... I'm a scholar of Sharia, too.

REZA ASLAN: Excuse me.

NONIE DARWISH: Sharia is the most oppressive system on earth. It encourages people to lie, if it's for the benefit of Islam. It doesn't allow Muslims to leave Islam, and there's a death penalty in all the schools of Sharia against those that leave Islam. Sharia defines what jihad is. Sharia is very clear. It's not …

REZA ASLAN: These are patterns of false statements. I'm confused.

NONIE DARWISH: I am speaking, I did not interrupt you.

JENNY BROCKIE: Nonie quickly, then I'll get a response from Reza.

NONIE DARWISH: Jihad is described as a war against non-Muslims, to establish the religion, the West is concerned, let's be open with them. Why this deception.

JENNY BROCKIE: Reza, a quick response from you.

NONIE DARWISH: Moderate Muslims are trying to convince the West that Sharia is good instead of trying to....

JENNY BROCKIE: I'll stop you there, there's a lot of other people that want to talk. Reza, quickly a response.

REZA ASLAN: I don't have a response to that, every word she says is factually incorrect. I don't really know what to say.[6]

What Sharia Really Is

He might have tried speaking the truth. For in fact, what Darwish said was factually correct. Islam, she said, "encourages people to lie, if it's for the benefit of Islam." The Qur'an says, "Let not believers take disbelievers as allies rather than believers. And whoever [of you] does that has nothing with Allah, except when taking precaution against them in prudence" (3:28).

Ibn Kathir's commentary on this verse explains that "believers who in some areas or times fear for their safety from the disbelievers" are "allowed to show friendship to the disbelievers outwardly, but never inwardly." For instance, al-Bukhari recorded that Abu Ad-Darda' said, 'We smile in the face of some people although our hearts curse them.' Al-Bukhari said that al-Hasan said, 'The Tuqyah [taqiyyah: deception for the promotion of Islam] is allowed until the Day of Resurrection.'"[7]

Al-Tabari, a mainstream and influential early Muslim chronicler and scholar, explained, "If you [Muslims] are under their [infidels'] authority, fearing for yourselves, behave loyally to them, with your tongue, while harboring inner animosity for them.... Allah has forbidden believers from being friendly or on intimate terms with the infidels in place of believers—except when infidels are above them [in authority]. In such a scenario, let them act friendly towards them."[8]

But is this a general permission for deception to further Islam, as Darwish said, or only permission to lie when in grave danger or fear of death? A hadith says that Muhammad forbade lying except in three cases: "in battle, for bringing reconciliation amongst persons and the narration of the words of the husband to his wife, and the narration of the words of a wife to her husband (in a twisted form in order to bring reconciliation between them)."[9] In light of the fact that Islamic jihadists and supremacists routinely claim that the United States is at war with Islam, however, the allowance for lying in battle may apply in any number of non-combat situations; there are, after all, many theaters of modern warfare.

Akin to this concept of taqiyya is another Islamic theological term: tawriya, a word that means dissimulation, equivocation, ambiguity. This can take the form of essentially any misleading statement—and according to the Saudi sheikh Mohammed Saleh al-Munajjid, Muslims can employ it whenever doing so may serve a "Sharia interest"—which was Darwish's point.[10]

Darwish also said that Sharia "doesn't allow Muslims to leave Islam, and there's a death penalty in all the schools of Sharia against those that leave Islam." That is also true. As we have seen, Islamic tradition holds that Muhammad said, "Whoever changes his Islamic religion, then kill him."[11] The *Tafsir al-Qurtubi*, a classic and thoroughly mainstream exegesis of the Qur'an, says this about Qur'an 2:217: "Scholars disagree about whether or not apostates are asked to repent. One group say that they are asked to repent and, if they do not, they are killed. Some say they are given an hour and others a month. Others say that they are asked to repent three times, and that is the view of Malik. Al-Hasan said they are asked a hundred times. It is also said that they are killed without being asked to repent."

Islam Online, a website manned by a team of Islam scholars and headed by the most respected and renowned Islamic scholar in the entire world, Sheikh Yusuf al-Qaradawi, explains, "If a sane person who has reached puberty voluntarily apostatizes from Islam, he deserves to be punished. In such a case, it is obligatory for the caliph (or his representative) to ask him to repent and return to Islam. If he does, it is accepted from him, but if he refuses, he is immediately killed." And what if someone doesn't wait for a caliph to appear and takes matters into his own hands? Although the killer is to be "disciplined" for "arrogating the caliph's prerogative and encroaching upon his rights," there is "no blood money for killing an apostate (or any expiation)"—in other words, no significant punishment for the killer.[12]

On Al Jazeera in February 2013, al-Qaradawi said, "If they had gotten rid of the apostasy punishment Islam wouldn't exist today." He quoted from the Qur'an: "Surah Al-Ma'idah 5:33 says: 'The punishment of those who wage war against Allah and His apostle is that they should be murdered or crucified."[13] He added, "And many hadiths, not only one or two, but many, narrated by a number of Muhammad's companions

state that any apostate should be killed. Ibn 'Abbas's hadith: 'Kill whom-
ever [sic] changes his faith [from Islam].'"[14]

On another occasion, Qaradawi confirmed Darwish's statement that
all the Muslim schools of jurisprudence endorsed the death penalty for
apostasy: "The Muslim jurists are unanimous that apostates must be
punished, yet they differ as to determining the kind of punishment to
be inflicted upon them. The majority of them, including the four main
schools of jurisprudence (Hanafi, Maliki, Shafi'i, and Hanbali) as well
as the other four schools of jurisprudence (the four Shiite schools of
Az-Zaidiyyah, Al-Ithna-'ashriyyah, Al-Ja'fariyyah, and Az-Zaheriyyah)
agree that apostates must be executed."[15]

Qaradawi has been praised as a "reformist" by academic John
Esposito of Georgetown University's Alaweed Center for Muslim-Chris-
tian Understanding.[16]

We saw in the last chapter that "war against non-Muslims, to establish the religion"—to quote Darwish—is a definition of jihad widely
believed and acted upon by Muslims.

Islamic Hypocrisy

The contrasts between Islamic society and Western society are
sharp. The Islamic moral critique of the West is familiar: we are a decay-
ing society reminiscent of the last days of the Roman Empire, a sink of
iniquity, exploiting women, obsessed with sex, drunk on earthly pleasure, soft, and selfish.

And there's no denying that there is a lot of truth to that. The question is whether the model Islamic society offers a genuine and viable
alternative. There are numerous indications that it doesn't.

This is because of some of the core features of Islamic morality,
including polygamy, which is sanctioned in the Qur'an: "And if you fear
that you will not deal justly with the orphan girls, then marry those that
please you of (other) women, two or three or four. But if you fear that
you will not be just, then (marry only) one or those your right hand
possesses. That is more suitable that you may not incline (to injustice)"
(4:3).

The idea that a man can have as many as four wives, as well as enjoy
sexual access to those his "right hand possesses," signifies that in Islam,

women are worth less than men as human beings. A woman may not have four husbands and slave men, but from the standpoint of Islamic law her husband is free to seek alternative female companionship.

Polygamy is not a relic of history. Like other aspects of sharia that are at variance with American law, it has come to America. The *New York Times* reported in March 2007 that "immigration to New York and other American cities has soared from places where polygamy is lawful and widespread, especially from West African countries like Mali, where demographic surveys show that 43 percent of women are in polygamous marriages."[17]

Muslims who practice polygamy in America don't seem concerned about breaking "manmade" American law. Ibrahim Hooper of CAIR stated, "Islamic scholars would differ on whether one could do so while living in the United States."[18] He was not reported to have said anything about discouraging this practice among American Muslims, despite its illegality. He may have calculated that the legalization of same-sex marriage would make it easier to change American law regarding polygamy—one reason why Muslims have allied with "progressives" with such alacrity.[19]

Unequal Divorce Laws

And Western feminists have not shown any notable indignation about Islamic divorce laws. A Muslim husband is completely free in regard to divorce; he can at any time announce to his wife, "You are divorced," and the deed is done.[20] The Qur'an only calls for a three-month waiting period to see if the wife is pregnant (65:1, 2:228).

To safeguard a man from repeatedly divorcing a useful wife in a fit of pique, the Qur'an stipulates that a husband may divorce his wife and then reunite with her at his word only twice. After he divorces her three times, his ex-wife must marry someone else, who must then divorce her, before she can go back to her first husband (2:229–30).

Islamic divorce laws are not the same for women: she should seek reconciliation with her husband and return her dowry to him: "And if a woman fears from her husband contempt or evasion, there is no sin upon them if they make terms of settlement between them—and settlement is best. And present in (human) souls is stinginess. But if you do good and fear Allah, then indeed Allah is ever, with what you do, acquainted" (4:128).

Muhammad's last and most favored wife, Aisha, explains in a hadith what form these "terms of settlement" might take. That Qur'an verse, she says, "concerns the woman whose husband does not want to keep her with him any longer, but wants to divorce her and marry some other lady, so she says to him: 'Keep me and do not divorce me, and then marry another woman, and you may neither spend on me, nor sleep with me.'"[21]

The "terms of settlement," then, involve the Muslim wife becoming a beggar, throwing herself at the mercy of a husband who does not want her.

Child Marriage

Aisha is most famous, however, for her age when Muhammad married her. A hadith has Aisha recounting,

> My mother, Umm Ruman, came to me while I was playing in a swing with some of my girl friends. She called me, and I went to her, not knowing what she wanted to do to me. She caught me by the hand and made me stand at the door of the house. I was breathless then, and when my breathing became normal, she took some water and rubbed my face and head with it. Then she took me into the house. There in the house I saw some Ansari [recent Muslim converts] women who said, "Best wishes and Allah's Blessing and a good luck." Then she entrusted me to them and they prepared me (for the marriage). Unexpectedly Allah's Messenger came to me in the forenoon and my mother handed me over to him, and at that time I was a girl of nine years of age.[22]

According to another Islamic tradition, Muhammad "married Aisha when she was a girl of six years of age, and he consummated that marriage when she was nine years old."[23] Tradition records that he was around fifty-three years old at the time.

The Qur'an says that Muhammad is the supreme example of conduct (cf. Qur'an 33:21)—and that holds for child marriage. In April 2011, Bangladeshi mufti Fazlul Haque Amini denounced attempts to ban child marriage: "Banning child marriage will cause challenging the marriage of the holy prophet of Islam … [putting] the moral character of the prophet into controversy and challenge." His denunciation came with a threat: "Islam permits child marriage and it will not be tolerated if any ruler will ever try to touch this issue in the name of giving more rights to women."[24] Haque claimed that two hundred thousand jihadists were ready to die fighting against laws restricting child marriage.

Allah Says Beat Her

Then there is the beating of disobedient women, which is largely tolerated and even encouraged in many Muslim cultures. This, too, has come to the West. In May 2012, Regime Ahmmad, a Muslim man in Scotland, pulled a knife and threatened to kill his eighteen-year-old daughter Shyvonne for sharing her bed with a young man to whom she was not married. Shyvonne recounted, "My father said a woman shouldn't share a bed with a man they are not married to. After that, there was a continuation of what he had been saying about how I shouldn't show my legs. An Islamic woman is not supposed to show her legs past the knees and stuff like that. After he showed the knife, there was about half a minutes [sic] conversation and then I ran out the room. He said I was supposed to be a Muslim and, if I wasn't, he would kill me and then himself. I didn't want to argue with him because he had a knife. He has always been very vocal. He would say he would chop my legs off and things like that."[25]

Of course, stories of domestic violence are not found only among Muslims. Violence, abuse, wayward wives, wayward daughters, outraged husbands, and furious fathers are found in all cultures. So, too, are men who threaten death, and kill. But only in Islam is such behavior given divine sanction. In August 2013, in Brandenburg, Germany, two Muslims from Chechnya broke into the home of a Muslim couple, beat the husband, and kicked his pregnant wife in the stomach, causing her to lose her child—as punishment for what the attackers believed to be the couple's "immoral behavior."[26]

Muslim women are sometimes beaten for failing to give birth to a male child. In September 2013, an Afghan physician noted that as many as eighty pregnant women came to him every day asking for tests to determine whether they were carrying a boy or a girl. "Those who don't have a son," he said, "beg doctors to abort the foetus if it is a girl. They say they will be beaten and subjected to psychological violence at home."[27]

Domestic violence is justified by the Qur'anic command to beat disobedient women: "Men are in charge of women by (right of) what Allah has given one over the other and what they spend (for mainte-nance) from their wealth. So righteous women are devoutly obedient, guarding in (the husband's) absence what Allah would have them guard. But those (wives) from whom you fear arrogance—(first) advise them; (then if they persist), forsake them in bed; and (finally), strike them" (4:34).

If it is in the Qur'an, it is the will of Allah. Accordingly, when law-makers in Chad tried to outlaw wife-beating in 2005, Muslim clerics led the charge against this initiative, saying it was un-Islamic.[28] A 2007 survey of hospital workers in moderate Turkey found 69 percent of women and 84.7 percent of men agreed that a husband was justified in beating his wife for, among other infractions, "criticising the male."[29]

In June 2013, Muslim states in the United Nations Council for Human Rights (UNCHR) rejected elements of a resolution opposing violence against women on the grounds that they violated Islamic law—including the statement that women had "the right to control matters concerning their sexual lives as well as their reproductive health without coercion, discrimination or violence."[30] Pro-lifers may object to the language about "reproductive health"—often a euphemism for abortion—but the objection to women being protected from "coercion, discrimination or violence" was uniquely Islamic.

That same month, Egyptian cleric Mahmoud al-Denawy explained that wife-beating should be limited: "When it comes to beating, he should never beat her harshly. He should never raise his hand. He should never beat her on her face. But he can use something very simple—like a siwak [dental stick] or something like this pen. The beat-ing should not lead to breaking her arm or a tooth. He should avoid this, because the Prophet urged us and told us that when you beat someone, you should never beat him or her on his or her face. This is because the face is owned by Allah."[31]

It is often claimed that Muhammad permitted beating of women only with an implement no larger than a toothbrush, but Muhammad himself contradicts that claim in a hadith in which Aisha recalls that he once caused her pain with a blow: "He struck me on the chest which caused me pain, and then said: Did you think that Allah and His Apostle would deal unjustly with you?"[32]

At another time, Aisha said, "I have not seen any woman suffering as much as the believing women."[33]

And even in America Muslim spokesmen do not deny that wife-beating is sanctioned in Islam, although they try to minimize its permissible extent. Former ISNA president Muzammil H. Siddiqi has said that "in some cases a husband may use some light disciplinary action in order to correct the moral infraction of his wife.... The Koran is very clear on this issue."[34]

Sharia Trumps British Law

Sharia courts have already been established in Britain—there are currently at least eighty-five around the country.[35] Ostensibly they are to deal only with matters of the Islamic faith that lie outside the purview of British civil law. However, spousal abuse is a foremost area in which the outlook of British law and Islamic law are markedly different. Were these sharia courts to accept the authority of British law, the courts would refer domestic violence cases to the civil courts; in all too many cases, however, they do not. In April 2013, the BBC's *Panorama* program ran a special report on the sharia courts, sending a reporter posing as a Muslim woman seeking divorce to the Leyton Islamic sharia council in east London.

Upon hearing the woman's complaint that her husband had beaten her, Dr. Suhaib Hasan at the council placed the blame on her: "I think that you should be courageous enough to ask this question to him. Just tell me why you are so upset, huh? Is it because of my cooking? Is it because I see my friends, huh? So I can—correct myself."

He told her not to contact the British police: "You involve the police if he hits you but you must understand this will be the final blow. You will have to leave the house. Where will you go then? A refuge? A refuge is a very bad option. Women are not happy in such places. Don't think about the police because if the police is involved then think, your family life is going to break."[36]

Family law barrister Charlotte Proudman remarked of the sharia courts, "There's no accountability and many of them are not operating in accordance with UK law."[37]

Despite the deleterious example of the Islamic law courts in Britain, anti-sharia measures in the United States have encountered stiff opposition.

North Carolina adopted an anti-sharia bill in August 2013, joining Kansas, Louisiana, Tennessee, Arizona, Oklahoma, and South Dakota as the seventh state to pass some form of anti-sharia legislation.[38] Over twenty states have introduced similar legislation.[39] Although they are variously worded, the primary intent of these statutes is to halt the use of Islamic law by American judges—a measure that many see as necessary, since sharia has already been involved in cases in twenty-three states.[40]

However, many conservatives, particularly religiously observant Jews and Christians, see anti-sharia initiatives as an alarming encroachment upon First Amendment protection of religion and stand with Islamic groups like CAIR against those initiatives.

Anti-Sharia Laws: A Threat to Religious Freedom?

But the idea that anti-sharia laws infringe upon religious freedom at all stems from some fundamental misapprehensions. In the March 2012 issue of the conservative Catholic publication *First Things*, law professor Robert K. Vischer equated anti-sharia laws with intrusions upon the religious freedom of Christians, such as laws that required "pro-life pharmacists to dispense the morning-after pill" and "Christian adoption agencies to place children with same-sex couples, and religious entities to pay for their employees' contraceptives." He asserted that "[t]he recent spate of 'anti-Sharia' initiatives" was "just the most politically popular example of such threats" to religious freedom.[41]

Vischer was not alone in objecting to anti-sharia legislation. The Associated Press claimed in 2012 that critics of anti-sharia laws viewed the drive to pass them as an "unwarranted campaign driven by fear of Muslims."[42] In criticizing an anti-sharia amendment to the Oklahoma state constitution that gained 70 percent of the vote in a state referendum but was later struck down by a federal judge, Daniel Mach, director of the American Civil Liberties Union's Program on Freedom of Religion and Belief, said, "This amendment did nothing more than target one faith for official condemnation. Even the state admits that there has never been any problem with Oklahoma courts wrongly applying religious law. The so-called 'Save Our State Amendment' was a solution in search of a problem, and a blatantly discriminatory solution at that."[43]

Ryan Kiesel of the ACLU's Oklahoma branch declared, "No one in Oklahoma deserves to be treated like a second-class citizen. This proposed amendment was an affront to the Constitution and everything it stands for."[44] One egregious example of the hysteria these laws aroused was Muslim author Reza Aslan's wild charge that "two-thirds of Americans don't think Muslims should have the same rights or civil liberties as non-Muslims."[45]

In reality, anti-sharia laws that are properly formulated neither infringe upon Muslims' civil liberties or religious freedom nor address a nonexistent problem. Vischer accurately stated some of reasons that Americans were concerned about sharia when he said that "proponents of this legislation tend to focus on manifestations of Sharia overseas: the stoning of adulterers, cutting off of the hands of thieves, and the denial of basic freedoms for women in some Islamic countries," and that "there are many schools of interpretation among Islamic legal scholars, and some interpretations stand in tension with the rights that we have come to take for granted in liberal democracies, including the rights of women, homosexual persons, religious minorities, and religious converts."

Vischer apparently assumed that Muslims in America had no intention, now or ever, of bringing "the stoning of adulterers, cutting off of the hands of thieves, and the denial of basic freedoms for women" to America, and that there are schools of interpretation among Islamic legal scholars that do not "stand in tension with the rights that we have come to take for granted in liberal democracies." In reality, however, there is no school of Islamic jurisprudence among either Sunnis or Shiites that does not mandate stoning for adultery, amputation of the hand for theft, and the subjugation of women. Stoning adulterers is in accord with the words and example of Muhammad, whom the Qur'an holds up as the supreme example of conduct for believers (33:21); amputation of the hand for theft is mandated in the Qur'an itself (5:38); and the oppression of women in numerous ways is amply attested by the words of both the Qur'an and the prophet of Islam.

And while there are individual Islamic legal scholars who have crafted interpretations of the Qur'an and Sunnah that are more compatible with Western pluralism and liberal democracy than is sharia in its classic formulations, these have never gained any significant traction among Muslims. Wherever sharia has been the law of the land, throughout Islamic history and today in Saudi Arabia, Iran, and other areas of the Islamic world, it has had the same character—never resembling liberal democracy by any stretch of the imagination. Sharia polities throughout history and today have denied the freedom of speech and the freedom of conscience, and they have mandated discrimination against women and non-Muslims.

Vischer says that "fears about the most extreme applications of Sharia need not prompt a categorical ban on Sharia," but he appeared to be unaware that the world has never seen a form of sharia that has not been "extreme" by the standards of liberal democracy. Many non-Muslims mistakenly believe that relatively free and Westernized majority-Muslim states—up until recently, principally Turkey, Tunisia, and Egypt—demonstrate the compatibility of sharia with understandings of human rights that are otherwise universally accepted. But this is a fundamental misapprehension: Turkey and other relatively Westernized Muslim countries have not been governed by sharia at all, but instead by legal codes imported from the West. In fact, the father of Turkish secularism, Mustafa Kemal Ataturk, established the modern-day Turkish republic as a defiant rejection of sharia and an explicit determination to establish a Western-style state, free from the strictures of Islamic law. Such states don't have a different, more expansive version of sharia;

they don't have sharia at all. (And today their freedoms are rapidly eroding, as Islamic supremacists assert political power and reintroduce elements of sharia all over the Islamic world).

Sharia is political and supremacist, mandating a society in which non-Muslims do not enjoy equality of rights with Muslims. And that is the focus of anti-sharia laws: to prevent an authoritarian and oppressive political and social system from eroding the freedoms we enjoy as Americans. It is plainly disingenuous to claim that anti-sharia laws would infringe upon Muslims' First Amendment rights to practice their religion. As Thomas Jefferson said, it doesn't matter whether my neighbor believes in one god or seventeen; it neither picks my pocket nor breaks my leg. It is only when my neighbor believes that his god commands him to pick my pocket or break my leg that his beliefs become a matter of concern for those who do not share them. No one wants to restrict individual Muslim religious practice. The purpose of anti-sharia laws is not to stop Muslims from getting married in Islamic religious ceremonies and the like, but to stop the political and supremacist aspects of Islam that infringe upon the rights and freedoms of non-Muslims.

The Islamic state, as delineated by sharia, encroaches on the basic rights of non-Muslims. It would be a sad irony for non-Muslims to oppose anti-sharia initiatives and thereby abet their own subjugation.

Excusing Islamic Oppression of Women

The failure of feminists to oppose sharia is particularly ironic. Even in the face of the evidence of Islam's oppression of women, Western feminists are largely indifferent.

Take, for instance, Dr. Laura Briggs, associate professor of women's studies and head of the department of women's studies at the University of Arizona. In a 2009 address, Briggs, author of *Reproducing Empire: Race, Sex, Science, and U.S. Imperialism in Puerto Rico*, praised the work of other professors, including Saba Mahmood, associate professor of social cultural anthropology at the University of California, Berkeley. Mahmood, said Briggs, "confronted one of the legacies of a long history of orientalism and the recent wars in the Middle East: the way we are invited to see Muslim women as hopelessly, painfully oppressed, without their own autonomy, will, or individual rights."

So, apparently the oppression of Muslim women has nothing to do with Islamic law or culture; instead it is a result of "orientalism and the recent wars in the Middle East." In other words, it is the West's fault. "If we sometimes notice other Middle Eastern women—women's rights activists, for example," Briggs continued, "it is only to reinforce the notion that the great mass of Muslim women are terribly oppressed by the rise of conservative religiosity, by their husbands, by the ways they are compelled to dress."

Briggs has good news. Mahmood spent two years—two years!—in Egypt and discovered that that oppression is just a mirage: "But after two years of fieldwork in the women's mosque movement in Egypt, Mahmood asks us to consider a new question: what if community, as much as or more than the notions of individual rights, is a route to living meaningfully? Perhaps we ought to rethink the idea that women's agency and personhood spring from resistance to subjection, and attend to the ways that in conservative religious communities, the cultivation of virtue and of closeness to God, of certain emotions and of forms of embodiment, are challenging but hardly one-dimensional ways of producing the self."

Clearing away the pseudo-intellectual gobbledygook, Briggs appeared to be saying that if women feel fulfilled in being subjugated as inferiors under sharia, then their good feelings outweighed their oppression and subjection. One wonders what Betty Friedan or Gloria Steinem might have said in the 1960s if this same argument-from-fulfillment had been posed to them regarding American women who were perfectly happy being housewives and not holding a job outside the home. But aside from their absolute inconsistency with what has been the feminist view of women's oppression for decades, Briggs's words also represented a betrayal of the Muslim women whose suffering is objective, ongoing, and largely unnoticed.

Consider the case of one Pakistani woman, Nasreen Bibi.

Islamic law forbids women to leave the home without permission from their male guardians, and Nasreen had repeatedly infuriated her husband, Muneer, by flouting this rule.

Muneer considered it an insult. His wife was humiliating him. She was shaking her fist in the very face of Allah. It could not be tolerated. It must not be tolerated. The last time it happened, he waited for her to come home. When she finally did, he began quizzing her about where she had been.

He did not find her answers satisfactory. There was no telling where she had been or what she had been doing. He told her—ordered her— to lie face down on the ground. Then he ordered her to recite the Six Kalimas, phrases from the Qur'an that express fundamental elements of Islamic faith. *There is no God but Allah Muhammad is the Messenger of Allah. I bear witness that no one is worthy of worship but Allah, the One alone, without partner, and I bear witness that Muhammad is His servant and Messenger. Glory be to Allah and Praise to Allah, and there is no God But Allah, and Allah is the Greatest. And there is no Might or Power except with Allah.* And so on.

Nasreen, no doubt terrified by this time and aware of what was to come, complied. As soon as he was finished, Muneer began swinging his axe. Raining blow after blow on Nasreen's prone body, he killed her, and he didn't stop hacking even then. He cut her body to pieces and threw the pieces into nearby fields.

When questioned by police, Muneer explained that he did it to provide a lesson to other Muslim women: that they must obey their husbands, as the Qur'an commands.[46]

But Linda Briggs and Saba Mahmoud would apparently turn a blind eye to the fate of Nasreen Bibi, and of so many others like her, as well as to genital mutilation, child marriage, honor killing, polygamy, and so much more that is sanctioned or tolerated by Islamic law—as long as the women involved were "living meaningfully." And our concern for them? "Orientalism"!

Ironically, in her address, Briggs also praised Saidiya Hartman, a professor of English and comparative literature and women's and gender studies at Columbia University. Hartman, according to Briggs, "sees everywhere around us and in us the legacies of slavery." Briggs asks, "Can we exorcise these ghosts by calling into memory the Middle Passage, the rapes, the slave raids, the fortresses of the Gold Coast and the betrayals of the obruni, the stranger, that made the commerce of slavery possible?" And she concludes, "In her books, *Scenes of Subjection* and *Lose Your Mother*, Women's Studies scholar Hartman writes brilliant prose that is full of heart and embodied, because she thinks that we as individuals and communities are not better off when we try to forget these things."

Fair enough. But if we are not better off when we try to forget slavery, why are we better off when we try to forget the oppression of women in Islam?

It's a question that Linda Briggs, and other feminists, would do well to consider. But they are just more exponents of the all-pervasive denial—as is the National Park Service, which was discovered in September 2013 to have produced a series of videos extolling Islam's contributions to women's rights. In one, a hijabbed young woman says, "In the 7th century A.D., Islam gave women the right to be involved in politics, the right to earn and keep her own money. Islam gave women the right to work outside of the home, Islam gave women the right to own property, Islam gave women the right to divorce, Islam gave women the right to choose who she marries. Islam gave women a whole bunch of rights that Western women acquired later in the 19th and 20th centuries and we've had these rights since the 7th century A.D. and it's just not acknowledged worldwide."[47]

The Park Service videos, needless to say, do not deal with the sanctioning of child marriage by Muhammad's example, or of spousal abuse, polygamy, or the devaluing of women's testimony and inheritance rights by the Qur'an, or with any of the other elements of Islam's institutionalized mistreatment of women. And they were paid for with your taxpayer dollars.

CHAPTER FOURTEEN

ANTI-SEMITISM AND OTHER ACCEPTABLE HATREDS

Those not so uncritical of Islam as the National Park Service were targeted and demonized. On September 11, 2013, a public information officer for Palm Beach County, Florida, named John Jamason posted a message on his personal Facebook page, "Never forget. There is no such thing as radical Islam. All Islam is radical. There may be Muslims who don't practice their religion, much like others. The Quran is a book that preaches hate."[1]

CAIR immediately complained and demanded that the county turn over to them everything that Jamason had written from a county computer over the previous month. County administrator Bob Weisman assured CAIR that Jamason had not written the offending Facebook message from a county computer and stated that county officials were determining whether or not to discipline him.

Qur'anic Hate: OK. Noticing It: Not OK.

Left unexamined in the controversy was whether or not what Jamason said was true. In light of the Qur'an's teachings about jihad and the subjugation of non-Muslims, he certainly had a case that "there is no such thing as radical Islam" and "all Islam is radical," for there is no mainstream sect of Islam or school of Islamic jurisprudence that does not teach that the Muslim community must wage war against unbelievers and subjugate them under its rule.

Jamason was also correct that "there may be Muslims who don't practice their religion, much like others." Indeed, there are many people who identify themselves as Muslims who have no interest in waging jihad against unbelievers but would prefer to hold down their jobs and take care of their families in peace, in the same way as there are millions of people who identify themselves as believers in other religions who are not particularly concerned with living out every teaching of the religion with which they identify.

But what CAIR was most outraged about was not that, of course, but Jamason's contention that the Qur'an teaches hate. They did not, however, provide any evidence showing that it doesn't.

So, does it?

War and Hate in the Qur'an

The Qur'an teaches that Muslims must fight and kill unbelievers "wherever you overtake them" until "religion is Allah's," that is, Islamic law rules all societies (2:190–93). They must fight unbelievers "until there is no fitnah and (until) the religion, all of it, is for Allah" (8:39). Muslims are to fight unbelievers and "prepare against them whatever you are able of power and of steeds of war by which you may terrify the enemy of Allah and your enemy and others besides them whom you do not know (but) whom Allah knows" (8:60).

Allah tells Muhammad to "fight against the disbelievers and the hypocrites and be harsh upon them. And their refuge is Hell, and wretched is the destination" (9:73). The followers of Muhammad should imitate him in this: "O you who have believed, fight those adjacent to you of the disbelievers and let them find in you harshness" (9:123). For

"Muhammad is the Messenger of Allah; and those with him are forceful against the disbelievers, merciful among themselves" (48:29).

As we have seen, Muslims should not befriend non-Muslims, unless it is to deceive them to save themselves from danger:

Allah says he will "cast terror into the hearts of those who disbelieve" (3:151). He tells his prophet: "(Remember) when your Lord inspired to the angels, "I am with you, so strengthen those who have believed. I will cast terror into the hearts of those who disbelieved, so strike [them] upon the necks and strike from them every fingertip."

Among "those who have disbelieved" are the Christians, who have made themselves into disbelievers by worshipping Christ as God: "They have certainly disbelieved who say, 'Allah is the Messiah, the son of Mary'" (5:17; 5:72). In worshipping Christ, they have associated a partner with Allah, thereby becoming polytheists, and "the polytheists are unclean" (9:28). Both Jews and Christians have ascribed a son to Allah, for which Allah should destroy them: "The Jews say, 'Ezra is the son of Allah'; and the Christians say, 'The Messiah is the son of Allah.' That is their statement from their mouths; they imitate the saying of those who disbelieved (before them). May Allah destroy them; how are they deluded?" (9:30).

Islamic Jew-Hatred

But the most despised unbelievers are the Jews. The Muslim holy book contends that Allah transformed disobedient Jews into "apes, despised" (2:65; 7:166), and "apes and pigs" (5:60). The Qur'an also says that Jews are accursed for rejecting the Qur'an, which they should have recognized as confirming their own Scriptures: "And when there came to them a Book from Allah confirming that which was with them— although before they used to pray for victory against those who disbelieved—but (then) when there came to them that which they recognized, they disbelieved in it; so the curse of Allah will be upon the disbelievers" (2:89).

The Jews "have been put under humiliation (by Allah) wherever they are overtaken, except for a covenant from Allah and a rope from the Muslims"—that is, except those who have accepted Islam or submitted to Muslim rule. "And they have drawn upon themselves anger from Allah and have been put under destitution. That is because they disbelieved in the verses of Allah and killed the prophets without right. That is because they disobeyed and (habitually) transgressed" (3:112). They killed the prophets because they disliked their messages: "Whenever there came to them a messenger with what their souls did not desire, a party (of messengers) they denied, and another party they killed" (5:70).

Contemporary Islamic jihadists take such verses very seriously and even teach their children to apply them to the Jews of today. Official Palestinian Authority television in July 2013 featured two girls reciting a poem that included this stanza:

> You who murdered Allah's pious prophets
> Oh, you who were brought up on spilling blood
> You have been condemned to humiliation and hardship
> Oh Sons of Zion, oh most evil among creations
> Oh barbaric monkeys, wretched pigs.[2]

This was a specifically Qur'anic imprecation. The verses about killing the prophets and spilling blood, as well as the idea that the Jews have been condemned to humiliation, echoed Qur'an 3:112; and the monkeys and pigs came from Qur'an 2:62–65; 5:59–60; and 7:166.

Meanwhile, the Qur'an also says that not only have the Jews disbelieved in revelations from Allah and killed the prophets, but they even dare to mock Allah himself: "And the Jews say, 'The hand of Allah is chained.' Chained are their hands, and cursed are they for what they say." They "strive throughout the land (causing) corruption, and Allah does not like corrupters" (5:64).

Allah gave food laws to the Jews because of their "wrongdoing," and for "for their averting from the way of Allah many (people)" (4:160), and by doing so, "repaid them for their injustice" (6:146). Some Jews are "avid listeners to falsehood" who "distort words beyond their (proper) usages." These are "the ones for whom Allah does not intend to purify their hearts," and they will be punished not just in hellfire but in this life as well: "For them in this world is disgrace, and for them in the Hereafter is a great punishment" (5:41).

According to the Qur'an, Jews dare to deny divine revelation, claiming that "Allah did not reveal to a human being anything," to which Muhammad is told to respond, "Who revealed the Scripture that Moses brought as light and guidance to the people? You (Jews) make it into pages, disclosing (some of) it and concealing much" (6:91).

In light of all this, it is understandable that Muslims should not get close to such people: "O you who have believed, do not take the Jews and the Christians as allies. They are [in fact] allies of one another. And whoever is an ally to them among you—then indeed, he is [one] of them. Indeed, Allah guides not the wrongdoing people" (5:51).

What's more, the Jews are "the most intense of the people in animosity toward the believers" (5:82). This, too, resonates in the contemporary Islamic supremacist consciousness. In a March 2012 interview, Kuwaiti Muslim Brotherhood leader Tareq al-Suwaidan declared, "The most dangerous thing facing the Muslims is not the dictatorships. The absolutely most dangerous thing is the Jews. They are the most dangerous. They are the greatest enemy."[3]

Al-Suweidan also exhorted Muslims to wage armed jihad against Israel as a religious duty, not just a political operation: "We must consolidate the position of the Palestinians within Palestine as much as possible. We must support the armed resistance in Gaza, and if possible, we must spread it to the West Bank, and even to Palestine [within the 1948 borders]. If we can, we should do that. Third, the countries bordering [Israel] must be serious in their resistance to the Zionist entity. Thanks to Allah, there are signs of this. Fourth, this must be a mission for the entire Islamic nation. Everyone should support this cause."[4]

We have seen that the Qur'an calls Muslims the "best of people" (3:110). On the other hand, "they who disbelieved among the People of the Scripture and the polytheists will be in the fire of Hell, abiding eternally therein. Those are the worst of creatures" (98:6). They are "like livestock" (7:179). "Indeed, the worst of living creatures in the sight of Allah are those who have disbelieved, and they will not [ever] believe" (8:55).

But when John Jamason called the Qur'an "a book that preaches hate," in the eyes of CAIR he was the one preaching hate, not the holy book of Islam. The hypocrisy of their harassment of Jamason was self-evident but only to those familiar enough with the Qur'an and honest enough to acknowledge the nature of all too much of its contents. That was a small group that did not include officials of Palm Beach County, who were—like so many other officials in the United States and elsewhere in the still marginally free world—all too ready to entertain the complaints about Muslim pressure groups despite being woefully ill-equipped to evaluate those complaints properly. Like Major Nidal Hasan's superiors, they knew that what was important above all was to avoid being labeled "bigoted" and "Islamophobic."

Islamic tradition is no kinder to the Jews than the Qur'an. The most notorious anti-Semitic passage among very many in Islamic tradition is the one in which Muhammad prophesies that Muslims will bring about the end times by killing Jews wholesale: "The last hour would not come unless the Muslims will fight against the Jews and the Muslims would kill them until the Jews would hide themselves behind a stone or a tree and a stone or a tree would say: Muslim, or the servant of Allah, there is a Jew behind me; come and kill him; but the tree Gharqad would not say, for it is the tree of the Jews."[5]

In 2008, the Saudi sheikh Muhammad al-Arefe explained that "studies conducted in Tel Aviv and in the Palestinian lands occupied by the Jews showed that they plant Gharqad trees around their homes, because the Prophet Muhammad said that when the Muslims fight the Jews, each and every stone and tree will say: 'Oh Muslim, oh servant of Allah, there is a Jew behind me, come and kill him.'" The Jews planted these trees, al-Arefe said, because they are "not man enough to stand and fight" the Muslims."[6]

In a similar vein, former Ohio resident and Muslim Brotherhood sheikh Salah Sultan said. "The stone which is thrown at the Jews hates these Jews, these Zionists, because Allah foretold, via His Prophet Muhammad, that Judgment Day will not come before the Jew and the Muslim fight. The Jew will hide behind stones and trees, and the stone and the tree will speak, saying: 'Oh Muslim, there is a Jew behind me, come and kill him.' The only exception will be the Gharqad tree.... The stone's self-awareness is such that it can distinguish Muslims from Jews."[7]

The Perennial Scapegoats

Islamic jihadists and supremacists make no secret of the fact that they take the Qur'an's numerous excoriations of the Jews to heart.

Sheikh Yusuf al-Qaradawi, Al Jazeera TV preacher and the most popular and renowned Muslim cleric in the world, said in 2009, "Throughout history, Allah has imposed upon the [Jews] people who would punish them for their corruption. The last punishment was carried out by Hitler. By means of all the things he did to them—even though they exaggerated this issue—he managed to put them in their place. This was divine punishment for them. Allah willing, the next time will be at the hand of the believers."

He hoped that he would be able to participate, despite being over eighty: "To conclude my speech, I'd like to say that the only thing I hope for is that as my life approaches its end, Allah will give me an opportunity to go to the land of Jihad and resistance, even if in a wheelchair. I will shoot Allah's enemies, the Jews, and they will throw a bomb at me, and thus, I will seal my life with martyrdom. Praise be to Allah, Lord of the Worlds. Allah's mercy and blessings upon you."[8]

Qaradawi's hostility to the Jews was not unique to him. In July 2013, the Australian sheik Sharif Hussein extrapolated from the Qur'an's teachings about the Jews to paint them as responsible for virtually every setback Muslims have suffered: "The Jews, always and everywhere, supply the hypocrites, lackeys, and traitors among the Muslims—whether presidents, ministers, or leaders of secular pan-Arab movements—with money, media outlets, weapons, and so on, in order to generate confusion and strife within Muslim societies."[9]

Other clerics' remarks contradicted the conventional wisdom that the Israeli-Palestinian conflict is over land and can be settled through negotiations. In the summer of 2013, as Barack Obama pressed Israel to resume peace talks with Palestinian Authority president Mahmoud Abbas, Sheikh Hammam Saeed, the leader of the Jordanian branch of the Muslim Brotherhood, thundered that eradicating all Jewish presence from the Holy Land was a matter of Islamic law. He termed the idea of a negotiated settlement "heresy, according to Islamic law, because Allah says that Palestine belongs to the Islamic nation, while they say that Palestine belongs to the Jews. Anyone who says that Palestine belongs to the Jews has no place in the religion of Allah, and no room in this creed. This is an issue of heresy and belief."

In another address, Saeed added, "This is what we say to the Jews: We will not accept you on the land of Palestine.... I say to you, oh Jews: The time of your reckoning has come. By Allah, we will hold you accountable for every drop of blood you have spilled, for every inch of land you attacked, and for every mosque-goer whose entry into the Al-Aqsa Mosque you have prevented." But he was not just talking about redressing perceived grievances: "Woe betide you, oh Jews, do you realize that this is mentioned in the Qur'an and the hadith?" And the crowd began chanting that Palestine was "the graveyard of the Jews."[10]

That genocidal vision has a surprisingly wide appeal. In June 2013, the Jordanian newspaper *Assawsana* published an article by Dr. Muhammad Qasem Batayena, chillingly and frankly entitled, "Let's Kill the Jews Everywhere." In it, Batayena insisted, "I'm not an extremist, nor racist ... I'm not bloodthirsty and not vengeful ... I'm not a terrorist and I've never been a killer." Nonetheless, he lamented that while "I am an Arab for sure," and "our blood is permitted," in contrast, "the blood of the apes and pigs is forbidden." In other words, he was angry that Muslims were not killing Jews, for "the Arab tyrants sold us for a cheap price and served us on golden plates as sacrifice for the Zionists."

But Batayena saw a brighter future ahead: "Yes, we will triumph, pray in Jerusalem and take revenge on the filthy murderers ... we will kill them wherever we find them, as the Holy Qur'an told us ... we will make them taste the taste of death, in which they became masters all over the Islamic and Arab lands.... Yes, we will kill them, and I swear that if I get the chance, I won't miss it ... since I believe in Allah and his Messenger, and I know that this world is nothing but the enjoyment of a delusion."[11] The exhortation to "kill them wherever you find them" appears three times in the Qur'an (2:191; 4:89; 9:5); and the statement "what is the life of this world except the enjoyment of delusion" is also Qur'anic (3:185).

Even Westernized Muslims

Even outwardly Westernized Muslims can see Jews behind every tree. Turkish prime minister Recep Tayyip Erdogan, for example, blamed Israel for the ouster of Egypt's Muslim Brotherhood president Mohamed Morsi in the summer of 2013.[12]

In fact, each side in Egypt that summer blamed the other for being a tool of the Jews. On August 14, 2013, Ahmad Taha al-Naqr of the Egyptian Association for Change said on Egyptian television, "I'd like to focus on the connection between the Jews and the Muslim Brotherhood. The MB have adopted the policy of the Jews, and they are implementing it to the letter, with respect to the invasion of the media, presenting an image of eternal victims.... They use violence and view others as Gentiles. The Jews always say that non-Jews are Gentiles and that it is permitted to kill them—Gentiles can be killed or banished, like they do to the Palestinians." The Muslim Brotherhood, he charged, acted just like the Jews: "The [August 14] Rabaa massacre was orchestrated in the same style as the historical Masada massacre of the Jews, so that the MB would be able to continue to harp on about it, thus justifying foreign intervention in the affairs of Egypt. They actually demanded such foreign intervention. Anyone demanding intervention in his country's affairs is committing high treason. They simply clone and implement the image of the Jews."[13]

On Al Jazeera three days later, Gamal Nassar, the former media secretary to the General Guide of the Muslim Brotherhood, countered that it was actually the opponents of the Muslim Brotherhood who were working with the Jews—and even that the head of Egypt's military (which had deposed the Brotherhood), Abdel Fattah el-Sisi, was himself a Jew: "I was surprised to learn, from the Algerian *Al-Watan* newspaper, that Al-Sisi [sic] is of Jewish origin. His mother is called Mulaika Titani, and her brother was a member of the Jewish Haganah organization. Thus, we see that this man, by any standard, is implementing a Zionist plan to divide Egypt.... This is a Zionist plot, and I am willing to be held responsible for what I say. Whoever reads *The Protocols of the Elders of Zion* and the writings of [the Jews], including those who were writing in the U.S., realizes that this plot was premeditated."[14]

Many Muslims take such accusations quite seriously. Another ostensibly Westernized Muslim, the former international cricket star Imran Khan, ex-husband of the glamorous heiress Jemima Goldsmith Khan and current leader of the principal opposition party in Pakistan, announced in August 2013 that he was planning to sue a Muslim cleric, Fazlur Rahman, for calling him an "agent for the Jewish lobby."[15]

Fashionable Jew-Hatred

While railing against the supposed "hate" of opponents of jihad terror, the moneyed Left had no trouble cozying up to Muslim anti-Semites.

On February 25, 2013, Muslim writer Reza Aslan, renowned as a hip, secular Muslim, tweeted, "Let the Third Intifada commence."

The First (1987–93) and Second (2000–05) Intifadas (literally "shakings off," or "uprisings") were escalations of the Palestinian jihad against Israel, resulting in numerous jihad attacks against Israeli civilians. To call for an intifada is tantamount to calling for Israelis to be murdered on buses, and in pizza parlors, and while sleeping in their beds—all features of the two previous Intifadas.

Nevertheless, on May 12, 2013, the Tanenbaum Center for Inter-religious Understanding, which describes itself as a "secular, non-sectarian organization that combats religious prejudice and promotes mutual respect," presented Reza Aslan with its Media Bridge-Builder Award at a gala celebration, at which ticket packages started at $350 and climbed as high as $50,000.[16]

The award was incongruous not solely because of Aslan's call for a new intifada. Reza Aslan is a board member of the National Iranian American Council (NIAC), which has been established in court as a lobbying group for the genocidally anti-Israel, anti-Semitic Islamic Republic of Iran.[17] Political analyst Michael Rubin has said, "Jamal Abdi, NIAC's policy director, now appears to push aside any pretense that NIAC is something other than Iran's lobby. Speaking at the forthcoming 'Expose AIPAC' conference, Abdi is featured on the 'Training: Constituent Lobbying for Iran' panel."[18]

According to investigative journalist Charles C. Johnson, "Iranian state-run media have referred to the National Iranian-American Council

(NIAC) since at least 2006 as 'Iran's lobby' in the U.S."[19] Iranian freedom activist Hassan Daioleslam "documented over a two-year period that NIAC is a front group lobbying on behalf of the Iranian regime."[20] NIAC had to pay him nearly $200,000 in legal fees after they sued him for defamation over his accusation that they were a front group for the mullahs and lost.[21] Yet Reza Aslan remains on their board.

Aslan has also tried to pass off Iran's genocide-minded former president Mahmoud Ahmadinejad—who boasted that jihadists would succeed in "removing the Zionist regime from the world scene" and once stated at the United Nations that the United States perpetrated the 9/11 attacks in order to help Israel—as a liberal reformer.[22] Aslan has called on the U.S. government to negotiate with Ahmadinejad himself, as well as with the jihad terror group Hamas, whose charter bears an epigraph from Muslim Brotherhood founder Hasan al-Banna: "Israel will exist and will continue to exist until Islam will obliterate it, just as it obliterated others before it."[23]

Aslan has even praised the jihad terror group Hizballah as "the most dynamic political and social organization in Lebanon." Hizballah's founder Hassan Nasrallah has said, "If they (Jews) all gather in Israel, it will save us the trouble of going after them worldwide."[24] Aslan has also had kind words for the Muslim Brotherhood in the wake of the toppling of Hosni Mubarak, writing, "The Muslim Brotherhood will have a significant role to play in post-Mubarak Egypt. And that is good thing [sic]."[25] (Millions of Egyptians obviously disagree.) And in the midst of all this praise for Islamic hardliners, Aslan frequently railed against "Islamophobia."

It is hard to see how all this enthusiasm for Islamic supremacists and terrorists, including vicious and violent-minded anti-Semites, constituted being a "Media Bridge-Builder," but of course for the well-heeled leftist elites of the Tanenbaum Center, admiring the Muslim Brotherhood, Hamas, Hizballah, and Mahmoud Ahmadinejad didn't place one outside the pale of acceptable discourse; it made one mainstream. Even leftist Jews didn't seem to mind: Temple Judea in Palm Beach Gardens, Florida, hosted Reza Aslan on October 8, 2013.[26]

The lionizing of Aslan was just one of innumerable examples of leftist foundations hailing a leftist pundit. And given Aslan's associations with the Islamic Republic–linked NIAC, his consistently anti-Israel stance, and his praise for Hamas and Hizballah, the Tanenbaum Center's award to Aslan also constituted a disturbing acceptance of anti-Semitism among those elites.

And that acceptance was in turn a byproduct of those elites' increasing enthusiasm about Islam and anxiousness to show that they welcome Muslims and Islam into the country. For Islamic jihadists have certainly made no secret of their hatred and contempt for Jews and every non-believer of whatever creed (or lack thereof) who resists their program of authoritarianism and supremacism.

That hatred has indeed come to America, as a horrifying incident of jihad mass murder in far-off Kenya illustrated. On September 21, 2013, Somali Islamic jihadists stormed an upscale mall in Nairobi, Kenya, murdering nearly seventy people and taking hostages. A witness inside the mall, Elijah Kamau, recounted that "the gunmen told Muslims to stand up and leave. They were safe, and non-Muslims would be targeted."[27] One of the freed hostages, a non-Muslim whom the jihadists took for a Muslim, recounted that the jihadists were quizzing the hostages to determine if they would live or die: "An Indian man came forward and they said, 'What is the name of Muhammad's mother?' When he couldn't answer they just shot him."[28]

The Kenyan military stormed the mall and battled the jihadists. And then it became clear that Al-Shabaab, the jihad group behind the massacre, was not made up solely of Somalis, even though it originated in that country. Also among the killers, Al-Shabaab claimed, were six Somali Americans. As the siege entered its second day, the jihad group released their names: Ahmed Mohamed Isse and Abdifatah Osman Keenadiid from Minneapolis and St. Paul, respectively; Gen Mustafe Noorudiin from Kansas City; Abdelkarem Ali Mohamed from Illinois; Abdishakur Sheikh Hassan from Maine; and Shafie Die from Tucson, Arizona.[29]

If this claim was true, it raised a key question: Where did these American Muslims learn the ideology that they put to bloody application in Nairobi? And why wasn't law enforcement right there to stop them from getting to Kenya? After all the pressure, all the charges of "Islamophobia" and "bigotry" from fashionable apologists for jihad like

Reza Aslan and the stripping of all realistic information about jihad from counterterror training materials, it wasn't surprising that Ahmed Mohamed Isse, Abdifatah Osman Keenadiid, Gen Mustafe Noorudiin, Abdelkarem Ali Mohamed, Abdishakur Sheikh Hassan, and Shafie Die made their way to Kenya and jihad mass murder; the only surprising thing was that there weren't many others like them.

But there will be. There is nothing in place to stop them. In the face of that hatred, the sentinels of Western freedom reached out their hands in friendship, temporized, ignored and denied the threat, and held $50,000-a-plate galas honoring the tuxedoed barbarians who were already within the gates.

CHAPTER FIFTEEN

WHERE WE ARE HEADED

Note: This chapter envisioning what could happen if America remains on the course it's on was written in late 2013 and early 2014. Events described below as happening in 2015, 2016, and 2017 are imaginary and hypothetical. Events happening in 2013 and earlier are actual. Where real people, publications, or organizations are quoted, the quotations are actual if footnoted, parodies if not.

Where is this all leading?

Imagine it is February 27, 2016.[1] Barack Obama awakens one morning to news that Muslims in Pakistan, Afghanistan, Indonesia, Egypt, and elsewhere are rioting and storming U.S. embassies, tearing down the American flag, and raising the black flag of jihad. They're in a rage over a book that depicts Muhammad as waging war against his enemies, consummating a marriage with a nine-year-old girl when in his fifties, and raining down curses upon Jews, Christians, and others. A grim-faced Obama immediately takes to the airwaves.

"This book is reprehensible and disgusting," Obama tells the world, his eyes flashing with indignation. "It does not represent the position of the government of the United States, and we condemn it in the strongest possible terms. This unseemly provocation of the noble believers in the Holy Qur'an has to end. This is America. We are better than this.

We are not a people who condone hate. We are a people who offer a welcoming, helping hand to those in need. And it is high time that we afford religious minorities the same protections that we strive so hard to offer to racial minorities."

The Obama administration quickly drafts a law that would criminalize the "use of any means to broadcast, write, produce, publish or distribute material that encourages or incites terrorism, including a website and public speaking, and of material that incites hatred that is likely to lead to violence against or stigmatization of a specific group."

The international community is thrilled. European heads of state rush to congratulate and thank Obama. The British prime minister David Cameron calls him "far-seeing." The German chancellor says he is "a true statesman." The Dutch prime minister opines that Obama is "richly deserving of his Nobel Peace Prize" and predicts that a new era of peace will soon dawn between the West and the Islamic world. The secretary general of the Organization of Islamic Cooperation (OIC) announces that he is "gratified" that the United States has finally recognized the "red lines that cannot be crossed regarding discussion of the holy figures of the world's great religions."[2]

The mainstream media is just as happy. An article appears on Slate congratulating Americans for finally coming around to the rest of the world's point of view, that there is "no sense in the First Amendment" and that we need not be "paralyzed by constitutional symbolism."[3] The *Los Angeles Times* hails the new clarity about the "distinction between speech that is simply offensive and speech that is deliberately tailored to put lives and property at immediate risk."[4] The *Washington Post* effuses that the United States has "recognized the power of our multiculturalism" and will finally "reach our true potential as a nation" now that "the voices of intolerance that wish to divide us along religious lines" have been "drowned out by overwhelming calls for pluralism and co-existence."[5]

Muslim spokesmen in the United States are enthusiastic as well. Haris Tarin of the Muslim Public Affairs Council heralds the imminent demise of the "hate-mongering industry in the United States that sees Islam as the problem."[6] Imam Husham al-Husainy of the Karbalaa Islamic Educational Center in Dearborn expresses his satisfaction that the United States has finally "put a law not to insult a spiritual leader."[7] Mohammad Qatanani of the Islamic Center of Passaic County, New Jersey, is likewise pleased that "we, as Americans, have put limits and borders on freedom of speech," recognizing that non-Muslims "have no *right* to talk about Muslim holy issues," as doing so will incite "hatred or war among people."[8]

A few roadblocks still remain on the road to peace. Some radio hosts object, but local stations drop their programs for fear of losing their advertisers and FCC licenses. A teary-eyed House minority leader John Boehner says at a press conference, "Look, I agree with the president that the Muhammad book is reprehensible and disgusting, and I don't condone hate speech in any way, shape, or form, but I am concerned about the First Amendment implications of this new bill." After a firestorm in the press, however, with charges flying that Boehner and the Republicans favor hate speech and are sowing division, Boehner backs down and agrees to support the bill. It passes and is signed into law. A Supreme Court challenge is quickly defeated when Justices Sotomayor, Kagan, and Sunstein lead a 6–3 majority vote in favor of the proposition that "hate speech" is not entitled to First Amendment protections and is lawfully subject to restrictions.

The change is immediate. Books critical of Islam and Muhammad disappear from the shelves. Websites tracking jihad terror activity are shut down, and, after vowing to continue to call attention to Islamization and the spread of sharia in the West, a few bloggers are quietly imprisoned. The mainstream media is unperturbed—these people were, after all, purveyors of "hate speech."

But when *Washington Post* executive editor is taken into custody over a story reporting new statements by the Taliban's Mullah Omar calling for jihad, *Post* publisher Katharine Weymouth is outraged. "The story," she urges in a front-page *Post* editorial, "was merely reporting on Mullah Omar's words. If there was any incitement to hatred, it was on the part of Omar, not the *Post*." In answer, White House press secretary Jay Carney explains, "The president feels that this kind of reporting can tend to stigmatize and increase suspicion of the Muslim community in the United States. The *Post*, and the rest of the media, has to learn to be more inclusive."

The media quickly learns to abide by the new rules. Jihad terror attacks in Thailand, Nigeria, and Chechnya are briefly noted in carefully circumspect terms in a few news articles that speak in warmly positive terms about Islam and explain that Muslims' struggle against non-Muslim oppression is justified in each particular case. Time goes by, and only the terror attacks with the very largest body counts are even reported in the United States.

Hot Dog and Beer? No, Tofu and Pepsi

Demands that Americans adhere to sharia begin to be issued regularly. Soon, pork and alcohol products disappear from grocery shelves. This is seen as a natural development after an increasing number of stores in the United States and Britain began setting up separate check-out lines for customers wishing to buy alcohol and pork products, so as to accommodate Muslim employees who refused to handle those items. One of the earliest reports of this phenomenon in the United States came in March 2007, when Muslim cashiers at some Target stores in the Minneapolis area refused to handle pork.[9] Then, in 2012, Wegmans supermarket in Rochester, New York, set up a special sharia-compliant checkout aisle, bearing the sign: "Attention customers: If your order contains pork or alcohol products, we respectfully ask that you choose another lane."[10] In December 2013, it came to light that the popular British chain Marks & Spencer was allowing Muslim employees to send customers who wanted to buy alcohol or pork to other lines.[11]

Both Wegmans and Marks & Spencer backed off and eliminated their original sharia-compliant policies after an outcry, but in 2015 and 2016 this solution begins to appear sensible to more and more retailers. And this time, there is no public outcry—because anyone expressing "Islamophobic" alarm about accommodations to sharia law would fall foul of the new hate speech law. As the immigration of Muslims into the United States and other Western countries continues at high levels, it is deemed economically advantageous to accommodate them, and, given the nature of sharia, there are always more demands to accommodate. Demands to be excused from checking out customers buying alcohol and pork, once met on a large scale, lead to demands that such noxious materials be removed entirely from the presence of Muslim employees, and severely restricted—and ultimately banned outright—on public health grounds. Those who object are derided as enabling alcoholism and obesity or at very least insensitive to the very real health issues posed by regular consumption of alcohol and pork products. The increasingly overbearing government concern for nutrition, which went hand in hand with the nationalization of the healthcare system after the Obamacare debacle of 2014, coalesces nicely with Islam's food laws, as sharia dietary restrictions are imposed upon the American people in the name of providing for the general welfare, with enthusiastic support from those who had pushed in years past for bans on trans fats and sugary sodas.

In the fall of 2016, a columnist for the *New York Post* writes what is meant to be a light-hearted piece about how hard it is to find a pork hot dog in New York City. "I went to sixteen pushcarts all over midtown and lower Manhattan," he wrote. "All were labeled 'halal.' I started out by asking a few of them if they had a pork frank, or if they knew where I could get one, but I got tired of the death stares and gave up." The piece continued,

> Weary, bewildered and thirsty, I retreated to a nearby bar. But there was something strange about it. Instead of bar nuts, the bowls were full of baby carrots. The place was nearly empty, but I still had a hard time catching the bartender's eye. Finally I got his attention and ordered a Heineken. The bartender looked at me like I was crazy. "Where the hell have you been, buddy?" he said to me. "Mayor de Blasio signed the executive order banning alcohol in public places, what, three days ago? You been visiting Mars or something?"
>
> Wrapped up in finishing my novel, I actually had been closed in my apartment and dead to the world for the previous week—and admittedly, I didn't pay too much attention to City Hall in the best of times. But this latest news dumbfounded me. "What?" I sputtered. "Are you telling me I can't get a drink in a bar in *New York City*?"

"Sugar-free root beer, sure," he responded. "Orange juice? I got plenty. But if I give you a beer, they'll haul me up on public health charges." I staggered out into the sunlight, thirstier than ever, and dazed. Was this New York? Was this America? A man can't relax with a frank and a beer?

This column sets off a firestorm. The *Post*'s offices are inundated with furious calls and emails denouncing the paper for publishing a piece that demonstrates such ignorant hostility toward the religious sensitivities of Muslim Americans, not to mention callous disregard for the general health and welfare. One emailer fumes, "Don't expect me to pay for health care for your fat a-- once you've gorged yourself on pork and addled your brains with beer." Another puts it a bit more fastidiously: "The *Post* was extremely irresponsible to run this column. All of us have to contribute our fair share for healthcare, and that means that every individual has to regard his own health as a matter of civic responsibility." The *New York Times* publishes a thoughtful op-ed by the Imam Faisal Abdul Rauf, of Ground Zero Mosque fame, gently pointing out how far-seeing Islam was to ban alcohol and pork, anticipating the realization by non-Muslim societies of how dangerous these substances are by fourteen hundred years.

Calls for the repeal of the Twenty-first Amendment and reinstatement of the Eighteenth, reimposing Prohibition on the United States, are greeted without much enthusiasm, but a large-scale campaign of education resembling the years-long effort to get Americans to quit smoking slowly begins to bear fruit. Finally, in 2018, a new law establishes that one can only buy alcohol with a government-issued permit, obtainable with a fee and proof that one is not Muslim and has no prior convictions and no record of alcoholic indiscretions.

The Death of Feminism

Meanwhile, Muslim groups begin to demand restrictions on women's rights, calling for women to cover their heads in public as a gesture of modesty and respect for their Muslim neighbors and defending those who brutalize women who venture out with heads uncovered as merely overzealous for a return to much-needed moral standards. Some

feminists object, but leading lights of the feminist movement, such as
Naomi Wolf, defend the hijab and denounce opposition to it as "Islamophobic."[12] Feminists who continue to speak out against the forced
covering and brutalization are swiftly arrested and prosecuted on the
grounds that they're promoting "Islamophobia."

New laws are enacted restricting the movements, educational
opportunities, and employment opportunities of women. All the new
laws are sold as preventing hatred against Muslims. And now no one
dares speak out. Those who do are reviled as "Islamophobes" in language reminiscent of a broadside published by the British feminist
Laurie Penny in the *Guardian* in late December 2013.

"Islamophobes," argued Penny with admirable certainty, only criticized sharia mistreatment of Muslim women because of their bigotry
and hatred. She complained, "misogyny only matters when it isn't being
done by white men." Penny added, "As a person who writes about
women's issues, I am constantly being told that Islam is the greatest
threat to gender equality in this or any other country—mostly by white
men, who always know best.... [T]he rhetoric and language of feminism has been co-opted by Islamophobes, who could not care less about
women of any creed or colour."[13]

Fearful of being tarred with the increasingly toxic "Islamophobia"
label—which can now bring prosecution and professional ruin, not to
mention threats of physical harm—both women and men who notice
the institutionalized mistreatment of women in Islamic law learn to
mute their concerns. Since Muslims' status is beyond criticism, the
public discourse begins to accord Muslim women, particularly those
who wear hijab and adhere to other Islamic restrictions, the presump-
tion of special wisdom and insight; the necessity of always portraying
them and their situation in a positive light begins to give them an aura
of secular twenty-first-century sanctity.

As this attitude becomes more deeply rooted, the Islamic critique
of the West's attitude toward women becomes more and more com-
monly aired in mainstream circles—and feminists who for years have
decried the objectification and commodification of women find new
allies in observant Muslims. Their concerns about polygamy, child marriage, divinely sanctioned wife-beating, forced marriage, honor killing,

and female genital mutilation, if they had any in the first place, fall by
the wayside as they devote themselves, under the banner of multicul-
turalist tolerance and respect for women, to cleaning up the public
square, banning pornography, shutting down businesses of all kinds
that traffic in suggestive imagery, and returning modesty to public
displays.

After the knockout game, the next urban horror to arise is gangs of
young men—whom the mainstream media, following the practice of
their European colleagues, describe only as "youths" beating and raping
young women who venture out without hijab. Like non-Muslim women
in many European cities in the previous decade, young American
women quickly learn that the best protection is not calling the police
or carrying a can of mace, but simply carrying a hijab in one's purse
and donning it when in public.

Despite the undertones of brutality in all this, at first non-Muslim
social conservatives are thrilled. They manage barely a demur when
laws begin to be enacted restricting the access of women to the workplace; it is all in the name of protecting the family and the dignity of
women, and after so many years of exploitation and objectification,
who could possibly be against that? Feminists and social conservatives
form an unlikely alliance in the name not of women's rights but of
women's dignity. Female Muslim activists write articles such as "The
Joy of the Hijab" and "My Family Comes before My Employer" that
celebrate modesty and what appear to be traditional values.

There are a few bumps in the road. In late 2016, a Muslim woman
named Farzana Hussein is run over by a car driven by her father for
the crime of having imbibed too deeply of Western ways—just like Faleh
Hassan Almaleki, who was murdered by being run over by *her* father
in Arizona in 2009 for the same reason.[14]

The few remaining "Islamophobes" who still dare to publish their
views try to make Farzana's murder into a women's rights issue, a
human rights issue, and a critique of a religious culture that mandates
the beating of disobedient women and thus creates an environment in
which a certain level of violence is not just tolerated but required. In
an effort to generate outrage over Farzana's mistreatment, some "anti-
Muslim" websites publish lurid photos of her broken body, only to find

themselves (like the pro-lifers who waved large photos of aborted babies in front of abortion clinics) excoriated for transgressing the parameters of good taste and public decency—and in legal trouble for engaging in speech that incites hatred. Ultimately these sites are shut down, and the outrage over the publication of the photos entirely overwhelms any debate on the sanctioning of the brutalization of women in Islamic law. The remaining voices of protest are drowned out by Muslim analysts explaining that Islam actually only allows for a "tap" of a disobedient woman, not anything that would cause her pain (knowing that their non-Muslim audience will be unaware of the hadith in which Aisha says that Muhammad, the supreme example of good conduct, struck her and caused her pain).[15]

The American Academy of Pediatrics, meanwhile, revives its policy of accommodating the desire of Muslim parents to excise their daughters' clitorises by recommending that doctors perform a "ritual nick"— a small excision designed to prevent parents from taking their daughters back to Muslim countries and having full clitoridectomies. The same policy had first been put in place in 2010 but then abandoned after "widespread denunciation."[16] This time, the denunciation is anything but widespread. The few dissenting voices are silenced by charges that they are criticizing Islamic culture and thereby exposing innocent Muslims to still more victimization—in other words, inciting hatred under the new speech law. After all, as far back as October 2103, a campaigner against female genital mutilation found Londoners ready and willing to sign a fake petition to legalize the practice, on the grounds that they did not want to appear "racist" or "Islamophobic." Three years later, the revulsion against these bogeys is all the stronger.[17]

At the same time, Muslim groups in the United States begin agitating for the legalization of polygamy, on the grounds of personal choice that were canonized in American jurisprudence by *Roe v. Wade* and the legalization of gay marriage. If choice is paramount and marriage is no longer a matter involving just one man and one woman, then why can't four women and one man enter freely into a marriage together?

It is, moreover, a matter of religious freedom. Social conservatives such as Pastor Rick Warren, who since around 2010 has been well known to be a warm friend of groups such as the Islamic Society of

North America, declare their support for the legalization of polygamy and campaign for it on the grounds that religious freedom must be upheld.

Enforcing the New Rules

Then the unthinkable happens. The scene is set when the polygamy issue splits the ranks of social conservatives. The Latter-Day Saints, the old mainline churches, and most big evangelical groups put their weight behind polygamy as a religious liberty issue. But in 2017, a small group of social conservatives, including the Family Research Council and the American Family Association, dissent from the majority of their colleagues, declaring their opposition to the legalization of polygamy on the grounds that it reduces women to possessions of men and denies their equality of dignity with men as fellow human beings. They are raked over the coals in the *New York Times* and the *Washington Post*, as well as on MSNBC and CNN—derided as ignoramuses, hatemongers, Islamophobes, and threats to America's multicultural harmony. The Southern Poverty Law Center sends out a fundraiser denouncing the AFA and FRC as "hate groups." And hordes of condescending commentators ridicule the "Bible thumpers" for not being aware that David, Solomon, and other biblical heroes were polygamists, and so how could it be wrong even in Christianity? Muslim polygamists, they assert, are more Christian than these judgmental and self-righteous evangelical rubes.

Under the avalanche of criticism, however, both organizations refuse to back down, and vow to fight against the legalization of polygamy all the way to the Supreme Court. This vow, however, goes unfulfilled. On February 27, 2017, a year to the day after Obama first announced his intention to implement hate speech laws, Muslim gunmen enter the offices of both organizations and open fire, killing a total of thirty-one people—mostly low-level clerical employees.

That is not the unthinkable incident—it comes when the *Times* and the *Post* and their lesser imitators publish editorials saying, "Yes, the killings were heinous, however, the gunmen could be forgiven for reacting in an understandable fashion to the grievous provocation that these organizations' hidebound and unrelenting Islamophobia had

represented." No one expresses anything more than glancing and per-
functory sympathy for the victims; the general tenor of all the coverage
is: *They had it coming. They should have known, they must have known,
what would happen if they stayed on the course they had taken. And so it
did happen, and they have no one to blame but themselves.*

The ever-present threat of violence behind Muslim demands for
accommodation, and leftist demands that those demands be heeded,
effectively quells any remaining opposition. And so America slips quietly and without anyone noticing except for an ever-diminishing circle
of derided and despised "Islamophobes," into general acceptance of the
assumption that Islam and Muslims must be accommodated at all
costs, and that if Muslims are violent, it is the fault of those who have
refused to come across with the desired accommodation or not done
so quickly enough or comprehensively enough.

It Can Happen Here—In Fact, It Already Is

This is not a vision of America as a sharia state. Not yet. This is a
vision of an America that is thoroughly cowed and subdued, and ready
to allow its society to be radically transformed in order to accommodate
Islam. This is a vision of an America that is simply staying on the course
it is now on, and following out today's controversies to the next logical
step.

Yes, this is a hysterical nightmare scenario—but those who dismiss
it as impossibly far-fetched would be well advised to consider what is
happening today in Europe, as detailed in chapter thirteen above. Most
people would assume that such things could never, ever happen in the
United States. In the first place, we will never enact hate speech laws,
and if we did, they would never be abused in this way. Would they?

Well, the quotations above from Slate, the *Los Angeles Times*, and
the *Washington Post*, applauding restrictions on the freedom of speech,
are all real. They were published in the wake of the jihad attack on the
U.S. consulate in Benghazi, Libya, and the murder of Ambassador Chris
Stevens and others. The Obama administration immediately ascribed
that violence to Muslim outrage over a YouTube video critical of
Muhammad, the prophet of Islam. It has now been definitively established that the administration knew that the video had nothing to do

with the attack (although the *New York Times* quixotically tried to revive the claim that it did in a "definitive study" published in December 2013), but administration officials chose, for reasons that are still unclear, to blame the filmmaker anyway.[18] In doing so, they put the onus on the freedom of speech, suggesting that such acts of violence wouldn't happen if only Americans would stop speaking critically of Islam.

Many Americans have long since stopped speaking out, no matter what temptations may be placed in front of them by the latest jihad terror attack, or the next hateful or supremacist or misogynistic imam. They have already learned the lesson that speaking critically of anything Islamic, under any circumstances, is ipso facto hateful—and simply not tolerable in a polite and multicultural society.

Conan Gets It

Where will it end? How can it end? When criticism of Islam is universally stigmatized, how can resistance possibly be mustered to the advance of Islamic jihad violence or to the institutionalized mistreatment of women and non-Muslims, as these elements of Islam become ever more familiar components of life in the United States?

It is already virtually impossible to speak out, as late-night comic Conan O'Brien discovered in November 2103, when he tweeted: "Marvel Comics is introducing a new Muslim Female superhero. She has so many more special powers than her husband's other wives."

O'Brien was referring to "Kamala Khan," Marvel Comics's new Muslim superhero, unveiled with great fanfare the previous week.[19] O'Brien's tweet was just a silly quip, but as the ayatollah Khomeini said, "There is no humor in Islam." One of those who were offended wrote on Twitter: "I didn't know that @ConanOBrien had Robert Spencer and Pamela Geller writing for him now. Interesting." A legion of leftists descended upon O'Brien's Twitter feed, accusing him of being a "f---ing racist scumbag" and "Islamophobic," and his joke of being "kinda tasteless," "really ignorant and terrible," "in very poor taste," and "f---ing gross and racist."

"Racist." What race Muslim polygamy is remains unclear.

O'Brien's joke has an obvious factual basis in the polygamy found in both the Qur'an and the lives of Muslims worldwide. But as O'Brien discovered, calling attention to uncomfortable truths about Islam is "racist" and wrong, even if they're undeniably … truths. O'Brien will not make this mistake again: almost immediately after people began criticizing him for it, he took the offending tweet down. After all, he wants to stay on television; bringing uncomfortable aspects of Islam to light is the quickest way to be read out of polite and decent society. Just ask Sam Harris and Richard Dawkins, formerly darlings of the leftist intelligentsia—until they touched that third rail of American public discourse and dared to criticize the violence and brutality that Islamic jihadists commit and justify by reference to Islamic texts and teachings.

Polygamy devalues women, reducing them to the status of commodities, and stands as an affront to their equality with men as human beings. But none of the enlightened leftists condemning Conan O'Brien for his little joke would dare speak out for the Muslim women who suffer in polygamous arrangements; to do so would be "Islamophobic," "racist," and probably "gross."

When Conan O'Brien calls attention to the reality of Muslim polygamy, even in the most light-hearted and glancing way, the attention of the fatuous and self-important Left (but I repeat myself) focuses not on the oppression of women under Islamic law, but on Conan O'Brien as "Islamophobic." The lesson has been reinforced so relentlessly and repeatedly over so long a period now that no Islamic supremacist entity had to utter a word condemning Conan O'Brien before Twitter lit up with condemnations of him from non-Muslim leftists.

They don't have to ask for instructions anymore. They know: any negative word about the oppression of women in Islam, and indeed, any negative word at all about jihad terror or Islamic supremacism in general, is "racist" and to be rejected with all the scorn and indignation one can muster.

Who Will Dare Speak Up?

I once had a very illuminating lunch with a leftist writer who had attacked me numerous times for "Islamophobia." In the course of conversation, I asked him if he thought there was a jihad threat at all. He admitted that there was but claimed that I had wildly exaggerated it.

Very well, I responded, and posited a hypothetical: What would he do if the jihadis really did start mounting attacks in the United States with the regularity of their attacks in, say, Nigeria or Thailand? What if Islamic supremacists began demanding accommodations to Islamic law that plainly contradicted Constitutional freedoms? He responded that he thought that if those things happened, people of good will on the Left would stand up and offer resistance.

But he was wrong. They won't. Because they have been taught for years that any criticism of Islamic jihad terror and oppression, no matter how accurate, no matter how mild, is that most abhorrent of things, "racism." And so they will most likely accept their subjugation with bland and self-satisfied complacency: they're subjugated dhimmis in the smoking ruins of a once-great society, but at least they aren't "Islamophobes."

If this happens, Conan O'Brien may be standing by with an apposite quip—right before he is led away to the reeducation camp.

WHAT MUST BE DONE

What must be done is very clear. The denial must end. The willful ignorance must end. The U.S. government must stop cooperating with its own enemies. The media must stop covering for Islamic jihadists and demonizing those who oppose them.

Tragically, none of this is likely to happen. That is because the United States today faces an even stronger enemy than the Islamic jihadists—and stronger than Russia and China as well. That enemy is the entrenched culture of self-hatred that denigrates anything and everything American and exalts the most inveterate America-haters as heroic underdogs struggling valiantly against a brutal and blind behemoth.

That culture is the foremost obstacle to our defense against jihad terror and Islamic supremacism, as this book has shown from beginning to end, in a never-ending tale of obfuscation of a genuine threat and slander of those who call attention to it.

And that culture is very deeply entrenched. It won't be going anywhere soon, no matter how many more lives are lost to Islamic jihad
and how much wanton destruction the jihadists leave in their wake. No
matter what, officials and opinion-makers will continue to wring their
hands over a largely non-existent "Islamophobia," while turning a blind
eye to the very real Muslim persecution of Christians and the advance
of jihad and sharia in the West.

The remaining free and aware citizens have to act, to call attention
to this problem before it is too late, and to call upon our elected officials
to do something about it, or elect new officials who will. But it is already
very, very late. And most people who are aware will not heed this call
to action, for they, too, fear being tarred and destroyed as "bigots" and
"Islamophobes."

If America had a sane and open-eyed political culture today, however, with an effective opposition to the ruling party, it would implement
measures such as these:

- *Tell the truth about Islamic jihad and supremacism.* It is
  now customary in American schools to hear about Muslims who have been oppressed because of 9/11 and how
  it is so important for non-Muslims to be accommodating
  and welcoming of them. That's all very well, but it should
  also be taught, and incorporated in public school curri-
  cula, that some Muslims are waging an ongoing Islamic
  jihad against the United States.
- *Enforce existing laws.* Section 2385 of the federal criminal code states that "whoever knowingly or willfully
  advocates, abets, advises, or teaches the duty, necessity,
  desirability, or propriety of overthrowing or destroying
  the government of the United States or the government
  of any State, Territory, District or Possession thereof, or
  the government of any political subdivision therein, by
  force or violence, or by the assassination of any officer
  of any such government … shall be fined under this title
  or imprisoned not more than twenty years, or both, and
  shall be ineligible for employment by the United States

or any department or agency thereof, for the five years next following his conviction."[1] It may be that the proviso in this statute that the overthrow of the government must be planned as taking place by "force and violence" prevents this law from being applied against Muslim Brotherhood groups intent on subverting America from within. Legal minds should study that issue. But surely—somehow—working toward "eliminating and destroying Western civilization from within," as the Muslim Brotherhood has stated its own strategic goal for America, ought to be a prosecutable offense.

- *Reclassify Muslim organizations.* The U.S. government should call upon Islamic advocacy groups in this country to renounce any intention now or in the future to replace the Constitution of the United States with Islamic sharia. This renunciation should be backed up with transparent actions in mosques and Islamic schools, which should teach against this intention, and against the elements of sharia that contradict American freedoms. Those that are found to be teaching sedition should be immediately closed and prosecuted where warranted.

- *End Muslim immigration into the United States,* as a simple matter of national security. This proposal will be condemned as "racist," but the harsh reality is that Muslims who are peaceful cannot be readily distinguished from Islamic jihadists. Can America really afford the national security risk of importing whole Muslim communities from Iraq and Somalia, as is happening now, without even trying to screen out potential jihadists?

- *Reconfigure our international alliances* so that no state that oppresses women or non-Muslims in accord with sharia provisions gets a penny of American aid or is considered a U.S. ally.

None of these recommendations will be adopted. No politician is willing to pay the political price for advocating them. Before too long, however, it will become apparent to everyone that the price of not adopting them was far, far steeper.

ACKNOWLEDGMENTS

As in most of my books, in this book I've used an English translation of the Qur'an produced by Muslims for Muslims so as to demonstrate that this is what mainstream Muslims themselves understand their holy text to be saying. I also try to use a different translation in every book to illustrate (at least to those who might chance to pick up more than one book that I've written) that these understandings of the Qur'anic text are general among Muslims, not restricted to one translation or a small group of them. In this book, I've mostly used the anonymous translation available at the Muslim website www.quran.com, an excellent resource for those who wish to study the Qur'anic text in both Arabic and English. Within the quotations from the Qur'an, there are sometimes words in parentheses; these are supplied by the translator to elucidate the meaning of the original Arabic.

Words in square brackets have been added by me for additional elucidation.

I am remarkably fortunate to be able to count many knowledgeable
scholars of Islam, counterterror analysts, human rights activists, and
exceptional human beings among my friends: so many people have
contributed to this book indirectly by helping me to understand the
larger significance of passing events and to place various incidents in
their proper context.

Specifically, I am indebted to Elizabeth Kantor, an editor of
immense acumen and insight, who improved this book immeasurably,
sharpening its focus and eliminating numerous infelicities. Harry
Crocker and the entire team at Regnery Publishing are, as always,
marvelously professional and at the very top of their field. My friend
and colleague Pamela Geller contributed several enormously helpful
suggestions regarding this book's content and presentation, for which
I am grateful.

Thanks also to the many whom I am, yet again, not at liberty to
name publicly in light of the threats from jihadis that are a daily reality
for them, but they know who they are.

And finally, a tip of the hat once again to the great Jeff Rubin, without whom none of this would have been possible.

NOTES

Introduction: Why It's So Hard to Find Out the Truth about the War We're In

1. "'Islam is Peace' Says President: Remarks by the President at Islamic Center of Washington, D.C.," White House, September 17, 2001.

2. George W. Bush, "Address to a Joint Session of Congress and the American People," White House, September 20, 2001.

3. Oren Kessler, "'Saudi Clerics Use Social Media to Spread Hate,'" *Jerusalem Post*, May 10, 2012.

4. "Catholic Men's Conference Opens Ticket Sales," Catholic Free Press, February 8, 2013.

5. Travis Andersen and Todd Feathers, "Bishop McManus of Worcester Arrested for Drunken Driving; Admits 'Terrible Error in Judgment'," *Boston Globe*, May 6, 2013.

6. Fred Lucas, "Obama Has Touted Al Qaeda's Demise 32 Times since Benghazi Attack," CNSNews.com, November 1, 2012, http://cnsnews.com;

Chris Megerian, "Obama Adviser Calls al Qaeda 'a Mortally Wounded Tiger That Still Has Some Life'," NJ.com, May 3, 2011.

Chapter 1: World War Who?

1. Rachel Cox, "Fort Hood Gunman Says Uniform 'Represents an Enemy of Islam'," KWTX.com, July 9, 2013.
2. Manny Fernandez, "Fort Hood Gunman Told Panel That Death Would Make Him a Martyr," *New York Times*, August 12, 2013.
3. Ibid.
4. "Hasan: 'Illegal war' Provoked Fort Hood Rampage," Associated Press, August 22, 2013.
5. "Doctor: Fort Hood Suspect Didn't Want Deployment," Associated Press, August 20, 2013.
6. "Hasan: 'I Switched Sides'," CNN, August 6, 2013.
7. Nick Allen, "Fort Hood Gunman Had Told US Military Colleagues That Infidels Should Have Their Throats Cut," *Telegraph*, November 8, 2009.
8. "Inside the Apartment of Nidal Malik Hasan," *Time*, http://www.time.com/time/photogallery/0,29307,1938378_1988330,00.html.
9. Dana Priest, "Fort Hood Suspect Warned of Threats Within the Ranks," *Washington Post*, November 10, 2009.
10. Tom Gjelten, Daniel Zwerdling, and Steve Inskeep, "Officials Begin Putting Shooting Pieces Together," National Public Radio, November 6, 2009.
11. Ibid.
12. Chelsea J. Carter, "Judge in Nidal Hasan Court-Bartial Bans al Qaeda–Linked E-mail, Other Evidence," CNN, August 19, 2013.
13. Fernandez, "Fort Hood Gunman Told Panel."
14. Allen, "Fort Hood Gunman Had Told US Military Colleagues."
15. James C. McKinley Jr. and James Dao, "Fort Hood Gunman Gave Signals Before His Rampage," *New York Times*, November 8, 2009.
16. Michael Graczyk, "No Defense from Suspect in Fort Hood Shooting," Associated Press, August 21, 2013.
17. Susan Crabtree, "Fort Hood Victims See Similarities to Benghazi," *Washington Times*, October 18, 2012.
18. "Hasan: 'Illegal war' Provoked Fort Hood Rampage."
19. Angela K. Brown, "Victims Want Hood Shooting Deemed Terror Attack, Associated Press, October 19, 2012.
20. Carter, "Judge in Nidal Hasan Court-Martial Bans al Qaeda–Linked E-mail."
21. "Judge Bars Most Motive Evidence in Fort Hood Trial," Associated Press, August 19, 2013.

22. "In Hasan Case, Superiors Ignored Own Worries," Associated Press, January 11, 2010.

23. Molly Hennessy-Fiske, "Ft. Hood Shooter Received Glowing Evaluations before Attack," *Los Angeles Times*, August 24, 2013.

24. "In Hasan Case, Superiors Ignored Own Worries." Associated Press.

25. "Islamophobia Reports and Other Documents," Council on American-Islamic Relations, November 21, 2013, http://www.cair.com/islamophobia/islamophobia-reports-other-documents.html.

26. Jason Ryan, Pierre Thomas, and Martha Raddatz, "How Alleged Fort Hood Shooter Slipped through the Cracks," ABC News, November 10, 2009.

27. "Final Report of the William H. Webster Commission on the Federal Bureau of Investigation, Counterterrorism Intelligence, and the Events at Fort Hood, Texas, on November 5, 2009," s3.amazonaws.com, 46, https://s3.amazonaws.com/s3.documentcloud.org/documents/779134/fort-hood-report.pdf.

28. Ibid., 52.

29. Ibid., 54.

30. Ibid., 57.

31. Ibid.

32. Ibid., 63.

33. Ibid., 65.

34. "Mueller: FBI Didn't Drop the ball on Ft. Hood Shooter," CBS News, August 22, 2013.

35. Daniel Bardsley, "Fort Hood Killer 'Does Not Represent Muslims': American Security Chief," *National*, November 9, 2009.

36. "General Casey: Diversity Shouldn't Be Casualty of Fort Hood," Reuters, November 8, 2009.

37. Paul von Zielbauer, "5 Men Are Convicted in Plot on Fort Dix," *New York Times*, December 22, 2008.

38. Brian Ross and Richard Esposito, "The Pizza Connection; Easy Access to Fort Dix," ABC News, May 8, 2007.

39. Tom Leonard, "Trial Starts for Muslims Accused of Plotting 'Jihad-Inspired' Attack on US Base," *Telegraph*, October 20, 2008.

40. Troy Graham, "Dix Informant 'Was Scared': Besnik Bakalli Said Three Terror Suspects Talked Only of 'Islam, Jihad, War, Guns'," *Philadelphia Inquirer*, December 2, 2008.

41. Jana Winter, "Clerk Rings Up N.J. Jihad Jerks," *New York Post*, May 13, 2007.

Chapter 2: Misunderstanding Islam with a Meat Cleaver

1. "Cameron: 'Woolwich Was a Betrayal of Islam,'" ITV News, June 3, 2013.
2. Tim Potter and Roy Wenzl, "Terry Lee Loewen Charged in Planned Suicide Bombing at Wichita Airport," *Wichita Eagle*, December 13, 2013; Andrew Grossman, "Man Arrested in Wichita Airport Bomb Plot," *Wall Street Journal*, December 13, 2013.
3. "Alleged Kansas Bomber Wanted to Be 'Obedient Slave of Allah'," Investigative Project on Terrorism, December 13, 2013, http://www.investigativeproject.org/4238/alleged-kansas-bomber-wanted-to-be-obedient-slave.
4. Pete Williams, "Feds Say They Disrupted Suicide Bomb Plot by Worker at Wichita Airport," NBC News, December 13, 2013, http://investigations.nbcnews.com/_news/2013/12/13/21891923-feds-say-they-disrupted-suicide-bomb-plot-by-worker-at-wichita-airport?lite.
5. "Saw" is a phrase Muslims utter after saying Muhammad's name or that of another prophet. It is an abbreviation for "salla Allahu alaihi wa-sallam," which means "May the peace and blessings of Allah be upon him," or literally, "May Allah pray for him and save him."
6. "Alleged Kansas Bomber Wanted to Be 'Obedient Slave of Allah,'" Investigative Project on Terrorism, December 13, 2013.
7. Tim Potter and Roy Wenzl, "Terry Lee Loewen Charged in Planned Suicide Bombing at Wichita Airport," *Wichita Eagle*, December 13, 2013, http://www.kansas.com/2013/12/13/3176861/wichita-news-conference-set-friday.html.
8. "Alleged Kansas Bomber Wanted to Be 'Obedient Slave of Allah,'" Investigative Project on Terrorism, December 13, 2013.
9. Andrew Grossman, "Man Arrested in Wichita Airport Bomb Plot," *Wall Street Journal*, December 13, 2013, http://online.wsj.com/news/articles/SB10001424052702303293604579256432689562234?mod=WSJ_WSJ_US_News_5.
10. "Eagle Editorial: Terrorism Threat Real, Present," *Wichita Eagle*, December 15, 2013, http://www.kansas.com/2013/12/15/3177504/eagle-editorial-terrorism-threat.html.
11. Barack Obama, "Remarks by the President on a New Beginning," June 4, 2009.
12. Charles P. Pierce, "Holy Mother of God," *Esquire*, April 15, 2013.
13. "CNN's Nat'l Sec Analyst Speculates 'Right-Wing Extremists' Could Be behind Marathon Bombing," Breitbart, April 15, 2013.
14. David Sirota, "Let's Hope the Boston Marathon Bomber is a White American," Salon, April 16, 2013.

15. Jake Tapper and Matt Smith, "Source: Boston Bomb Suspect Says Brother Was Brains behind Attack," CNN, April 22, 2013.

16. "Boston Bombings Suspect Dzhokhar Tsarnaev Left Note in Boat He Hid in, Sources Say," CBS News, May 16, 2013.

17. Robert Spencer, "Boston Jihad Bomber Tsarnaev's Social Media Page Shows His Interest in Islam and Bombs," Jihad Watch, April 19, 2013; Tsarnaev's page at http://vk.com/id160300242 was altered to remove the bomb image sometime between April 19 and July 22, 2013: Robert Spencer, "Who Edited Boston Marathon Jihad Murderer's Social Media Page?," Jihad Watch, July 22, 2013.

18. Tamerlan Tsarnaev, YouTube channel, http://www.youtube.com/user/muazseyfullah/videos?flow=grid&view=15.

19. Simon Kearney and Tracy Ong, "Police Seize Muslim 'Kill Enemies' Videos," *Australian*, January 20, 2007.

20. Timothy Burke, "Everything We Know about Tamerlan Tsarnaev, Dead Bombing Suspect," Deadspin, April 19, 2013.

21. Sally Jacobs, "Tsarnaev Friend Tells of Beliefs in Conspiracies," *Boston Globe*, August 8, 2013.

22. Megan Garber, "The Boston Bombers Were Muslim: So?," *Atlantic*, April 19, 2013.

23. Katharine Q. Seelye, Eric Schmitt, and Scott Shane, "Boston Bombs Were Loaded to Maim," *New York Times*, April 16, 2013; John Sexton, "Pressure Cooker Bomb Construction Detailed in al Qaeda Magazine," Breitbart, April 16, 2013.

24. "Manhunt: The Boston Bombers," PBS Nova, July 15, 2013.

25. Jonathan Dienst and Erin McClam, "Bombing Suspects: Brothers with Foreign Roots, American Lives," NBC News, April 20, 2013.

26. Chelsea J. Carter and Greg Botelho, "'CAPTURED!!!' Boston Police Announce Marathon Bombing Suspect in Custody," CNN, April 19, 2013.

27. Garber, "The Boston Bombers Were Muslim: So?."

28. "Chris Matthews on Bombers: 'What Difference Does It Make Why They Did It?,'" Real Clear Politics, April 23, 2013.

29. "Bashir: Suspected Boston Bombers Hurt 'Peace-Loving Religion' of Islam," Real Clear Politics, April 22, 2013.

30. "Boston Bombers' Family 'Was on the Run from Russian Mob': Gangsters BEHEADED Their Dog and Tortured Their Dad before Brothers Became Gun-Toting Drug Dealers in America, Claims Report," *Daily Mail*, December 15, 2013.

31. Christine McConville, "O'Malley: Don't Focus on Hatred, Revenge," *Boston Herald*, April 22, 2013.

32. Qur'an 2:190–93, 4:89, 9:5, 9:29, 47:4, etc.

33. Patrick Goodenough, "Al-Qaeda Propagandist Called for Attacks on Sports Events," CNS News, April 16, 2013.

34. Paul Wood, "Face-to-Face with Abu Sakkar, Syria's 'Heart-Eating Cannibal,'" BBC, July 5, 2013, http://www.bbc.co.uk/news/magazine-23190533.

35. Candice M. Giove, "Smitten Teen Girls Stir Up #FreeJahar Mania for Boston Marathon Bombings Suspect," *New York Post*, May 12, 2013.

36. "'Free Jahar' Chant as Boston Bombing Suspect Heads to Court," CBS Boston, July 10, 2013.

37. Marie Szaniszlo and John Zaremba, "Mayor, Top Cop Blast *Rolling Stone* over Tsarnaev Cover," *Boston Herald*, July 17, 2013.

38. David S. Bernstein, "Menino's Mosque," *Boston Phoenix*, November 24, 2008.

39. Ibid.

40. Noreen S. Ahmed-Ullah, Sam Roe, and Laurie Cohen, "A Rare Look at Secretive Brotherhood in America," *Chicago Tribune*, September 19, 2004.

41. Mohamed Akram, "An Explanatory Memorandum on the General Strategic Goal for the Group in North America," May 22, 1991, Government Exhibit 003-0085, U.S. vs. HLF, et al., 7 (21).

42. Matt Viser and Bryan Bender, "Obama Says FBI Acted Properly in Bombing Case," *Boston Globe*, April 30, 2013.

43. "Obama Administration Corrects Clapper's Claim That Muslim Brotherhood Is 'Secular,'" Fox News, February 10, 2011.

44. Viser and Bender, "Obama Says FBI Acted Properly in Bombing Case."

45. "Russia Had Tamerlan Tsarnaev under Surveillance," *USA Today*, April 30, 2013.

46. "EXCLUSIVE: Saudi Arabia 'Warned the United States IN WRITING about Boston Bomber Tamerlan Tsarnaev in 2012,'" *Daily Mail*, April 30, 2013; David Martosko and American Media Institute, "Saudi Arabian Ambassador in Washington now DENIES His Nation Warned the United States about Tamerlan Tsarnaev in 2012," *Daily Mail*, May 1, 2013.

47. Viser and Bender, "Obama Says FBI Acted Properly in Bombing Case."

48. "Obama's Snooping Excludes Mosques, Missed Boston Bombers," *Investor's Business Daily*, June 12, 2013.

49. Noah Rothman, "GOP'er Louie Gohmert and FBI's Robert Mueller Explode over Investigation into Boston Bombers," Mediaite, June 13, 2013.

Chapter 3: We Wuz Framed!

1. Paul Harris, "The Ex-FBI Informant with a Change of Heart: 'There Is No Real Hunt. It's Fixed'," *Guardian*, March 20, 2012.

2. Trevor Aaronson, "The Informants," *Mother Jones*, September/October 2011.

3. Matt Coker, "Craig Monteilh and the FBI Entrapment of Local Muslims Explored in Anaheim Friday Night," *OC Weekly*, June 6, 2013.

4. Aaronson, "The Informants."

5. Malia Wollan and Charlie Savage, "Holder Calls Terrorism Sting Operations 'Essential'," *New York Times*, December 11, 2010.

6. Farhana Khera, "Americans Should Be Free to Pray without FBI Snooping," *Progressive*, April 13, 2010.

7. Ibid.

8. Aaronson, "A South Florida Muslim Leader Refused to Be a Snitch, So the Feds Tried to Destroy Him," *New Times Broward-Palm Beach*, October 8, 2009.

9. Ibid.

10. "Amended Judgment in Criminal Case," *United States v. Imran Mandhai*, October 29, 2002.

11. Foad Farahi, Facebook page, http://www.facebook.com/people/Foad-Farahi/542716898.

12. "Free To Pray," ISNA Convention, conference session, Chicago, IL, July 3, 2010.

13. Ibid.

14. "Muslim Advocates, ADC, CAIR, MPAC: Senate Homeland Security Report Lacks Substantive Analysis, Contradicts Own Recommendations," Muslim Advocates Press Release, June 23, 2008, http://www.muslimadvocates.org/press_room/muslim_advocates_adc_cair_mpac.html.

15. "FBI Betrayed Us: Iowa Muslims," OnIslam, February 4, 2012.

16. "Mosque Informants Infuriate US Muslims," OnIslam, February 28, 2009.

17. Daniel Pipes and Sharon Chadha, "CAIR: Islamists Fooling the Establishment," *Middle East Quarterly*, Spring 2006.

18. Todd Starnes, "CAIR Says Poster Warning Against Helping FBI Is Misinterpreted," Fox News, January 13, 2011.

19. Robert Spencer, "Hamas-Linked CAIR Thug Cyrus McGoldrick Again Threatens 'Snitches'," Jihad Watch, December 26, 2012.

20. Allie Shah and James Walsh, "Somalis Take to the Street to Protest Group's Actions," *Star Tribune*, June 12, 2009.

21. "CAIR Impeded FBI Probe of Somali Terrorist Group in Kenya Attack," quotes within by Abdirizak Bihi, Judicial Watch, September 23, 2013.

22. Council on American-Islamic Relations, *Legislating Fear: Islamophobia and Its Impact in the United States* (September 19, 2013): 95–96.

23. Charles C. Johnson, "Somali-American Leader: 'I Tried to Warn America' about Homegrown Radicalization," Daily Caller, September 23, 2013.

24. "EMAIL: Islamic Society of Boston Tells Members to Call ACLU," Breitbart, April 25, 2013.

25. "Obama Drone Speech Delivered at National Defense University (FULL TRANSCRIPT)," Huffington Post, May 23, 2013.

26. "Fight Terrorism: Mosque Guidelines Recommendations," Muslim Public Affairs Council.

27. "Fight Terrorism: Frequently Asked Questions about MPAC's National Anti-Terrorism Campaign Mission," Muslim Public Affairs Council, http://www.mpac.org/ngcft/faqs/.

28. Aaronson, "The Informants."

29. Benjamin Weiser, "Convictions in Synagogue Bombing Plot Upheld," *New York Times*, August 23, 2013; Trevor Aaronson, "Inside the Terror Factory," *Mother Jones*, January 11, 2013.

30. Weiser, "Convictions in Synagogue Bombing Plot Upheld."

31. Ibid.

32. Aaronson, "Inside the Terror Factory."

33. Ibid.

34. Arnold Ahlert, "Thwarted Fed Bomber Wanted 'Whole World' Ruled by Islam," FrontPageMagazine.com, October 19, 2012.

35. Robert Spencer, "What Would It Take for You to Go on Jihad?," Atlas Shrugs, October 22, 2012.

36. "Bangladeshi Held in Plot to Bomb N.Y. Federal Reserve," *Awramba Times*, October 18, 2012.

37. "Fort Dix Conviction Upsets Muslims," *Record*, December 23, 2008.

38. "5 Men Found Guilty of Plotting to Kill Fort Dix Soldiers," Associated Press, December 22, 2008.

39. Ibid.

40. Tom Leonard, "Trial Starts for Muslims Accused of Plotting 'Jihad-Inspired' Attack on US Base," *Telegraph*, October 20, 2008.

41. "Fort Dix Plot Unravels," CBS News, December 22, 2008.

42. Howard Koplowitz, "Justin Kaliebe, New York Teen, to Get 30-Year Sentence for Trying to Join Al-Qaeda," *International Business Times*, June 26, 2013.

43. Ibid.

44. "Lawyer: N.Y. Terror Suspect Teen Has Autism, Is Mixed Up," Associated Press, July 11, 2013.

45. Ibid.

46. Koplowitz, "Justin Kaliebe, New York Teen, to Get 30-Year Sentence for Trying to Join Al-Qaeda."

47. "Lawyer: N.Y. Terror Suspect Teen Has Autism, Is Mixed Up," Associated Press.

48. Koplowitz, "Justin Kaliebe, New York Teen, to Get 30-Year Sentence for Trying to Join Al-Qaeda."

49. "Lawyer: N.Y. Terror Suspect Teen Has Autism, Is Mixed Up," Associated Press.

50. Ibid.

51. Koplowitz, "Justin Kaliebe, New York Teen, to Get 30-Year Sentence for Trying to Join Al-Qaeda."

52. Mosi Secret, "Man Sentenced for Role in Plot to Blow Up Subways," *New York Times*, December 14, 2012.

53. Henrick Karoliszyn and Samuel Goldsmith, "Muslim Advocates Charge NYPD Is Racial Profiling in Queens Raids Tied to Alleged Zazi Terror Plot," *New York Daily News*, October 10, 2009.

54. Secret, "Man Sentenced for Role in Plot to Blow Up Subways."

55. "Mosque Informants Infuriate US Muslims," OnIslam, February 28, 2009.

56. "NY Police Grilled over Muslim Surveillance," OnIslam, October 7, 2011.

57. Ibid.

Chapter 4: The Jihad against Counterterrorism

1. Patrik Jonsson, "Muslim Group Sues FBI over Surveillance at California Mosques," *Christian Science Monitor*, February 23, 2011.

2. Ibid.

3. Paul Harris, "The Ex-FBI Informant with a Change of Heart: 'There Is No Real Hunt. It's Fixed,'" *Guardian*, March 20, 2012.

4. Julie Cannold, "Muslim Group Files Lawsuit against Feds," CNN, April 13, 2012.

5. Ibid.

6. Ryan Devereaux, "Civil Liberties Groups File Lawsuit over NYPD Surveillance of Muslims," *Guardian*, June 18, 2013.

7. Ibid.

8. Ibid.

9. Muhammad Hisham Kabbani, "Islamic Extremism: A Viable Threat to U.S. National Security," U.S. State Department Open Forum, January 7, 1999, http://www.generalfiles.org/download/gs469b3f6ch32i0/Kabbani-Testimony-1999-US-State-Department.pdf.html.

10. "Saudi Publications on Hate Ideology Fill American Mosques," Center for Religious Freedom, Freedom House, 2005, http://crf.hudson.org/files/publications/SaudiPropoganda.pdf; "Study: 3 in 4 U.S. Mosques Preach Anti-West Extremism," World Net Daily, February 24, 2008.

11. Mordechai Kedar and David Yerushalmi, "Shari'a and Violence in American Mosques," *Middle East Quarterly*, Summer 2011.

12. John Rossomando, "Pro-Morsi Demonstrations Make MB Ties Harder to Hide," IPT News, August 12, 2013.

13. Chelsea Schilling, "Shocking Terror Ties to Christian Girl's Family Mosque,' World Net Daily, August 31, 2009.

14. Khalid Sheikh Mohammed, Walid bin 'Attash, Ramzi bin As-Shibh, 'Ali 'Abd Al-'Aziz 'Ali, and "Mustafa Ahmed Al-Hawsawi, "The Islamic Response to the Government's Nine Accusations," Jihad Watch, March 11, 2009.

15. "Pakistan Taliban Vow More Violence," BBC, January 29, 2007.

16. Kristina Goetz, "Memphian Drifted to Dark Side of Islamic Extremism, Plotted One-Man Jihad vs. Homeland," Memphis Commercial Appeal, November 24, 2010.

17. Ibid.

18. "Texas Resident Arrested on Charge of Attempted Use of Weapon of Mass Destruction," U.S. Department of Justice, February 24, 2011.

19. Shelley Terry, "Easter Sunday Ashtabula Murder Case Bound over to Grand Jury," Star Beacon, April 10, 2013.

Chapter 5: The Jihad against Talking about Jihad

1. Lydia Polgren, "Nigeria Counts 100 Deaths over Danish Caricatures," New York Times, February 24, 2006.

2. Rukmini Callimachi, "Defame Islam, Get Sued?," Associated Press, March 14, 2008.

3. "'Offensive Cartoons Like 9/11 of Islamic World,'" Journal of Turkish Weekly, February 14, 2006.

4. Callimachi, "Defame Islam, Get Sued?"

5. Ibid.

6. Doudou Diène, "Racism, Racial Discrimination, Xenophobia and Related Forms of Intolerance: Follow-Up to and Implementation of the Durban Declaration and Programme of Action," United Nations Human Rights Council, August 21, 2007.

7. Ekmeleddin Ihsanoglu, "Speech of Secretary General at the Thirty-Fifth Session of the Council of Foreign Ministers of the Organisation of the Islamic Conference," Council of Foreign Ministers, June 18, 2008.

8. "Muslims Condemn Dutch Lawmaker's Film," CNN, March 28, 2008.

9. "Geert Wilders Receives Summons: A Sledgehammer Blow to the Freedom of Speech," Jihad Watch, December 4, 2009.

10. Pamela Geller, "Geert Wilders Verdict: Not Guilty All Counts! Eureka! 'Today Is a Victory for Freedom of Speech'," AtlasShrugs.com, June 23, 2011.

11. "UN Resolution against Islamophobia, Judeophobia and Christianophobia," Reuters, November 24, 2010.

12. Patrick Goodenough, "New Name, Same Old Focus for Islamic Bloc," CNSNews.com, June 30, 2011.

13. "Full Text: President Barack Obama's Speech to the Muslim World," *Time*, June 4, 2009.

14. Jonathan Turley, "Just Say No to Blasphemy: U.S. Supports Egypt in Limiting Anti-Religious Speech," *USA Today*, October 19, 2009.

15. Ibid.

16. Eugene Volokh, "Is the Obama Administration Supporting Calls to Outlaw Supposed Hate Speech?," Huffington Post, October 1, 2009.

17. Daniel Greenfield, "The Cartoonphobia War Rages On," FrontPageMagazine.com, July 22, 2011.

18. Abigail R. Esman, "Could You Be A Criminal? US Supports UN Anti-Free Speech Measure," *Forbes*, December 30, 2011, http://www.forbes.com/sites/abigailesman/2011/12/30/could-you-be-a-criminal-us-supports-un-anti-free-speech-measure/.

19. Goodenough, "New Name, Same Old Focus for Islamic Bloc."

20. Matthew Lee, "Clinton: Islam, West Can Agree on Tolerance," Associated Press, July 15, 2011.

21. Greenfield, "The Cartoonphobia War Rages On."

22. Patrick Goodenough, "Obama Administration Welcoming Islamic Group to Washington for Discussion on 'Tolerance'," CNS News, December 9, 2011.

23. Steve Rendall, Isabel Macdonald, Veronica Cassidy, and Dina Marguerite Jacir, "Smearcasting: How Islamophobes Spread Fear, Bigotry and Misinformation," Fairness & Accuracy in Reporting (FAIR), October 2008.

24. Max Blumenthal, "The Great Islamophobic Crusade," Huffington Post, December 20, 2010.

25. Ibid.

26. Robert Steinback, "Jihad Against Islam," Southern Poverty Law Center Intelligence Report, Summer 2011; Steinback, "The Anti-Muslim Inner Circle," Southern Poverty Law Center Intelligence Report, Summer 2011. For a response, see Robert Spencer, "SPLC Fronts for the Jihad, Smears Freedom Fighters," Jihad Watch, June 22, 2011.

27. "Challenging Islamophobia: The Role of Civic and Faith Groups in Combating Anti-Muslim Hate Speech and Crimes," Center for American Progress, October 4, 2010.

28. Wajahat Ali, "America's 'Detainee 001'—the Persecution of John Walker Lindh," GOATMILK, July 11, 2011.

29. "Muslim Public Affairs Council (MPAC)," Discover the Networks, http://www.discoverthenetworks.org/printgroupProfile.asp?grpid=6177.

30. Wajahat Ali, Eli Clifton, Matthew Duss, Lee Fang, Scott Keyes, and Faiz Shakir, *Fear, Inc.: The Roots of the Islamophobia Network in America* (Washington, D.C.: Center for American Progress, 2011).
31. Ibid.
32. See the comments field at Robert Spencer, "Dutch Mosque: Girls Must Be Circumcised," Jihad Watch, April 8, 2004.
33. Ali, Clifton, Duss, Fang, Keyes, and Shakir, *Fear, Inc.*
34. Ibid.
35. Andrew Berwick, *2083: A European Declaration of Independence* (Anders Behring Breivik, 2011), 743.
36. Ibid., 1348.
37. Ibid., 948.
38. Ibid., 949.
39. Daniel Greenfield, "In Defense of Robert Spencer," FrontPage Magazine.com, July 26, 2011.
40. Robert Spencer, "Mass Murderer Breivik Details His Plan to Destroy Counter-Jihad Movement: The Full Document," Jihad Watch, January 28, 2014.
41. Fjordman, "Breivik's Confession and the Media's Silence," FrontPageMagazine.com, January 27, 2014.
42. "Iran's New President Glorifies Martyrdom," Middle East Media Research Institute, July 29, 2005.
43. "Leading Sunni Sheikh Yousef Al-Qaradhawi and Other Sheikhs Herald the Coming Conquest of Rome," Middle East Media Research Institute, December 6, 2002.
44. Art Moore, "Did CAIR Founder Say Islam to Rule America?," World Net Daily, December 11, 2006.
45. Laura L. Rubenfeld, "Democrats Embrace Siraj Wahhaj: Supporter of Cop-Killer, Al Qaeda and Hamas," FrontPageMagazine.com, August 29, 2012.
46. Ali, Clifton, Duss, Fang, Keyes, and Shakir, *Fear, Inc.*
47. Ibid.
48. Robert Spencer, "Blessing from a Tyrant," FrontPageMagazine.com, January 6, 2009.
49. Abdur-Rahman Muhammad, "Whether or Not Ground Zero Mosque Is Built, U.S. Muslims Have Access to the American Dream," *New York Daily News*, September 5, 2010.
50. Callimachi, "Defame Islam, Get Sued?."
51. *Same Hate, New Target: Islamophobia and its Impact in the United States, January 2009–December 2010*, Council on American-Islamic Relations, June 2011, 29.

52. Blumenthal, "The Great Islamophobic Crusade."

53. "Los Angeles Police Plan to Map Muslims," Associated Press, November 9, 2007.

54. Joe R. Hicks and David A. Lehrer, "Hyperbole Rules in Muslim Debate," *Los Angeles Daily News*, December 26, 2010.

55. "Blacks, Jews Most Likely Victim of US Hate Crimes: FBI," Agence France-Presse, November 22, 2010.

56. Daniel Pipes and Sharon Chadha, "CAIR's Hate Crimes Nonsense," Front-PageMagazine.com, May 18, 2005.

57. "Obama: 'The Future Must Not Belong to Those Who Slander the Prophet of Islam'," *Washington Post*, September 26, 2012.

58. Ahmed ibn Naqib al-Misri, *Reliance of the Traveler* ('*Umdat al-Salik*): *A Classic Manual of Islamic Sacred Law*, trans. Nuh Ha Mim Keller (Amana Publications, 1999), R2.2.

Chapter 6: Not Just in Egypt Anymore

1. Cairo Declaration on Human Rights in Islam, August 5, 1990.

2. "Hamas Charter (1988)," http://www.thejerusalemfund.org/www.thejerusalemfund.org/carryover/documents/charter.html.

3. "Washington's Schizophrenic Approach toward the Muslim Brotherhood," IPT News, September 28, 2010.

4. Brynjar Lia, *The Society of the Muslim Brothers in Egypt* (Ithaca: Ithaca Press, 1998), 79.

5. Clare M. Lopez, "History of the Muslim Brotherhood Penetration of the U.S. Government," Gatestone Institute, April 15, 2013.

6. Mohamed Akram, "An Explanatory Memorandum on the General Strategic Goal for the Group in North America," May 22, 1991, Government Exhibit 003-0085, U.S. vs. HLF, et al.,7 (21).

7. Ibid.

8. Ibid.

9. Michael Waller, "Testimony before the United States Senate Committee on the Judiciary," *Terrorist Recruitment and Infiltration in the United States: Prisons and Military as an Operational Base*, October 14, 2003.

10. Helen Kennedy, "Israel Foe's Donation Draws Flak," *New York Daily News*, January 10, 2002.

11. Ibid.; Kate O'Beirne, "The Chaplain Problem," *National Review*, October 27, 2003.

12. "Rally at Lafayette Park: Alamoudi," Investigative Project on Terrorism, October 28, 2000.

13. Matt Continetti, "Mueller's Misstep: The FBI Director Befriends Apologists for Terror," *National Review*, June 12, 2002.

14. Mary Beth Sheridan and Douglas Farah, "Jailed Muslim Had Made a Name in Washington: Alamoudi Won Respect as a Moderate Advocate," *Washington Post*, December 1, 2003.

15. "Abdurahman Alamoudi Sentenced to Jail in Terrorism Financing Case," Department of Justice, October 15, 2004.

16. "Alamoudi Sentence Cut by Six Years," IPT News, July 25, 2011.

17. Scott Shane and Souad Mekhennet, "Imam's Path from Condemning Terror to Preaching Jihad," *New York Times*, May 8, 2010.

18. Massimo Calabresi, Timothy J. Burger, and Elaine Shannon, "Why Did the Imam Befriend Hijackers?," August 4, 2003.

19. "Yemeni Muslim Brotherhood Leaders Sheltered Anwar al-Awlaki," Global Muslim Brotherhood Report, October 10, 2011, http://globalmbreport.org/?p=5136.

20. Laurie Goodstein, "A Nation Challenged: The American Muslims; Influential American Muslims Temper Their Tone," *New York Times*, October 19, 2001.

21. Catherine Herridge and Pamela Browne, "FBI Tracked Radical American Cleric to Defense Dept. lunch, Documents Show," Fox News, September 12, 2013.

22. "Introduction to CSID," Center for the Study of Islam and Democracy, https://www.csidonline.org/about-csid.

23. Steven C. Baker, "Who's Protecting the President?," FrontPageMagazine.com, May 5, 2003.

24. "Muslims in Fed Terror Probe Making Donations to Obama," World Net Daily, August 29, 2008.

25. "About Us," Muslim American Society, http://www.muslimamericansociety.org/main/content/about-us.

26. "Frequently Asked Questions about MAS," Muslim American Society http://muslimamericansociety.org/main/content/frequently-asked-questions-about-mas.

27. Noreen S. Ahmed-Ullah, Sam Roe, and Laurie Cohen, "A Rare Look at Secretive Brotherhood in America," *Chicago Tribune*, September 19, 2004.

28. "IPT Exclusive: Under Oath, Alamoudi Ties MAS to Brotherhood," IPT News, March 14, 2012.

29. "AAH Demands Congressman Keith Ellison Denounce Islamist Group or Resign," Americans Against Hate, June 6, 2007.

30. James Osborne, "Clinton Invites Controversial Muslim Leader on Conference Call," Fox News, June 8, 2009.

31. "Islamic Association For Palestine (IAP)," Discover the Networks, http://www.discoverthenetworks.org/printgroupProfile.asp?grpid=6215.

32. Ibid.

33. Daniel Pipes and Sharon Chadha, "CAIR: Islamists Fooling the Establishment," *Middle East Quarterly* (Spring 2006).

34. Ibid.

35. "Holy Land Founders Get Life Sentences," JTA, May 28, 2009.

36. "HLF's Financial Support of CAIR Garners New Scrutiny," Investigative Project on Terrorism, October 12, 2007.

37. "What They Say About CAIR," Council on American-Islamic Relations, http://www.cair.com/about-us/what-they-say-about-cair.html.

38. Ibid.

39. "The State Department's Poor Choices of Muslim Outreach Emissaries," IPT News, August 27, 2010.

40. Ibid.

41. Erick Stakelbeck, "Muslim Brotherhood Gaining Foothold in U.S. Gov't?," CBN News, October 12, 2011.

42. "Islamic Society of North America (ISNA)," Discover the Networks.

43. Josh Gerstein, "U.S.: Facts Tie Muslim Groups to Hamas Front Case," *New York Sun*, July 11, 2008.

44. "ISNA Admits Hamas Ties," IPT News, July 25, 2008.

45. "Islamic Society of North America (ISNA)," Discover the Networks.

46. Stephen Brown, "Polishing An Image—Islamic-Style," FrontPageMagazine. com, September 29, 2006.

47. "VP Biden Meets with MB Linked Leader of Islamic Society of North America Mohamed Magid on Gun Violence," Militant Islam Monitor, May 10, 2013, http://www.militantislammonitor.org/article/id/5827.

48. "Why Islam? 'Why Not Islam?' Should Be the Campaign," barenakedislam.com, August 17, 2011, http://www.barenakedislam. com/2011/page/73/.

49. "The State Department's Poor Choices of Muslim Outreach Emissaries," IPT News.

50. "DHS Official Daniel Sutherland Spoke at Recent ISNA Conference," Militant Islam Monitor, September 23, 2008.

51. "Valerie Jarrett and Ingrid Mattson, "White House Opens Wider to Islam," *Maggie's Notebook*, blog, July 23, 2009, http://maggiesnotebook.blogspot. com/2009/07/valerie-jarrett-ingrid-matton-white.html.

52. "ISNA Approves of Meeting with DHS Secretary; U.S. Muslim Brotherhood Likely in Attendance," Global Muslim Brotherhood Daily Report, February 4, 2010.

53. "ISNA President Opens Townhall Meeting on the Nation's Security with John Brennan," Islamic Society of North America, February 16, 2010.

54. Neil Munro, "Obama's Iftar Guest List Omits Controversial Attendees," *Daily Caller*, August 11, 2011.

55. Marc Ambinder, "'Brotherhood' Invited to Obama Speech by U.S.," *Atlantic*, June 3, 2009.
56. Stakelbeck, "Muslim Brotherhood Gaining Foothold in U.S. Gov't?"
57. Franklin Foer, "Grover Norquist's Strange Alliance with Radical Islam," *New Republic*, November 1, 2001.
58. Frank Gaffney, "A Troubling Influence," FrontPageMagazine.com, December 9, 2003.
59. Ibid.
60. Ibid.
61. Ibid.
62. Pamela Geller, "Grover Norquist's Jihad," *American Thinker*, March 4, 2010.
63. Kenneth R. Timmerman, "Grover Norquist's New Muslim Protégé," FrontPageMagazine.com, September 26, 2011.
64. Paul Sperry, "A GOP 'Moderate Muslim'—or Not," *New York Post*, January 9, 2011.

Chapter 7: Islamic Infiltration? McCarthyism!

1. Chris Lisee, "Rep. Michele Bachmann's Muslim Brotherhood Claims Draw Fierce Fire," Religion News Service, July 18, 2012.
2. Ibid.
3. Ibid.
4. Alex Seitz-Wald, "John Brennan's Awesome Bachmann Putdown," Salon, August 8, 2012.
5. Ibid.
6. "CAIR 'Grateful' Constitution Limits Michele Bachmann's McCarthyism," Council on American-Islamic Relations, July 19, 2012.
7. Patrick Poole, "BREAKING: Homeland Security Adviser Allegedly Leaked Intel to Attack Rick Perry," PJ Media, October 26, 2011.
8. Maggie M. Thornton, "Napolitano Says Texas Lying about Mohamed Elibiary: She's Offended at Louie Gohmerts 'Insinuations'," Maggie's Notebook, July 21, 2012, http://www.maggiesnotebook.com/2012/07/napolitano-says-texas-lying-about-mohamed-elibiary-shes-offended-at-louie-gohmerts-insinuations/.
9. Robert Spencer, "Dallas: A Tribute to the Great Islamic Visionary, Ayatollah Khomeini," Jihad Watch, December 14, 2004.
10. Spencer, "Dallas Muslim Leader to Columnist: 'Expect Someone to Put a Banana in Your Exhaust Pipe," Jihad Watch, June 10, 2006.
11. Spencer, "Muslim Brotherhood Supporter Mohamed Elibiary Gets Promotion on Homeland Security Advisory Council," Jihad Watch, September 14, 2013.

12. "ISNA Admits Hamas Ties," IPT News, July 25, 2008.

13. Andrew Gilligan and Alex Spillius, "Barack Obama Adviser Says Sharia Law Is Misunderstood," *Telegraph*, October 8, 2009.

14. Tomer Ovadia, "Rep. Keith Ellison: Michele Bachmann 'Wanted Attention'," Politico, July 20, 2012.

15. Chris Lisee, "Rep. Michele Bachmann's Muslim Brotherhood Claims Draw Fierce Fire," Religion News Service, July 18, 2012.

16. Jennifer Bendery, "Keith Ellison: Michele Bachmann Thinks Muslims 'Are Evil'," Huffington Post, July 19, 2012.

17. Ovadia, "Rep. Keith Ellison: Michele Bachmann 'Wanted Attention'".

18. "Democrats' Dilemma," *Washington Times*, September 24, 2006.

19. Patrick Poole, "Rep. Keith Ellison Rewrites History on His Muslim Brotherhood, CAIR Ties," PJ Media, July 21, 2012.

20. Ibid.

21. Mitch Anderson, "Ellison: Hajj Was Transformative," *Minneapolis/St. Paul Star Tribune*, December 18, 2008.

22. Joseph Abrams, "Group That Funded Rep. Ellison's Pilgrimage to Mecca Called a Front for Extremism," Fox News, January 8, 2009.

23. Ryan Mauro, "Congressman Promotes Fear Inc. 'Islamophobia' Event," FrontPageMagazine, September 12, 2011.

24. Matthew Shaffer, "Rep. Keith Ellison's 'Bigotry'," *National Review*, March 10, 2011.

25. Nick Wing, "Michele Bachmann Not Worthy of Intelligence Committee Role, 178,000 Say in Petition to John Boehner," Huffington Post, January 14, 2013.

26. Ibid.

27. Ahmed Shawki, "A Man and 6 of the Brotherhood in the White House!," *Rose El-Youssef*, December 22, 2012, http://www.investigativeproject.org/3868/a-man-and-6-of-the-brotherhood-in-the-white-house.

28. Ibid.

29. Spencer, "Dhimmitude and Stealth Jihad at Fort Hood," Jihad Watch, December 2, 2009; Brooks Egerton, "Terrorist Links Led U.S. Military to Cut Ties with Syrian Opposition Leader," *Dallas Morning News*, September 5, 2013.

30. Ben Hubbard, "Islamist Rebels Create Dilemma on Syria Policy," *New York Times*, April 27, 2013.

31. Adam Kredo, "Muslim Brotherhood Official, Former Clinton Foundation Employee Arrested," *Washington Free Beacon*, September 18, 2013.

32. Ibid.

33. Eileen F. Toplansky, "The Muslim Brotherhood and Weiner," *American Thinker*, June 19, 2011.

34. "Huma Abedin & Hillary Clinton—Abedin Family Ties to Al-Qaeda," *Free Republic*, November 11, 2007.

35. Ed O'Keefe, "John McCain Defends Huma Abedin against Accusations She's Part of Conspiracy, *Washington Post*, July 18, 2012.

36. Ibid.

37. "Michele Bachmann's Letter to Keith Ellison," FrontPageMag.com, July 20, 2012.

38. O'Keefe, "John McCain Defends Huma Abedin against Accusations She's Part of Conspiracy."

39. Arnold Ahlert, "More Secrets From Huma Abedin," FrontPage Magazine, May 20, 2013.

40. O'Keefe, "John McCain Defends Huma Abedin against Accusations She's Part of Conspiracy."

41. Andrew C. McCarthy, "The Huma Unmentionables," *National Review*, July 24, 2013.

42. For a case in which Hiss was not guilty, see "The Alger Hiss Story: Search for the Truth," NYU.edu, https://files.nyu.edu/th15/public/who.html. For the consensus on Hiss, see Carl T. Bogus, *Buckley: William F. Buckley Jr. and the Rise of American Conservatism* (New York: Bloomsbury Press, 2011).

43. Gilbert R. Cherrick, "Dinner with Eleanor Roosevelt," The Alger Hiss Story, NYU.edu, https://files.nyu.edu/th15/public/cherrick.html.

44. O'Keefe, "John McCain Defends Huma Abedin against Accusations She's Part of Conspiracy."

45. Lauren Williams, "McCain Crosses Paths with Rebel Kidnapper," *Daily Star*, May 30, 2013.

46. See, for example, Stephen Jones, "Allen Weinstein's Scholarship," *Oklahoma Law Review* 31, no. 3 (1978).

47. Bradley Klapper, "Hillary Clinton Meets Egypt's New Islamist President, Mohammed Morsi," Associated Press, July 14, 2012.

48. Sharona Schwartz, "'Hey Obama, You Are Stupid, Bad Man': Viral Egyptian Music Video Accuses Obama of Supporting Terrorism, Muslim Brotherhood," Blaze, August 5, 2013.

Chapter 8: Marginalizing Freedom Fighters

1. Francine Knowles, "Terror Task-Force Trainer's Class Canceled after Group Calls Him 'Bigot'," *Chicago Sun-Times*, August 19, 2013.

2. Ibid.

3. Sophia Tareen, "Suburban Police Cancel Anti-Terrorism Trainings," Associated Press, August 18, 2013.

4. Knowles, "Terror Task-Force Trainer's Class Canceled after Group Calls Him 'Bigot'."

5. Ibid.

6. Ibid.

7. "CAIR Asks Illinois Law Enforcement to Drop Anti-Muslim Trainer," Council on American-Islamic Relations press release, August 15, 2013.

8. Ibid.

9. Matt Sedensky, "Muslims Say Group's Police Training Maligns Faith," Associated Press, July 11, 2012.

10. James D. Davis, "Muslim Organizations Say Police Training Teaches Bigotry," *South Florida Sun-Sentinel*, July 11, 2012.

11. Tareen, "Suburban Police Cancel Anti-Terrorism Trainings."

12. Davis, "Muslim Organizations Say Police Training Teaches Bigotry."

13. Sedensky, "Muslims Say Group's Police Training Maligns Faith."

14. Martin E. Comas, "UCF Prof Accused of Anti-Muslim Teachings Blasted Again by America-Islamic Advocacy Group," *Orlando Sentinel*, August 10, 2013.

15. Denise-Marie Ordway, "Islamic group says UCF professor promotes anti-Muslim hate," Orlando Sentinel, June 20, 2013.

16. Comas, "UCF Prof Accused of Anti-Muslim Teachings Blasted Again by America-Islamic Advocacy Group."

17. "CAIR Asks Kansas Rep. Pompeo to Correct 'False and Irresponsible' Attack on Muslims," Council on American-Islamic Relations, June 12, 2013.

18. "Same Hate, New Target: Islamophobia and Its Impact in the United States, January 2009–December 2010," Council on American-Islamic Relations and University of California, Berkeley, Center for Race & Gender.

19. "International Conference on Islamophobia ends," World Bulletin, September 14, 2013.

20. Terry Davidson, "York Regional Police Threaten Rabbi's Role as Chaplain over Pamela Geller Speech," *Toronto Sun*, May 1, 2013.

21. Pamela Geller, "Free Speech under Fire in Canada," American Thinker, May 3, 2013.

22. Brian Stillman, Georgett Roberts, Jennifer Fermino, and David K. Li, "EXCLUSIVE VIDEO: Woman Defaces 'Anti-Jihad' Ad in Times Square Station," *New York Post*, September 25, 2012.

23. Robert Spencer, "Cyrus McGoldrick of Hamas-Linked CAIR Applauds Mona Eltahawy's Fascist Vandalism," Jihad Watch, September 26, 2012.

24. Spencer, "Christina Abraham, 'Civil Rights Director' at Hamas-Linked CAIR-Chicago, Calls for More Fascist Vandalism of AFDI Pro-Freedom Ads," Jihad Watch, September 26, 2012.

25. Sam Nunberg, "Iranian Regime Loses to Legal Project in Federal District Court," Legal Project, September 18, 2012.

26. Spencer, "Reza Aslan Calls for Fascist Vandalism of AFDI Pro-Freedom Ads," Jihad Watch, September 26, 2012.

27. Faria Mardhani, "Have We Taken Free Speech Too Far?," *Washington Square News*, September 26, 2012.

Chapter 9: Banned in the Land of Hope and Change

1. "FBI Removes Hundreds of Training Documents after Probe on Treatment of Islam," Fox News, February 21, 2012.

2. "CAIR: Jesse Jackson, ICNA Endorse Letter on Anti-Islam FBI Training," Council on American-Islamic Relations, August 6, 2010.

3. Andrew C. McCarthy, "Director Mueller, Say No to CAIR: A Muslim Brotherhood Tentacle Targets Robert Spencer," *National Review*, August 10, 2010.

4. Roger L. Simon, "Real Blog War: CAIR Goes After Robert Spencer," PJ Media, August 9, 2010.

5. Spencer Ackerman, "FBI Teaches Agents: 'Mainstream' Muslims Are 'Violent, Radical'," Wired, September 14, 2011.

6. McCarthy, "Why They Can't Condemn Hamas," *National Review*, August 28, 2010; "Nihad Awad," Investigative Project on Terrorism, August 4, 2010.

7. "Hizballah's Brash U.S. Supporters," IPT News, November 18, 2010; Reza Aslan, "Obama's Middle East Policy Is a Failure," Huffington Post, October 29, 2010.

8. Josh Gerstein, "Mag Says W.H. Islam Envoy Misquoted; Writer Denies," Politico, February 16, 2010; Joel Mowbray, "Islamic Hall of Shame," FrontPageMagazine.com, May 30, 2005.

9. Muhammed Ibn Ismail Al-Bukhari, trans. Muhammad M. Khan, *Sahih al-Bukhari*: *The Translation of the Meanings* 9, bk. 88, no. 6922 (1997).

10. A. Guillaume, *The Life of Muhammad*: *A Translation of Ibn Ishaq's Sirat Rasul Allah* (New York: Oxford University Press, 1955), 674–76.

11. Ackerman, "FBI Teaches Agents: 'Mainstream' Muslims Are 'Violent, Radical'."

12. Ibid.

13. Ibid.

14. "FBI Drops Lecture That Was Critical of Islam," Associated Press, September 16, 2011.

15. Salam al-Marayati, "The Wrong Way to Fight Terrorism," *Los Angeles Times*, October 19, 2011.

16. "Community to Brennan Re FBI Training," Muslim Advocates, October 19, 2011.

17. Ibid.

18. Ibid.

19. Ibid.

20. Ibid.

21. Federal Bureau of Investigation, "The Radicalization Process: From Conversion to Jihad," May 10, 2006.

22. "Community to Brennan Re FBI Training," Muslim Advocates.

23. Ian Fisher, "A Tale of War: Iraqi Describes Battling G.I.'s," *New York Times*, December 5, 2003.

24. "Commander of the Khobar Terrorist Squad Tells the Story of the Operation," Middle East Media Research Institute, Special Dispatch no. 731, June 15, 2004.

25. "Al-Qa'ida Internet Magazine Sawt Al-Jihad Calls to Intensify Fighting During Ramadan—'the Month of Jihad,'" Middle East Media Research Institute, Special Dispatch no. 804, October 22, 2004.

26. AlMaghrib Institute et al, "Letter to John Brennan," October 19, 2011.

27. Letter of John Brennan to Farhana Khera, November 3, 2011, in AWR Hawkins, "Emerson, IPT Expose Brennan Letter: FBI Training 'Substandard and Offensive' to Muslims," Breitbart, February 8, 2013.

28. Ibid.

29. Ibid.

30. Ibid.

31. Ibid.

32. "U.S. Wants to Build up Hezbollah Moderates: Adviser," Reuters, May 18, 2010.

33. John Brennan, "The Conundrum of Iran: Strengthening Moderates without Acquiescing to Belligerence," *Annals of The American Academy of Political and Social Science* (July 2008), http://www.investigativeproject.org/documents/misc/743.pdf.

34. Ibid.

35. Haviv Rettig Gur, "America Increases Pressure on EU to Designate Hezbollah a Terror Organization," *Times of Israel*, December 11, 2012.

36. Salam al-Marayati, "Muslims in America," *NewsHour with Jim Lehrer*, PBS, November 24, 1999.

37. Brennan, "A New Approach For Safeguarding Americans," Center for Strategic and International Studies, August 6, 2009, http://csis.org/files/attachments/090806_brennan_transcript.pdf.

38. Steven Emerson and John Rossomando, "Obama CIA Nominee John Brennan Wrong for the Job," IPT News, February 5, 2013.

39. "Counterterror Adviser Defends Jihad as 'Legitimate Tenet of Islam,'" Fox News, May 26, 2010.

40. Brennan, "Securing the Homeland by Renewing America's Strengths, Resilience, and Values," Center for Strategic and International Studies, May 26, 2010, http://www.whitehouse.gov/the-press-office/remarks-assistant-president-homeland-security-and-counterterrorism-john-brennan-csi.

41. "CAIR Welcomes New Security Strategy's Focus on Confronting Al-Qaeda," Council on American-Islamic Relations, May 27, 2010.

42. "Report: Non-Muslims Deserve to Be Punished," Fox News, April 1, 2008.

43. "WH Counter-Terrorism Adviser Brennan Storms out of TWT Offices," Washington Times, August 23, 2010.

44. Ibid.

45. Ibid.

46. Ibid.

47. Brennan, "A New Approach For Safeguarding Americans."

48. "ISNA President Opens Townhall Meeting on the Nation's Security with John Brennan," Islamic Society of North America, February 16, 2010.

49. Emerson and Rossomando, "Obama CIA Nominee John Brennan Wrong for the Job."

50. "ISNA Admits Hamas Ties," IPT News, July 25, 2008.

51. "British National Arrested for Assisting Hamas," Israeli Ministry of Foreign Affairs, May 29, 2006; "British Aid Worker Deported from Israel," Israeli Ministry of Foreign Affairs, May 30, 2006.

52. "British National Arrested for Assisting Hamas," Israeli Ministry of Foreign Affairs.

53. Victor Davis Hanson, "The Obama Nominations," National Review, January 7, 2013.

Chapter 10: Taking Aim at the Real Danger

1. Todd Starnes, "US Army Labeled Evangelicals, Catholics as Examples of Religious Extremism," Fox News, April 5, 2013.

2. Ibid.

3. Matthew Vadum, "Conservative Enemies of the State," FrontPageMagazine.com, September 2, 2013.

4. Todd Starnes, "Does Army Consider Christians, Tea Party, a Terror Threat?," Fox News, October 23, 2013.

5. Starnes, "The Army's List of 'Domestic Hate Groups'," Fox News, April 10, 2013.

6. Starnes, "Does Army Consider Christians, Tea Party, a Terror Threat?"
7. "Napolitano Defends Report on Right-Wing Extremist Groups," CNN, April 15, 2009.
8. Matt Viser and Bryan Bender, "Obama Says FBI Acted Properly in Bombing Case," *Boston Globe*, April 30, 2013.
9. "Obama Administration Corrects Clapper's Claim That Muslim Brotherhood Is 'Secular'," Fox News, February 10, 2011.
10. Viser and Bender, "Obama Says FBI Acted Properly in Bombing Case."
11. "Russia Had Tamerlan Tsarnaev under Surveillance," Associated Press, April 30, 2013.
12. Robert Spencer, "Hillary Clinton on Muhammad Filmmaker: 'We're Going to Have That Person Arrested and Prosecuted,'" Jihad Watch, October 25, 2012.
13. Byron Tau, "Feds Suggest Anti-Muslim Speech Can Be Punished," Politico, May 31, 2013.
14. Ibid.
15. Ibid.
16. Ibid.

Chapter 11: Do the Jihadis Have a Case?

1. "Education in Islam," Al-Islam.org, http://www.al-islam.org/education-Islam-rizvi/1.htm.
2. Ahmed ibn Naqib al-Misri, *Reliance of the Traveller* (*'Umdat al-Salik*): *A Classic Manual of Islamic Sacred Law*, trans. Nuh Ha Mim Keller (Amana Publications, 1999), xx, section o4.9.
3. Sultanhussein Tabandeh, *A Muslim Commentary on the Universal Declaration of Human Rights*, trans. F. J. Goulding (1970).
4. Jalalu'd-Din al-Mahalli and Jalalu'd-Din as-Suyuti, *Tafsir al-Jalalayn*, trans. Aisha Bewley (Dar Al Taqwa Ltd., 2007), 1359.
5. Muslim ibn al-Hajjaj al-Qushayri, *Sahih Muslim*, vol. 1, bk. 10, no. 31, trans. Abdul Hamid Siddiqi.
6. A. Guillaume, *The Life of Muhammad*: *A Translation of Ibn Ishaq's Sirat Rasul Allah*, Oxford University Press, 1955, 314.
7. Ibn Kathir, *Tafsir Ibn Kathir*, vol. 1 (Darussalam, 2000), 531.
8. Muhammad Aashiq Ilahi Bulandshahri, *Illuminating Discourses on the Noble Qur'an* (*Tafsir Anwarul Bayan*), vol. 1, trans. Afzal Hussain Elias and Muhammad Arshad Fakhri (Karachi: Darul-Ishaat, 2005), 235.
9. al-Mahalli and as-Suyuti, *Tafsir al-Jalalayn*, 385.
10. al-Qushayri, *Sahih Muslim*, vol. 3, bk. 17, no. 4294.
11. "Surat at-Tawba: Repentance, Tafsir," http://ourworld.compuserve.com/homepages/ABewley/tawba1.html.

12. Ibid.
13. Bulandshahri, *Illuminating Discourses on the Noble Qur'an* (*Tafsir Anwarul Bayan*), vol. 1, 235.
14. Sayyid Abul A'la Mawdudi, *Towards Understanding the Qur'an*, vol. 3, trans. Zafar Ishaq Ansari, (The Islamic Foundation, 1999), 202.
15. Ibid., 275–76.
16. A. Guillaume, *The Life of Muhammad: A Translation of Ibn Ishaq's Sirat Rasul Allah*, (New York: Oxford University Press, 1955), 212–13.
17. Ibid.
18. Ibid.
19. 'Abdullah bin Muhammad ibn Humaid, "The Call to Jihad (Holy Fighting for Allah's Cause) in the Qur'an," *Sahih Bukhari* 9, appendix III, 462.
20. Sayyid Qutb, *Milestones* (The Mother Mosque Foundation, n.d.), 53.
21. Ibid., 57.
22. S. K. Malik, *The Qur'anic Concept of War* (Adam Publishers, 1992), 11.
23. Ibn Arabi, in Suyuti, *Itqan* iii, 69. Cf. John Wansbrough, *Quranic Studies*, (Prometheus, 2003), 184.
24. "Surat at-Tawba: Repentance," *Tafsir al-Jalalayn*, trans. anonymous, http://ourworld.compuserve.com/homepages/ABewley/tawba1.html.
25. Kathir, *Tafsir Ibn Kathir*, vol. 4, 377.
26. "Surat at-Tawba: Repentance," *Tafsir Ibn Juzayy*.
27. Majid Khadduri, *War and Peace in the Law of Islam* (Baltimore: Johns Hopkins University Press, 1955), 51.
28. Imran Ahsan Khan Nyazee, *Theories of Islamic Law: The Methodology of Ijtihad*. (The Other Press, 1994), 251–52.
29. Abu Bakr Jabir al-Jaza'iri, *Minhaj al-Muslim: A Book of Creed, Manners, Character, Acts of Worship and Other Deeds* (Darussalam, 2001), 165.
30. Ibid., 182.
31. Ibid., 184.
32. Ahmed ibn Naqib al-Misri, *Reliance of the Traveller* ('*Umdat al-Salik*): *A Classic Manual of Islamic Sacred Law*, trans. Nuh Ha Mim Keller (Amana Publications, 1999), xx, section o9.0.
33. Ibid., 602, section o9.8.
34. Ibid., 602, section o9.6.
35. "Al-Qaeda Cleric Praises Tsarnaev Brothers as Models for Muslim Children," Middle East Media Research Institute, September 6, 2013.

Chapter 12: Free Society or Caliphate?

1. Caroline Fourest, *Brother Tariq: The Doublespeak of Tariq Ramadan* (Encounter Books, 2008), 19.

2. "Hamza Tzortzis," Stand for Peace, September 9, 2011, http://standforpeace. org.uk/hamza-tzortzis/.
3. Elad Benari, "Top IDF Official Warns: Global Jihad Is at Our Doorstep," Israel National News, July 24, 2013.
4. "Syrian Rebel Commander Ahmad 'Issa: Iran Will Always Be Our No. 1 Enemy, Syrian People Will Decide about Israel," Middle East Media Research Institute, June 12, 2013.
5. "Founder of Hizb Al-Tahrir in Chicago: The Caliphate Is Coming, and Britain and America Can Go to Hell," Middle East Media Research Institute, June 21, 2013.
6. David Lev, "PA Arabs Fete 'New Mahdi,' Establishment of Calpihate [sic]," Israel National News, June 5, 2013.
7. "Pro-Morsi Demonstration at Al-Aqsa Mosque: U.S., France, Britain to Be Destroyed, Rome to Be Conquered," Middle East Media Research Institute, July 12, 2013.
8. "British Islamists Protest French Campaign in Mali: Hollande Is a 'Son of Pharoah', Islam Will Dominate France and England," Middle East Media Research Institute, January 12, 2013.
9. Ibid.
10. Ibid.
11. "Ten Years Later, Radical Islam Still a Taboo Subject," IPT News, September 8, 2011.
12. "Australian Islamist Musa Cerantonio: We Must Fight the Infidels by Physical Warfare until the Caliphate Is Restored," Middle East Media Research Institute, November 30, 2012.
13. Ibid.
14. "Damascus Demonstration: To Hell with Freedom, We Want an Islamic Caliphate and Weapons," Middle East Media Research Institute, September 14, 2012.
15. "Islamic Militant Group Claims Attack on Egyptian-Israeli Border," Al Arabiya, June 19, 2012.
16. "Arrested Indonesian Describes Plot on Police Video," Associated Press, September 6, 2012.
17. Amy Chew, "Militant Laskar Jihad Group Disbands," CNN, October 16, 2002; Daniel Pipes, "What Is Jihad," *New York Post*, December 31, 2002; Rod Dreher, "Do Christians Bleed?," *National Review*, September 16, 2002.
18. Raymond Ibrahim, "Muslim Brotherhood: 'Yes, We Will Be Masters of the World'," Jihad Watch, July 28, 2012.
19. "Report: Brotherhood Has Egyptian Caliphate Plans," IPT News, June 24, 2010.

20. Tulin Daloglu, "Davutoglu Invokes Ottomanism as a New Order for Mideast," Al-Monitor, March 10, 2013.
21. "Hamas MP and Cleric Yunis Al-Astal in a Friday Sermon: We Will Conquer Rome, and from There Continue to Conquer the Two Americas and Eastern Europe," Middle East Media Research Institute, clip no. 1739, April 11, 2008.
22. "New Muslim Brotherhood Leader: Resistance in Iraq and Palestine is Legitimate; America is Satan; Islam Will Invade America and Europe," Middle East Media Research Institute, special dispatch series no. 655, February 4, 2004.
23. Ibid.
24. Arnie Cooper, "Is Islam 'Worse' Than Any Other Religion?," Miller-McCune, December 3, 2010.
25. Daniel Pipes, "The Danger Within: Militant Islam in America," Commentary, November 2001.
26. Aaron Klein, "Soda, Pizza and the Destruction of America," World Net Daily, March 18, 2003.
27. Lisa Gardiner, "American Muslim Leader Urges Faithful to Spread Islam's Message," San Ramon Valley Herald, July 4, 1998. See also Daniel Pipes, "CAIR: 'Moderate' Friends of Terror," New York Post, April 22, 2002.
28. Ibid.
29. Lou Gelfand, "Reader Says Use of 'Fundamentalist' Hurting Muslims," Minneapolis Star Tribune, April 4, 1993.
30. Robert Spencer, "DC Imam Wants to Establish an 'Islamic State of North America No Later Than 2050'," Jihad Watch, November 9, 2007.
31. Steven Stalinsky, "Kuwaiti Muslim Brotherhood Leader and Director of Saudi Al-Risala TV Tareq Al Suwaidan Tours West, Promoting Restoration of Caliphate and New Era of Cyber Jihad," Middle East Media Research Institute, June 14, 2012.
32. "Mixed Messages from Touring Muslim Lecturer," Australian, June 7, 2012.
33. "PRESS RELEASE: Mohammad صلى الله عليه وسلم Mercy to Mankind: Messenger, Leader & Statesman," Hizb ut-Tahrir America, June 9, 2013, http://www.hizb-america.org/index.php/mediacenter/pressreleases/173-press-release-mohammad-mercy-to-mankind-messenger-leader-statesman. The caliphate was abolished on March 3, 1924—26 Rajab 1342 according to the Islamic Hijri calendar. June 9, 2013, corresponds to 30 Rajab and was the first Saturday after the anniversary.
34. Ibid.
35. "Frequently Asked Questions," Hizb ut-Tahrir America, http://www.hizb-america.org/index.php/aboutus/faqs.

Chapter 13: Life under Sharia

1. Nicolai Sennels, "Sharia Police in 'Small Caliphate' in The Hague: Neighborhood in The Hague Dominated by Orthodox Muslims," Jihad Watch, May 27, 2013.
2. "'Muslim Patrol' Vigilantes Attempt to Control London Streets," *Commentator*, January 16, 2013.
3. "'Christianity Can Go to Hell' Says NEW Muslim Patrol Video," *Commentator*, February 4, 2013.
4. Dominic Holden, "Police Arrest Musab Mohamed Masmari in Neighbours Arson Case," SLOG News & Arts, February 1, 2014.
5. Vicky Allan, "Ground Zero Imam Gives Scotland His Recipe for Successful Multiculturalism," *Sunday Herald*, August 28, 2011.
6. "Fear of Islam," SBS Insight, November 2, 2010.
7. Ibn Kathir, *Tafsir Ibn Kathir*, vol. 2 (Darussalam, 2000), 142.
8. Raymond Ibrahim, "Islam, War, and Deceit: A Synthesis (Part I)," Jihad Watch, February 14, 2009.
9. Muslim ibn al-Hajjaj al-Qushayri, *Sahih Muslim*, vol. 4, bk. 30, no. 6303, trans. Abdul Hamid Siddiqi.
10. Raymond Ibrahim, "Tawriya: New Islamic Doctrine Permits 'Creative Lying'," Gatestone Institute, February 28, 2012.
11. Muhammed Ibn Ismail Al-Bukhari, *Sahih al-Bukhari: The Translation of the Meanings*, vol. 9, bk. 88, no. 6922, trans. Muhammad M. Khan (Darussalam, 1997).
12. Robert Spencer, "Death to the Apostates," FrontPageMagazine.com, October 24, 2006.
13. Surah al-Maida, or the Chapter of the Table, is the Qur'an's fifth chapter.
14. Nicole Lafond, "Gore, Current Silent as Cleric Affirms Death Penalty for Leaving Islam on Al-Jazeera," *Daily Caller*, February 12, 2013.
15. Rebecca Bynum, "Qaradawi on Apostasy," Jihad Watch, April 14, 2006.
16. John L. Esposito, "Practice and Theory: A Response to 'Islam and the Challenge of Democracy,'" *Boston Review* (April/May 2003).
17. Nina Bernstein, "In Secret, Polygamy Follows Africans to N.Y.," *New York Times*, March 23, 2007.
18. Maryclaire Dale, "Pa. Bigamist Slain Hours before Trip," Associated Press, August 8, 2007.
19. Lornet Turnbull, "Opponents of Gay-Marriage Law Get Unexpected Aid: From Muslims," *Seattle Times*, May 24, 2012.
20. Some Muslim sources render this as "I divorce you."
21. Al-Bukhari, *Sahih al-Bukhari: The Translation of the Meanings*, vol. 7, bk. 67, no. 5206.
22. Ibid., vol. 5, bk. 63, no. 3894.

23. Ibid., vol. 5, book 63, no. 3896; Ibid., vol. 7, bk. 67, no. 5158.

24. "Islamist Leader Threatens of Waging Jihad," *Weekly Blitz*, April 20, 2011.

25. "Sheriff Fears for Teen after Muslim Dad Who Pulled a Knife on His Daughter Walks Free," *Daily Record*, June 4, 2013.

26. Nicolai Sennels, "Germany: Muslims Break In to Home of Couple and Beat Unborn Child to Death to Enforce Sharia," Islam Versus Europe, August 4, 2013.

27. Kreshma Fakhri, "Sex Determination Test Adds to Women's Woes: Interviews by Killid Confirm There Is Greater Violence against Women at Home When They Have Daughters," Killid Group, RAWA News, September 2, 2013, http://www.rawa.org/temp/runews/2013/09/02/sex-determination-test-adds-to-women-s-woes.html#ixzz2eoJAo2zK.

28. "Chad Struggles to Pass New Family Law," *VOA News*, April 15, 2005.

29. "Turkish Health Workers Condone Wife Beating," Physorg.com, December 13, 2007.

30. "Islamic States Frown on Islam-Opposing Paragraphs of UNHCR Violence against Women Resolution," Kuwait News Agency, June 14, 2013.

31. "Egyptian Cleric Mahmoud Al-Denawy Instructs European Muslims on Wife Beating," Middle East Media Research Institute, June 17, 2013.

32. al-Qushayri, *Sahih Muslim*, vol. 2, bk. 4, no. 2127, trans. Abdul Hamid Siddiqi.

33. Abu Dawud, *Sunan Abu Dawud, English Translation with Explanatory Notes*, trans. Ahmad Hasan, (Kitab Bhavan, 1990), bk. 11, no. 2141.

34. Steven Stalinsky and Y. Yehoshua, "Muslim Clerics on the Religious Rulings Regarding Wife-Beating," *Middle East Media Research Institute*, special report no. 27, March 22, 2004.

35. James Fielding, "Sharia Court Tells 'Abused Wife' to Stay," *Express*, April 7, 2013.

36. Ibid.

37. Ibid.

38. William Bigelow, "North Carolina Passes Anti-Sharia Law," Breitbart, August 28, 2013.

39. Annalise Frank, "NC Senate Passes 'Sharia Law' bill," *Raleigh News & Observer*, July 19, 2013.

40. David N. Goodman, "Muslim Rights Group Urges Bill in Michigan Legislature Be Stopped," Associated Press, December 12, 2012.

41. Robert K. Vischer, "The Dangers of Anti-Sharia Laws," *First Things*, March 2012.

42. "Florida Weighs Ban on Shariah Law in Domestic Courtrooms," Associated Press, March 2, 2012.

43. "Court Upholds Ruling Blocking Oklahoma Sharia and International Law Ban," American Civil Liberties Union, January 10, 2012.

44. Ibid.

45. Amanda Golden, "Best-Selling Author Reza Aslan Lectures on Islamophobia," *Colgate Maroon-News*, February 16, 2012.

46. "In Cold Blood: Killed for Stepping Out," *Express Tribune*, June 8, 2013.

47. "National Park Service Produces Videos Praising Islam's Contributions to Women's Rights," *Independent Journal Review*, September 18, 2013.

Chapter 14: Anti-Semitism and Other Acceptable Hatreds

1. Jennifer Sorentrue, "Muslim Group Demands Public Records after County Communications Staffer Posts Anti-Islamic Message," *Palm Beach Post*, September 13, 2013.

2. Itamar Marcus and Nan Jacques Zilberdik, "Little Girls on PA TV: Jews Are the 'Most Evil among Creations, Barbaric Monkeys, Wretched Pigs,' Condemned to 'Humiliation and Hardship'," Palestinian Media Watch, July 7, 2013.

3. Steven Stalinsky, "Kuwaiti Muslim Brotherhood Leader and Director of Saudi Al-Risala TV Tareq Al-Suwaidan Tours West, Promoting Restoration of Caliphate and New Era of Cyber Jihad," Middle East Media Research Institute, June 14, 2012.

4. Ibid.

5. Muslim ibn al-Hajjaj al-Qushayri, *Sahih Muslim*, trans. Abdul Hamid Siddiqi (Kitab Bhavan, 2000), vol. 4, bk. 41, no. 6985.

6. Benjamin Weinthal, "Switzerland Bans Cleric for Anti-Semitic Rhetoric," *Jerusalem Post*, May 28, 2013.

7. "As Gaza Fighting Continues, Egyptian Clerics Intensify Antisemitic Statements; Columbus, Ohio Muslim Scholar/Leader Dr. Salah Sultan: Muhammad Said That Judgment Day Will Not Come until Muslims Fight the Jews and Kill Them; America Will Suffer Destruction," Middle East Media Research Institute, December 30, 2008.

8. "Sheik Yousuf Al-Qaradhawi: Allah Imposed Hitler upon the Jews to Punish Them—'Allah Willing, the Next Time Will Be at the Hand of the Believers'," Middle East Media Research Institute, January 28–30, 2009.

9. "Australian Sheik Sharif Hussein to Obama: Oh Enemy of Allah, You Will Be Trampled upon by Pure Muslim Feet," Middle East Media Research Institute, July 3, 2013.

10. "Leader of Jordanian Muslim Brotherhood Hammam Saeed: Peace Negotiations Are Heresy," Middle East Media Research Institute, n.d.

11. "Jordanian Newspaper: 'Let's Kill the Jews Everywhere,'" Elder of Ziyon, June 16, 2013.
12. "Turkish PM Accuses Israel of Orchestrating Egypt Coup," AGI, August 20, 2013.
13. "Egyptian Association for Change Spokesman: Muslim Brotherhood Implements the Methods of the Jews," Middle East Media Research Institute, August 14, 2013.
14. "Al-Jazeera Commentator, Former MB Official, Gamal Nassar: Al-Sisi Is Jewish, Implementing Protocols of Elders of Zion in Egypt," Middle East Media Research Institute, August 17, 2013.
15. Palash Ghosh, "Anti-Semitism in a Country with No Jews: Pakistan's Imran Khan Sues Cleric for Calling Him 'Jewish Agent'," *International Business Times*, August 6, 2013.
16. "The 2013 Tanenbaum Awards Honor New York Times Bestselling Author and Activist Reza Aslan and Philanthropic Leader FJC," Tanenbaum Center for Interreligious Understanding, April 29, 2013.
17. National Iranian American Council, "Staff and Board of Directors," http://www.niacouncil.org/site/PageServer?pagename=About_staff_board; Sam Nunberg, "Iranian Regime Loses to Legal Project in Federal District Court," Legal Project, September 18, 2012.
18. Michael Rubin, "Is NIAC the Iran Lobby?," *Commentary*, February 8, 2013.
19. Charles C. Johnson, "Documents: Hagel Staffers Met with 'Front Group' for Iranian Regime," *Daily Caller*, February 20, 2013.
20. Sam Nunberg, "A Response to NIAC's Deceitful Fundraising Letter," FrontPageMagazine.com, January 9, 2013.
21. Adam Kredo, "Sanctioning Iran's American Allies: NIAC Ordered to Pay Nearly $200K in Legal Fees," *Washington Free Beacon*, April 22, 2013.
22. "Ahmadinejad Predicts the Removal of 'Zionists' from the World," *Telegraph*, September 3, 2010; "US Walks out on Ahmadinejad UN Speech," Associated Press, September 23, 2010; Reza Aslan, "Do We Have Ahmadinejad All Wrong?," *Atlantic*, January 13, 2011.
23. Reza Aslan, "Ahmadinejad Returns to Chaos," *Daily Beast*, September 28, 2010; Aslan, "Obama's Middle East Policy Is a Failure," Huffington Post, October 29, 2010; "The Covenant of the Islamic Resistance Movement," Yale University, August 18, 1988, http://avalon.law.yale.edu/20th_century/hamas.asp.
24. "Hizballah's Brash U.S. Supporters," IPT News, November 18, 2010; "Hassan Nasrallah: In His Own Words," Committee for Accuracy in Middle East Reporting in America (CAMERA), July 26, 2006.
25. Reza Aslan, "Do Egyptians Want Both Democracy and a Role for Religion in Their Government?," *Washington Post*, January 30, 2011.

26. "Member Appreciation Event, Dr. Reza Aslan in Honor of Rabbi Joel and Susan Levine," Temple Judea, n.d., http://templejudeapbc.org/News/15/member-appreciation-event-dr-reza-aslan-in-honor-of-rabbi-joel-and-susan-levine.

27. Jason Straziuso, "Witness: Kenya Mall Attackers Target Non-Muslims," Associated Press, September 21, 2013.

28. Guy Alexander, "Kenyan Mall Shooting: 'They Threw Grenades like Maize to Chickens'," *Observer*, September 21, 2013.

29. Bridget Johnson, "Al-Shabaab: Three Americans among Gunmen in Kenya Mall," PJ Media, September 22, 2013; "Illinois, Maine, Arizona Muslims among Kenyan Mall Massacre killers," Creeping Sharia, September 23, 2013.

Chapter 15: Where We Are Headed

1. The eighty-third anniversary of the Reichstag fire that Adolf Hitler used as a pretext to arrogate dictatorial powers to himself.

2. "Speech of Secretary General at the Thirty-Fifth Session of the Council of Foreign Ministers of the Organisation of the Islamic Conference," Organization of the Islamic Conference, June 18, 2008.

3. Eric Posner, "The World Doesn't Love the First Amendment: The Vile Anti-Muslim Video Shows That the U.S. Overvalues Free Speech," Slate, September 25, 2012.

4. Sarah Chayes, "Does 'Innocence of Muslims' Meet the Free-Speech Test?," *Los Angeles Times*, September 18, 2012.

5. Nathan Lean, "Sept. 11: Eleven Years Later, American Muslims Are Victims," *Washington Post*, September 11, 2012.

6. Jerome Socolovsky, "Anti-Islam Film Linked to 'Islamophobic Industry,'" Voice of America, September 14, 2012.

7. Niraj Warikoo, "Protesters to Rally in Dearborn against Anti-Islam Film," *Detroit Free Press*, September 21, 2012.

8. Tiffany Gabbay, "Free Speech That Mocks Islam Is National Security Threat for U.S., Prominent NJ Imam Tells TheBlaze," Blaze, September 20, 2012.

9. Chris Serres, "Some Muslim Workers at Target Refuse to Handle Pork," Buzz.mn, March 13, 2007.

10. Ray Levato, "Sign at Wegmans draws attention," WHEC.com, March 30, 2012.

11. Sophie Jane Evans, "M&S Tells Muslim Staff They CAN Refuse to Serve Customers Buying Alcohol or Pork," *Daily Mail*, December 22, 2013.

12. Naomi Wolf, "Behind the Veil Lives a Thriving Muslim Sexuality," *Sydney Morning Herald*, August 30, 2008.

13. Laurie Penny, "This Isn't 'Feminism.' It's Islamophobia," *Guardian*, December 22, 2013.

14. Sarah Netter, "Arizona Police Hunt for Dad Accused of Running Over Daughter: Police Say Faleh Hassan Almaleki Believed His Daughter Was 'Too Westernized,'" ABC News, October 22, 2009.

15. Muslim ibn al-Hajjaj al-Qushayri, *Sahih Muslim*, trans. Abdul Hamid Siddiqi (Kitab Bhavan, 2000), vol. 2, bk. 4, no. 2127.

16. Katie Drummond, "'Compromise' on Female Circumcision Ignites Debate," AOL News, May 10, 2010.

17. Anna Davis, "What Happened When Anti-FGM Campaigner Asked People in the Street to Sign a Petition in Favour of Mutilating Girls," *London Evening Standard*, October 28, 2013.

18. David D. Kirkpatrick, "A Deadly Mix in Benghazi," *New York Times*, December 28, 2013.

19. George Gene Gustines, "Mighty, Muslim and Leaping Off the Page," *New York Times*, November 5, 2013.

Epilogue: What Must Be Done

1. United States Code Title 18, Part I, Chapter 115, Section 2385, "Advocating Overthrow of Government."

INDEX